# GOD SPEAKS!
## The Flying Spaghetti Monster
### in His Own Words

Jon Smith

www.lulu.com/stress

Copyright Statement

**GOD SPEAKS!**
**The Flying Spaghetti Monster**
***In His Own Words***

ISBN: 978-1-4116-8276-4

Edited by Janice M. Frum

# Basic Information: Angelic Omniscience Ends

# FSM Iconography

What does the Flying Spaghetti Monster (FSM) really look like? This deep question has perplexed humanity since the very beginning (specifically, 2005). Bobby Henderson's website (www.venganza.org), which everyone must visit, includes visions others have had. Some appear on coffee cups. Some on hats. Some on dinner plates. However, all historical images, including Henderson's rendering, have certain fundamental defining charateristics. Meatball eyes are small and placed on stalks. Pupils are centered or absent, leaving the eyes blank. Noodly appendages point away and are jagged, complex, and asymmetrical. The body is either formless, like primal pasta, or a variation of the Jesus fish.

My vision of the FSM, printed on the cover, page 1, and throughout this text, breaks all traditions of FSM iconography. Note that the eyes are large, to see more of the world. They are firmly placed in the body, as in advanced thinking animals; eyes on stalks are characteristic of primitive insects. The pupils no longer stare blankly ahead, but diverge, revealing the subtlety of the FSM's inner thoughts. Indeed, the perceptive student may discover that this ocular placement resembles tossed dice, a reference to the role of randomness in FSM thinking. It is significant that the body is not fishlike, but an encompassing oval with inward-turning appendages, symbolizing that the FSM embraces all religions. Simplicity and symmetry are central to body and limb, reflecting the classic perfection of the revealed truths in this volume. Indeed, each verse is very much a direct reflection of the FSM. To summarize, the revolutionary (not evolutionary) new FSM icon symbolizes a new FSM message, good news for us all.

How did I have my vision of the FSM? It was one of the most profound religious experiences of my life. I was meditating with my pet Burmese cat Moco on my lap. (Legend has it that the Burmese breed is favored by Buddhist monks.) Suddenly Moco started scratching her ear with some urgency. Then the FSM image sort of jumped out at me.

**DEDICATION**

I wish to thank Bobby Henderson for his encouragement, and for sharing his vision and insight with the world. My book is a scholarly theological analysis of the Flying Spaghetti Monster construct inspired by Bobby's wit and wisdom. It is obligatory that everyone take a pilgrimage to his website (www.venganza.org), buy his book, and purchase all related FSM products.

# CONTENTS

# CHAPTER 1
# In the Beginning

*In the beginning was the word.*
*And the word was with God.*
*And the word was God.*
*–John 1:1*

The first words of the Bible speak of creation. They are words that have inspired humanity for thousands of years. But what do they mean? Let me share an amazing journey of words, one that led me to revelations that must be viewed as coming directly from God. Furthermore, I offer indisputable proof (which you can replicate) that this is so.

## The Game of Anagrams

My journey began with a children's game, **anagrams**. An anagram involves rearranging the letters in a word and words into a phrase. "Elvis" can be rearranged into the anagram "Lives." "Lemon" becomes "Melon." Here are some other anagrams of words and phases:

*"Debit card" = "Bad credit"*
*"Slot machines" = "Cash lost in 'em"*
*"Dormitory" = "Dirty Room"*
*"Astronomer" = "Moon starer"*

One day I decided to take the first six words of the Biblical creation story and, just for fun, look for anagrams. Generally, for a phrase of five or six words, any good computer anagram generator (I use Anagram Genius) can find thousands of anagrams. Astonishingly, the very first anagram that emerged for "In the beginning was the word" was:

*"Then God threw in a big new sin."*

Confused and hoping for further edification, I searched for more anagrams, and found the equally disconcerting recombination:

*"Intertwined benign hogwash."*

Now desperate, I tried the final words, "and the word was God." One emerged:

*"Warthogs now added"*

## The Flying Spaghetti Monster

It was time to take a new look at the meaning of life and God's message for us all. Where to begin? Should I start with the world's oldest religion? The world's biggest religion? The world's richest religion? The world's most aggressive religion? The noisiest religion?

After much deliberation, the answer came to me in a flash. When considering deep questions about origins, I must start fresh and begin with the world's youngest religion, the one also most invested in its theory of creation. Here there is only one candidate, one for which over 70 percent of its scriptural writing is about its view of creation. The religion: Pastafarianism. Its creation theory: The universe was created by the Flying Spaghetti Monster. The insights of this volume are a chronicle of my remarkable journey.

-----------------

Discussion of anagrams adapted from *The Anagram Dictionary* by Michael Curl (Robert Hale & Company, 1996) and *Words at Play: Quips, Quirks & Oddities* by O.V. Michaelsen (Sterling Publishing Company, Inc., 1998)

# CHAPTER 2

## The Flying Spaghetti Monster

The World's most recent religion started in June, 2005. In a small town in Oregon, Bobby Henderson (age 24) had enough. Frustrated with the Kansas Board of Education's debate on teaching supernatural theories of intelligent design (such as the Biblical 7-day creation myth) side-by-side with Darwin's theory of natural selection, he wrote an open letter formally requesting that his deity, the Flying Spaghetti Monster (FSM), be given equal time. Here is his request:

> Let us remember that there are multiple theories of Intelligent Design. I and many others around the world are of the strong belief that the universe was created by a Flying Spaghetti Monster. It was He who created all that we see and all that we feel. We feel strongly that the overwhelming scientific evidence pointing towards evolutionary processes is nothing but a coincidence, put in place by Him. (www.venganza.org)

Bobby backed his request with the threat of legal action. Three members of the Board replied and strongly sympathized with his position (they were the dissenting votes in the debate). A supporter of Biblical creation theory warned "It is a serious offense to mock God."

Bobby's religion, "Flying Spaghetti Monsterism," or "Pastafarianism," caught on. His website, venganza.org, received many thousands of hits, and noted scholars wrote providing support for his vision that the universe was created by the Flying Spaghetti Monster. Scientists proclaimed: "Prove that it didn't happen!" Theologians provided logical evidence. ("The Flying Spaghetti Monster is a being with every perfection. Existence is a perfection. Therefore, the Flying Spaghetti Monster exists.")

Soon the nation's media noticed, and the Flying Spaghetti Monster appeared in *Wired News*, the *New York Times*, and *Scientific American.*

The initial beliefs of Flying Spaghetti Monsterism were sketchy. An invisible and undetectable Flying Spaghetti

Monster created the universe, starting with a mountain, trees, and "midgit." Evidence pointing toward Darwin's theory was intentionally planted by the FSM to distract and test us. However, the existing evidence clearly shows that "global warming, earthquakes, hurricanes, and other natural disasters are a direct effect of the shrinking numbers of Pirates since the 1880s." As the number of pirates have declined, warming and disasters increased. This fact has yet to be challenged by scientists or theologians.

Bobby has enunciated a few additional beliefs and practices:

1. The FSM guides human affairs with His "Noodly Appendage."
2. The official ending for prayers to the FSM is "Ramen," not "Amen."
3. In heaven there's a stripper factory and a beer volcano.
4. Every Friday is a religious holiday.
5. FSM teachers must be "baptized" by "holy meat sauce."

6. It is disrespectful to teach of the FSM without wearing His chosen outfit, full pirate regalia.
7. It is polite to end conversations with the words “May you be touched by His noodly appendage.”

Flying Spaghetti Monsterism has already inspired a rich artistic tradition, as can be seen on its website.

Initial revelations are supplemented by *The Gospel of the Flying Spaghetti Monster* (Henderson, 2006).

**Reference**

Henderson, B. (2006). *The Gospel of the Flying Spaghetti Monster.* New York: Villard Books.

# CHAPTER 3

## The Inner Wisdom of the Spaghettigram

Flying Spaghetti Monsterism might seem like a prank or a spoof. But sometimes viewing things through the eyes of a child helps us to see the truth. Indeed, using the tool of anagrams helped me realize that in the form of the Flying Spaghetti Monster, God is speaking to us through humor. To chuckle or scoff is to miss the point. God is testing us to look past the humor to the truth. Indeed, we shall see that the FSM in His Spaghettigrams states in no uncertain terms His disdain for parody (*"ignorant, empty, flippant, moth-eaten spoofing"*). The anagram is the divine tool of revelation.

All anagrams generated in an attempt to seek knowledge about the Flying Spaghetti Monster are called ***Spaghettigrams***. They are properly organized into four-line verses, or quatrains. Here are the rules.

**Angelic Omniscient Spaghettigrams** are anagrams of the phrase "Flying Spaghetti Monster" with no words added. These are the most prized and important anagrams. They are Angelic in purity and direct from the all-knowing, omniscient FSM. They are nothing less than the infallible, authoritative word of the Deity.

**Wisdom Spaghettigrams** are anagrams that add any topic, name, or phrase to the phrase "Flying Spaghetti Monster." Thus, "sexuality and the Flying Spaghetti Monster" can produce a proper Wisdom Spaghettigram. A Wisdom Spaghettigram is often a question, as one might ask an oracle, "Does the Flying Spaghetti Monster permit polygamy?"

**Illuminary Spaghettigrams** include at least one key word or phrase from the FSM lexicon, for example:

*Noodle or Noodly Appendage*

*Pirate*

*Fish*

*Kansas School Board*

*Beer Volcano*

The key word or phrase must be logically a part of the phrase to be submitted to anagrammatic analysis. Thus, "Noodles are food" would not be acceptable, where as "May you be blessed by His Noodly Appendage" (*"Debasingly moneyless, baboon-headed yuppy"*) is fine.

Finally, the FSM prefers to communicate in terms of quatrains, or four-line verses, like the quatrains of Nostradamus, the 16th century French physician, astrologer, and prophet. Nostradamus created a total of 942 quatrains. Here are a few examples:

*The human realm of Angelic offspring*
*Appearing at the time of the great games of slaughter*
*It will be seized and plunged into the Vat*
*High price unguarded none will have provided for it*

*The gods will make it appear to the humans*
*The bird of prey offers itself to the heavens*
*Everlasting captive times what lightning on the top*
*Late and soon comes the awaited help*

*When the fish that travels over both land and sea*
*is cast up on to the shore by a great wave,*
*its shape foreign, smooth and frightful.*
*From the sea the enemies soon reach the walls.*

The astute reader will readily see that the quatrains of Nostradamus often sound like Spaghettigram quatrains. This is evidence of the validity of the Spaghettigram.

Finally, all religious scriptures require interpretation. Typically, such interpretative literature is more extensive than the volume of primary scriptures. That branch of interpretative scholarship for Pastafarianism is termed "noodlology." This book presents Spaghettigrams and noodlological analysis.

# CHAPTER 4

## The Angelic Omniscient Spaghettigrams

All of the gems of inner wisdom presented in this chapter are anagrams of "***Flying Spaghetti Monster***." As such, they are truly words of wisdom that come *directly from* the Flying Spaghetti Monster. No other world religion can make such a provable claim about its scriptures.

First, let me explain a few things about how this book is set up. Anagrams are printed in a *special font*, preceded by the pest-like FSM icon:

Thus, rearranging the letters of "Flying Spaghetti Monster" gives:

*Almighty pestering fonts.*

We begin with the most central of Spaghettigrams, the Original Spaghettigram Quatrain, "*Finest Might, Sporty*

*Angel.*" The FSM proclaims the wisdom of this quatrain (*This strong, if empty, Angel.*) We see the FSM symbolized as an "Angel," a reference that appears frequently in Pastic Quatrains. Once again, all Spaghettigrams in this chapter are anagrams of the words "Flying Spaghetti Monster."

*Finest Might, Sporty Angel*
*(Ghastly Omnipresent Gift)*

*This strong, if empty, Angel.*
*Fine, strong, almighty pest.*
*Temptingly fights reason.*
*Strong, hasty, fleeting, imp.*

Scholarly analysis, noodlology, explains that the FSM is a mighty angel, one given to the sport of fighting close-minded logic and reason. He is an omnipresent gift, always there to be considered. Note the element of impish playfulness; the FSM is a hasty, ghastly pest to those lacking a sense of humor.

## The Four Noodly Truths

The body of Angelic Omniscient Spaghettigrams comprise four groups: (1) The Nature of Illusion and Folly, (2) Sources of Ignorance and Folly, (3) Noodly Virtues, and (4) Spiritual Exercises.

### THE NATURE OF ILLUSION AND FOLLY

What are truth and illusion? What are wisdom and folly? The Angelic Omniscient Quatrains reveal that often illusion is omnipresent and tempts us like a star; however, we should see that following the path of error exposes us to the sting of the powerful serpent of a false angel. Illusion is a fog, a flimsy ghost, nothing more than an empty slot in the game of life.

*Oh! Star feigns temptingly.*
*Fleeting myths or apt sign?*
*Sting of almighty serpent.*
*This sporty angel figment.*

- *Ghastly if pertinent smog.*
- *Frighten temptingly as so.*
- *Flimsy penetrating ghost.*
- *Frightening as empty slot.*

## SOURCES OF ILLUSION AND FOLLY

The Angelic Omniscient Spaghetti-grams teach us how to detect illusion and folly. Quatrains direct our attention to Love and Sex, the Self-Tormenting Ego, the Chains of Desire, and the Problem of Anger.

### Love and Sex

- *Tempting 'n' faithless orgy.*
- *Phony flirt gets steaming.*
- *Self-pitying tenth orgasm.*
- *Hot self-pity G-string. Amen!*

- *Finest porn gets almighty.*
- *Niftiest, ghastly porn gem.*
- *If mighty angel tests porn,*

- Porn feigns stately might.
- Filthy G-string poets. Amen!

**The Self-Tormenting Ego**

- Self-tormenting, hasty pig.
- Self-rating egotist nymph.
- Self-pitying hag torments.
- Smother self-pitying gnat.

**The Chains of Desire**

- Fetish groans temptingly.
- Penalty of thirsting gems.
- This frosty pig gentleman.
- Satisfying, rotten phlegm.

**The Problem of Anger**

- This petty gem of snarling.
- Self-tormenting, pithy gas.
- This flimsy, potent nagger.
- Strongest, filthy, mean pig.
- Snotty if angriest phlegm.

## NOODLY VIRTUES

Every religion has its favorite catalog of virtues. The FSM favors Cleanliness, Courage, Humor, Bearing Witness, and Renunciation. Again, the quatrains, and quatrain fragments, speak for themselves.

### Cleanliness

- *Filth torments sane piggy.*
- *Filthy, strong pest enigma.*

### Courage

- *Mighty saint, flog Serpent.*
- *Frighten stagy simpleton.*
- *Fate so implying strength . . .*
- *of a serpent's mighty glint.*

### Humor

- *Penalty of tight grimness.*
- *Honest, grim self-pity gnat.*

### Bearing Witness

- *My! The self-rating posting.*
- *Salty might of presenting.*

### Renunciation

- *Thrifty, penniless maggot.*
- *Not thrifty, pleasing gem.*

## SPIRITUAL EXERCISES

The FSM encourages all forms of prayer and devotion. However, He teaches us to engage in three core techniques: Pastation, Noodlation, and Saucery.

### Pastation

One practices pastation by simply thinking positive feelings or having positive fantasies about the most positive aspects of the FSP. One "pastates" oneself (or becomes "pastate") before the deity. For example, one might entertain a fantasy about the "noodly appendages of love that bind the universe" or the "warm flowing sauce that embraces all."

### Noodlation

Noodlation is a way of emptying the mind. It is expressed in the following Noodlation Quatrain:

- *Forget simplest anything.*
- *Ghost-empty self-training.*
- *Angel's empty of thirsting.*
- *Angel hits strong, if empty.*

One practices noodlation by meditatively repeating the mantra "nooooo" (pronounced "nuu") slowly, over and over and over. Whenever your mind wanders, don't get upset, or "spill the pasta." Gently and easily return to repeating "noooo." At first this may seem a bit mechanical. As your emptying skills grow, your focusing skills strengthen and you find yourself forgetting all distraction. The sounds "noooo... nooooooo" become more and more elongated. This is the phase of "stretching the noodle." Eventually, the sounds begin to blend together, so the beginning becomes the end and the end becomes the beginning and the middle is everywhere, just as in very well cooked pasta:

"nooooonoooooonoooooonoooooooooooo"

In deeper levels of noodlation, only the "oooo" remains, and gently dissolves into the great sauce of the universe:

"o o o o o o o o o o o o o o o o o o o o o o o o o o o o o o o . . . . "

Often this stage of noodlation feels extremely pleasant, evoking a sigh of "ooooooooo." This can be enjoyed in itself, or as distraction to be put aside *"Forget simplest anything."*

**Saucery**

When one engages in "saucery," or "sauces it," one simply savors each moment as it comes and goes, like savoring every drop of spaghetti sauce. Do not linger on any drop, or think about how the sauce was created. Instead, simply attend to each drop of sauce that comes and goes. The universe is the "great sauce that is everywhere."

## STRUGGLES

Pastation, noodlation, and saucery are not easy. They take time, effort, and diligence. Many barriers can emerge along the path. The following Spaghettigrams poetically describe some of the struggles of the path. For each there is no concrete correct interpretation. When you practice pastation, noodlation, or saucery, let your mind dwell upon one of these quatrains. Do not try to deliberately figure it out. Let your subconscious speak to you. All you have to do is listen with an open mind.

Lightning-fast, remote spy,
spy something flattering.
Fragment this tiny gospel.
Finest ghostly tampering.

Floating, mighty serpents.
From angel's petty insight
Thrifty poem stings angel.
Often angel strips mighty.
Serpent of almighty sting.

Poets rant shiftingly. Gem.
Patient ogres fling myths.
Stylish poet fragmenting.
Atoms step frighteningly.

Ghastly, impenitent frogs.
Fine, strong almighty pets,
tempting of ghastly snore.
Angel's gift or inept myths.
Forget anything misspelt.

- Angel's often mighty trips.
- If angel's mighty portents.
- Saintly, top gem frightens.
- Plotting far-seeing myths.

- Mighty farts not sleeping.
- Fart hissingly potent gem.
- Gosh! Tiny, tempting flares.
- Gritty feelings . . .phantoms?

# CHAPTER 5

## The Meaning of Love

Love is central to all religion. What does the Flying Spaghetti Monster really think of love? His sole omniscient words on the topic, perhaps, subtle, defy easy interpretation. Recall the "Love Quatrain":

- *Tempting 'n' faithless orgy.*
- *Phony flirt gets steaming.*
- *Self-pitying tenth orgasm.*
- *Hot self-pity G-string! Amen!*

In this chapter we turn to the Wisdom Spaghettigrams in search of further insight into the subtleties of this quatrain. We examine Love, Abstinence, Compassion, Service, Heterosexuality, and Homosexuality. We now explore the beautiful Wisdom Spaghettigrams, anagrams in which a key word is added to the phrase "Flying Spaghetti Monster." Thus the Love Quatrains are all Spaghettigrams of the phrase, "Love and the Flying Spaghetti Monster."

## LOVE (and the FSM)

The first Love Quatrain warns of false love, "favored, tempting angel." Although the angel of false love may be pleasing and fervent, he in fact tests us.

- *Honestly! This favored, tempting angel.*
- *Soothingly venerated tempting flash.*
- *Oh My God! This fervent, pleasing talent.*
- *God In Heaven! Ample fortnightly tests.*

The second Quatrain shows us more of the angel of false love. He is handsome, hot, and shapely. But tempting as this type of love might be, the quatrain hints at a warning; the tempting angel is negligent, a flirt, stealthy, and a nymph. Partaking in love with this angel presents one with a test ("test drive").

- *Top-heavy, handsomest, negligent flirt.*
- *Test-driving of shapely, hot gentleman.*
- *Permanently invested of a ghost-light.*
- *God-given nymph of stealthier talents.*

The third and fourth quatrains reveal the true nature of the angel of false love. It is indeed Satan. And what makes this love Satanic is its filthiness and violence ("hot-tempered," "angry," "hothead," "dogfight," and "malevolent"). Indeed, the violence of false love promises a living death that can fragment even the love poets.

*Slovenly fighting hot-tempered Satan.*
*Stifling, over-the-top, shady gentleman.*
*Grindingly moth-eaten loveshaft pest.*
*O My God! Splattering heaven-sent filth.*

*Self-violent, angry, tempting hotheads.*
*Snottily avenging hot-tempered flash.*
*Malevolent, spiny dogfight threatens.*
*Honestly! Poets fragment living death.*

The final quatrain offers a glimmer of hope. The victim of false love must realize, loathe, hate his or her depravity, and recognize that false love renders one a self-tormenting ghost (sexually obsessed by his "top-heavy dangle"). Only then is true forgiveness possible. The quatrain ends with an exuberant "Tally-ho!" Of course, "Tally-ho!" is a hunting cry. When fox hunters sight a fox, they shout "tally-ho" to urge their hounds for a vigorous chase. Thus we learn that forgiveness is not an end in itself, but a "tally-ho" that urges us to pursue the hunt for Satan and his false love.

- *Strangely hating of this development.*
- *Ghost self-loathing, tiny depravement.*
- *This self-tormenting, top-heavy dangle.*
- *Forgiveness and the tempting tally-ho.*

**ABSTINENCE (and the FSM)**

One might reasonably surmise that the FSM advises abstinence. However Wisdom Spaghettigrams for "Abstinence and the Flying Spaghetti Monster" revealed a different message. Abstinence is a frightening, stony-faced, flashy, misbegotten, pedantic, and disenchanting bonehead.

Frightening bonehead attempts incessantly.
Stony-faced, bantering, tempting healthiness.
Flashiest, misbegotten, enchanting pedantry.
This beast of prey -disenchanting tanglement.

**COMPASSION (and the FSM)**

In His Compassion Quatrains, the FSM makes an unexpected distinction, between compassion and parody. The first quatrain celebrates the poetry and strength of compassion, its "fetching, important pleasantness."

Almighty poet's fine strength and compassion,
hypermodest neat, lightning-fast compassion,
is fetching, important pleasantness.
Oh My God!
Forthcoming, happiest and saintly gemstones.

Sharpness of temptingly magnetic sainthood.
Contrast stampedingly spoofing heathenism.
Pig self-tormented, sycophantish antagonism.
Fragment opinionated mightless sycophants.

The saintliness of compassion is contrasted with "the heathens" who parody or spoof saintly compassion. Spoofers are condemned as "pigs," "self-tormented," "opinionated," and "mightless."

- Softest idea man enchants grippingly smooth,
- hot-tempered Satanism snatchingly spoofing.
- Sad spoofing nightmare impotently chastens.
- Oh My God! Hesitant flippantness grimaces not.
- Oh My God! Ignorant pittances flash emptiness.

- Goodness! This moth-eaten, smarting flippancy.
- Hypocrite's stinging. Madman's elephant's-foot.
- Lightning-fast, moody, moth-eaten scrappiness.
- O My God! Smashing pretentions flash pittance.

Those who spoof flippantly eventually face the torment of the dogfight they have created. They are sycophants to spoofery. Their softheadness becomes chastened as they moan in penitence.

- *Pessimal dogfight torments inane Sycophant.*
- *Fat lemmings dishearten stooping Sycophant.*
- *Moaningly stropping softhead chastisement.*
- *Compassion! Moans ghastly frighted penitent*

**SERVICE (and the FSM)**

The FSM teaches us to express compassion through service to humanity.

- *Fetching, persevering, stealthy saintdom.*
- *Festively championing dearest strength.*
- *Assertive strength if gently championed.*
- *Farsightedly enchant sportive meetings.*

The five saintly qualities of good "fetching" service: *assertive, persevering, quiet (stealthy, gentle), farsighted,* and *enchanting.*

*Assertive:* Be bold in helping others. Don't wait to be asked. Offer your assistance the moment you see a need.

*Persevering:* Once you make a promise to help, follow-through and follow-up. Continue in spite of frustration and lack of recognition.

*Quiet:* Don't boast about how virtuous you are in serving others. Above all, never, **never**, say that you are performing service because of the Flying Spaghetti Monster (or that you want to share the Flying Spaghetti Monster with others, or share the Sauce.) Service is its own reward.

*Farsighted:* When you offer help, get the big picture. Offer assistance that will last. It is better to teach a woman to fish than to give her a bowl of pasta.

*Enchanting.* Don't forget to have fun. And by all means do not lose your sense of humor. If necessary, ask the FSM for "the gift of humor."

## HETEROSEXUALITY (and the FSM)

The FSM's concern with heterosexuality is not particularly lofty. Reminiscent of the health-based restrictions of the book of Leviticus, the FSM gives specific restrictions on heterosexual practices. The First Straight Quatrain notes that young heterosexuals experiment, often hastily, with various sexual practices at times seen as taboo.

- Softheartedly experimental,
  hastiest young thing.
- Toughish anal-sex torments,
  hyperelegant fetidity .
- Frightened, naughty oral-sex
  hesitates impotently.
- Youngest faintheart threatens,
  explodes mightily.

There are risks to this experimentation. Sex hygiene and the advice of sexology get “thrown out of the window” (defenestrate). Such risk-taking is essentially defeatist.

- False-heartedly snotty,
  thuggish experimentation.
- Triumphantly defenestrating
  heathiest sexology.
- Stoutheartedly hating self-important
  sex hygiene.
- Expertly soothing defeatism
  threatens naughtily.

Self-proclaimed sex experts often compound the problem. Experts with their own sexual conflicts may utter threats. Poor advice may seem flashy. Advice from well-meaning female mother-figures may be uninformed, and further agitate the problem. Even expert professionals contribute to the problem with exhortations that often seem excessively sentimental to young heterosexuals.

- *Oh My God! Filthiest expert threatens nauseatingly.*
- *Tauntingly threaten flashiest expertise. Oh My God!*
- *Inexpertly enthusing motherly softheads agitate.*
- *Hypersentimental egghead exhortations stultify .*

This can end in exhaustion and drug abuse, as vividly and poignantly portrayed on the following page.

- *Hyperemotionally exhausting defeatist strength.*
- *Goodnight! Shiftily exasperate ethylene tantrums.*

**HOMOSEXUALITY (and the FSM)**

Unlike many of the world's deities, the FSM is quite sympathetic to homosexuality and is fully attuned to the current struggles of gays and lesbians. The first Gay Quatrain begins with an exuberant celebration of those who experiment with their homosexual inclinations. The quatrain ends with an observation that of all the sources of morality-figures in the world, mothers provide explanations that truly satisfy. Indeed, gays often "come out" to their mothers, receiving support that strengthens and toughens their resolve to be true to themselves.

- *O My God! Healthful, tasty, astonishing experiment.*
- *My exponential, sought-after, almighty hedonists.*

*Handsomely satisfying to experimental thought.*

*Motherly-toughened explanations might satisfy.*

The second Gay Quatrain provides an observation of the long sad history of oppression of gays and lesbians, and an exhortation to gay liberation. It begins with the image of the mental hospital, an obvious reference to ancient condemnations of homosexuality as a mental illness. With a weary, sad, cry of encouragement ("Heigh-ho!"), the quatrain notes that even in the dark past, examples of tolerance of homosexuality surprisingly (mystifyingly) exist. The third pastic verse triumphantly rejects oppression ("Goodnight!") and proclaims militancy, as long as it is expertly and healthily pursued. This quatrain ends with a goal: breaking out of the closet ("exposing almighty stealthy hedonism") and freely embracing the rights gays have long sought.

*I'm sexy, softhearted*
*young thing mental hospital.*

- Heigh-ho! Outstanding, tolerant
  examples mystify.
- Goodnight! Famously expert,
  heathy militantness.
- Dashingly sexy, sought-after,
  hot implementation.
- Exposing almighty fortunate,
  stealthy hedonism.

# CHAPTER 6

## The Seven Deadly Sins Revisited

The Seven Deadly Sins were first articulated in the sixth century by St. Gregory the Great and have served as a bedrock for human morality. Gregory listed the sins according to seriousness, the degree to which they offended against God. The least serious sin is Lust, the most serious, Pride. Remember that this chapter contains Wisdom Spaghettigrams ("Lust and the Flying Spaghetti Monster," etc)

### LUST (and the FSM)

If you need proof of the existence of the FSM, consider the vivid and honest quatrains on the perils of lust.

- *Harlot's deftly tempting naughtiness.*
- *Genital's snotty, thumping self-hatred.*
- *Strongest, ill-fated, naughtiest nymph.*
- *Fat, thrusting, smelling spotted hyena!*

- *Fellations steady thumping strength.*
- *Unpretty delight of smashing talents.*
- *Painfully gnashed tightest torments.*
- *Ungently spitting fathomless hatred.*

- *Tightest, stealthy superman fondling.*
- *Ghastly, dishonest, tempting flaunter.*
- *Half-shy, spurting, dottiest gentleman.*
- *Spendthrift genitals molest naughty.*

## GLUTTONY (and the FSM)

The Flying Spaghetti Monster has much to say about the temptations and "tanglements" of Gluttony. Indeed, one might speculate that the FSM is particularly sensitive to gustatory abuses of His noodly appendages and accompanying meatballs. In a style perhaps reminiscent of earlier books of the Old Testament, He refers to overeaters as "fat," "pigs," "hogs," "stupid," "fatheads," "simpletons," "filthy," "toads," and "thugs." Indeed, the sheer passion of the following quatrains is remarkable. If the FSM were not a deity, one might suspect He has issues.

Goodnight! Stupefying tasty enthrallment.
Damn-fool, petty thug threatens stingingly.
hoggishly taunting and petty self-torment.
Honestly! Gratifying, hot, stupid tanglement.

Goodnight! Filthy, unpretty, gentle Satanism.
Petty self-torment and hoggishly taunting.
Ungently frightens ghastly impotent toad.
This old-fogyish, unpretty, giant tanglement.

Goodnight! Fat nymph stutters inelegantly.
Deftly steaming snaringly potent thought.
Maggot's snotty, deathly, unrepenting filth.
Torpidity of ghastly enthusing tanglement.

Goodnight! Smelly, petty, unhesitant farting.
Fool tempting turgently nasty nightshade.
Maggot's snotty, deathly, unrepenting filth.
Hot grunting toadyish self-pity tanglement.

Goodnight! Surely stealthy, tempting infant.
Farsightedly spouting hot tiny tanglement.

## GREED (and the FSM)

The words of the FSM concerning greed are subtle and difficult. Noodologists still ponder their meaning.

- *Spendthrift egotism = deathly gangrene.*
- *Tight-fisted ape-men strangle hydrogen.*
- *A frightened, strengthened polygamist.*
- *Emptiest Neanderthal frightens doggy .*

## SLOTH (and the FSM)

Here the FSM is clear. To be slothful is to be a filthy, petty, filthy, strange, and ghastly demon. He clearly admonishes us to avoid the frightening path of the simpleton and renounce the delights of stagnation and listlessness.

- *Goodnight! Threaten fat, listless nymph.*
- *Stagnate – Petty filth or slashing demon?*
- *Strangest, half-shy, omnipotent delight.*
- *Ghastly (not hated) simpleton frightens*

## ANGER (and the FSM)

Anger leads to hatemongering and dogfights. No matter how justified ("prettified") anger may seem, it is ultimately the haggling nonsense of a mad hatter, the threats of someone with the mind of the Gestapo. Indeed, it is Satan himself who frightens with his pesty, ranting, pedantic, temper. The FSM makes brief reference to the link between sexual frustration and anger, possibly an early prophecy of the works of Sigmund Freud.

- *Lightning-fast present-day hatemonger.*
- *Prettify mad hatter nonsense haggling.*
- *Damn Gestapo threatens frighteningly.*
- *Seethingly transparent, mean dogfight.*

- *Hot-tempered Satan nags frighteningly.*
- *Oh Man! Rantingly stage-frightened pest.*
- *Amen! This pedantry threatens flogging.*
- *Frighten straggly and moth-eaten penis.*

## JEALOUSY (and the FSM)

Noodlological excavations have unearthed a fragment of FSM's insights concerning jealousy. But His intent is clear. Jealousy is an entanglement and fetish. The jealous person is a filthy goat.

- *Filthy jeopardy goatishness tanglement.*
- *Oh My God! Stagnant fetishes jeer pliantly.*

## PRIDE (and the FSM)

The sin of pride may seem quite innocent. In our self-indulgent society, it is right-minded to be happy over that which glitters and gleams. We pridefully boast of our virtues and possessions. Our lives become poems in which we spend lavishly on self-aggrandizement.

- *Right-minded happy neatness of glitter.*
- *Happy! Finest red-hot, strident gleaming.*
- *Handiest, gleaming spendthrift poetry.*
- *Sharpest dignity of permanent delight.*

But the sin of pride is flashy and shallow. Pride is ghastly, petty, posing, ignorant, and degrades one's deepest humanity. Pride leads to anger and grim disheartenment.

- *The petty-minded, pig-ignorant flashers.*
- *Ghastly frighted and impenitent poser.*
- *Angry of tight-lipped disheartenments.*
- *This floppy, degrading man-in-the-street.*

Pride in its worst form is a "grim pedantry," a narrow ostentatious adherence to formal rules, the "me first" rules of an indulgent society. But ultimately pride is "pestilent nightshade," the detested poison that should frighten all of us.

- *Grim pedantry of pestilent nightshade.*
- Detested . . . *rampantly frighting phonies.*

# CHAPTER 7
## World Religions and the Flying Spaghetti Monster

World religions offer many paths to salvation from sin and evil. The FSM's observations of this eternal human struggle provide important guidance to us all. Again, this chapter presents Wisdom Spaghettigrams ("Salvation and the Flying Spaghetti Monster," etc.).

### SALVATION (and the FSM)

In the Salvation Quatrains, the FSM reminds us of the reality of sin and evil, the frightening "pestilence" of Satan. We may suffer the illusion that we are enslaved by a strong and omnipotent evil. But the Satan that frightens is not all-powerful; in mocking tones, the FSM exposes the true weakness of Satan; he is "flailing," "smarty-pants," "fathead," and "idiot savant."

- *Oh My God! Valiant, pestilent Satan frightens.*
- *God In Heaven! Hottest flailing smarty-pants.*
- *Omnipotently enslaving straight fatheads.*
- *Manly strength of the pleasing idiot savant.*

However, the bondage of evil is not to be slighted. A life of sin is nothing less than a "stagnant living death," one that enslaves our spontaneity with madness, phoniness, and shrill defeatism.

- *Masterly, stagnant of phoniest living death.*
- *Stifling ornament delights top-heavy Satan.*
- *Half-mad or enslaving tightest spontaneity.*
- *Not shrilling top-heavy, stagnant defeatism.*
- *Flashingly. Nightmare's potent devastation.*

What then is the promise of salvation? Salvation is the finest, safest, right path, which to the righteous is tempting. Only through salvation one can attain "hot gladness." And the key to salvation is vigilance, innovation, and honesty ("fine, sharp statements"). That is, be ever alert to the possibility of sin. Be creative in combating sin. And above all, live with courageous honesty.

- *Oh My God! Finest tantalising relevant paths.*
- *Right and safest halo innovates temptingly.*
- *Hypervigilant attainments of hot gladness.*
- *Valiantly fine, sharp statements. Goodnight!*

**CHRISTIANITY (and the FSM)**

Christianity is an ancient, rich, and complex religion, with many factions, denominations, and sects. FSM quatrains on a person who can at times be found in all of Christianity, the follower who seeks favor from the Almighty through self-serving, slavishly submissive, flattery – the Sycophant. The FSM sees the strident and "high-and-mighty" Sycophant as a threat to the true meaning and deep "enigma" of Christianity. Fueling the passion of the Sycophant is a defeatist nightmare of an imagined threat of godless hedonism. In language strangely reminiscent of the Book of Revelation, the third quatrain likens the Sycophant to a filthy piranha or a spotted hyena. The point is clear; although the Sycophant's attempts at "strident, tight-fisted tyranny" to dominate Christendom may superficially seem "nifty" or "trendy," they are ultimately destructive. The FSM even likens the Sycophant to the "Almighty-hating" Antichrist.

The final quatrain offers hope. FSM sees the virtue of chastity as an answer to strident sycophantry. It is through chastity that the Almighty inspires strength, "mightily shattering the hyperconfident Satanist." Here are the pastic quatrains for "Christianity and the Flying Spaghetti Monster."

- Almighty Sycophant is threatening, if strident
- This mortifying pittance threatens dashingly.
- Craftily nastiest high-and-mighty pretentions.
- Sycophantly thirsting in defeatist nightmare.

- Nightmares prettify itchingly hedonist Satan.
- Moth-eaten tidy Satanist frightens chirpingly.
- Shirt-lifting sycophants threaten tidy enigma.
- Fine Antichrist thrashes temptingly toadying.

- Tight-fisted tyrannies champion shatteringly.
- Nifty, earth-shattering, diligent sycophantism.
- Filthy piranhas dominate tightest stringency.
- Spotted hyena Antichrist malignity frightens

- Almighty to inspire fine strength and chastity
- Inspire mightily of chastity and neat strength.
- Thriftily endearing potent, smashing chastity.
- Mightily shattering hyperconfident Satanist.

- This deftest, inspiratory, enchanting Almighty.
- Hot might gently inspire handiest, crafty saint.
- The might enchants giftedly inspiratory saint.
- Perfect! Transmit healthy, astonishing dignity.

**CATHOLICISM (and the FSM)**

The FSM is remarkably prolific in His consideration of the Roman Catholic Church. I was surprised at the number of Spaghettigrams that emerged that make reference to the scandal of pedophilia in the priesthood. It is rare that so many quatrains emerge on a single theme.

The Priestly Quatrains begin with a prelude, one that notes that true and "farsighted contemplation" reveals a deep problem in the Church. It is a problem that indeed evokes a direct complaint from the Flying Spaghetti Monster himself ("mighty tentacles" = "noodly appendages"). The problem involves a sickening ("stomach ache") and frightening temptation, one that is so short-sighted that it is unaware of long-term consequences.

*Farsighted contemplation chastens mightily.*
*Frostiest high and mighty tentacles complain.*
*Temptation frightens slidingly. Stomach ache.*
*Genital's filthy, short-sighted accompaniment.*

The FSM proclaims a "mightily fondling chastisement catastrophe" – the crisis of pedophilia in the priesthood. It is also a crisis of leadership, which has too often responded with chastisement. Although church officials foolishly succumb to the temptation of responding with scathing chastisements, the worst of the pedophiles still persist with tenacity.

- *Almighty chastisements or pathetic fondling?*
- *Mightily fondling chastisement catastrophe,*
- *Foolhardily tempting, scathing chastisement.*
- *Ghastliest fondlers might champion tenacity.*

Those charged of pedophilia were first admonished to maintain their priestly vows of chastity. But such pedantic pledges create "torment," and are ultimately "toothless," a mere pittance and easily faked.

- *Chastity champions a self-tormenting delight*
- *Hammer-flinging, pedantic, toothless chastity.*
- *Fetching diplomat malingers honest chastity.*
- *Not self-loathing, shamming, decrepit chastity.*
- *Smallest high and mighty of corniest pittance.*

In the judgement of the FSM, church officials have "splotched" their response. Often, through misguided empathy, they have simply looked the other way. Sometimes their lack of response was a result of ignorance of the extent of the problem. The FSM correctly notes that dogmatic proclamations have shifted incompetently, at times blaming priests, the media, or the sin of homosexuality. The comments of the Church have often been both hair-splitting and softheaded. In the omniscient eyes of the FSM, this is nothing less than cheating, a "faithless and slighting pantomime."

- *Empathetic Almighty not chastising fondlers.*
- *If ignorant, Almighty splotched chastisement.*
- *Dogmatical shifting thrashes incompetently.*
- *Hair-splitting softhead comments cheatingly.*
- *Faithless, crotchety and slighting pantomime.*

The FSM concludes with an ominous warning. The "chastisement catastrophe" threatens the church itself. As the "inane" Church hierarchy continues to be frightened by its distorted view of the source of the problem ("mythical splotches"), for example, the intrinsic moral evil of homosexuality or the temptation of secularism, they respond with dogmatism. Dogmatism brings with it fascist intolerance, sycophantic obedience, and "tight-fisted name-calling." When church leaders see themselves as perfect and "high and mighty," the church itself is contaminated.

This response of "slashing filth" through dogmatism is doomed to failure. The FSM sees it as a "pathetic, mightless anarchist deformation." If the church continues on this path, forces of evil (the "Anachist") will prevail, and "filth" will massacre the insincere, ineffective "mythical" penitent.

*Mythical splotches frighten inane dogmatist.*
*Complete, intolerant high and mighty fascists.*
*Sycophantism or the tight-fisted name-calling.*
*Still-perfect high and mighty contaminates so.*

*Slashing filth threatens dogmatic impotency.*
*Snatchingly pathetic, mightless deformation.*
*Anarchist's half-completed tightest ignominy.*
*Filth, massacres mythical penitent. Goodnight!*

Although the passion of these Spaghettigrams comes through clearly, some ambiguity remains concerning their intent. Seeking further illumination, I continued my pastic discourse with the FSM. Given that priests appear to be the primary concern, I decided to seek Spaghettigrams for "priests, Catholicism, and the Flying Spaghetti Monster." To my horror, the FSM replied with these Spaghettigrams. I offer the Antichrist Quatrain for your consideration.

**Priests, Catholicism, and the FSM**

*Speedingly Storming, Fathomless, Pathetic Antichrist*

*Antichrist pleases,*
*temptingly comforting shitheads.*

*Self-tormented pigsties*
*champion ghastly Antichrist.*

*Plainest, farsighted Antichrist*
*smooches temptingly.*

*Shapeless, dogmatic Antichrist*
*frightens impotently.*

## PROTESTANTISM (and the FSM)

Rearranging the letters of "Protestantism and the Flying Spaghetti Monster" gives:

- *Impotently spendthrift nightmare stagnates so.*
- *Madman's pottiest ghastly pretentions frighten.*
- *Dogfight smothers rampantly nastiest penitent.*
- *Pottiest fragmentation strengthens dampishly.*

This historical quatrain offers a simple summary of the Christian reformation, in which Protestantism broke away from Catholicism. The FSM views the pre-reformation Catholic church as a "stagnant, impotent, spendthrift, nightmare." The presiding pope, Leo X, had a somewhat unchaste love for pleasure and was responsible for many church-led deceptive money-making schemes. Perhaps this is the source of the FSM's less than flattering appraisal, "madmans, pottiest, ghastly pretensions." The reformation itself is seen as a strengthening dampish fragmentation. The term "dampish" is archaic, dating back to 1590 for being "confused, bewildered, or shocked." This appears to refer to the response of the Catholic church or early protestant leaders. Noodlological scholarship speculates that because the meaning of "dampish" dates back to about the time of the reformation itself, the Protestant Quatrain is actually an old prophesy.

## RELIGIOUS FUNDAMENTALISM (and the FSM)

- *Goddamnit! Moth-eaten frightfulness imperils nauseatingly.*
- *Maggot's frumpish defamation disheartens unintelligently.*
- *Maggot's different-shaped ornament humiliates insultingly.*
- *Filthiest, intemperate dogfight slanders unmagnanimously.*

- Hatemongering threatens smudgily
  self-pitiful damnations.
- Defamation sputters unintelligently
  god-fearing mishmash.
- Off-putting, earth-shattering demonism
  misleads ungenially.
- Oh Dear Me! Ungentlemanly,
  faultfinding, poserish stigmatist.

- Nauseatingly pummeling
  stiffish, death-dealing tormentors.
- Goddamnit! Mutteringly profligate,
  inhumane faithlessness.

Some have charged the FSM of being biased against Christianity, especially its conservative manifestations. The classic FSM mural of celestial Adam touching a noodly appendage of the FSM has by some been interpreted as an oblique reference to Michelangelo's famous painting of the Creation of Adam. However, to be fair to Pastafarians, many devout believers have seen the Holy Mother in a grilled cheese sandwich.

In an unprecedented demonstration that puts to rest all questions of bias, the FSM offers His wisdom concerning the world of religion outside of Christianity. We conclude with His quatrains on Scientology, agnosticism, and atheism.

## SCIENTOLOGY (and the FSM)

Like the Church of the FSM, Scientology is a relatively new world religion. Created in the 1952 by the great humanitarian and author L. Ron Hubbard, Scientology offers beliefs, practices, and devices dedicated to the development of the human spirit. The methods of Scientology are extremely precise. The church has evoked some controversy, and has been accused of harassing critics and former members, perhaps a reference in the following quatrain.

- *Delightsomely gratifying, topnotch neatness.*
- *Omnipotently God-fearing, ghastly tetchiness.*
- *Incompetently threatens toadyish floggings.*
- *Goodnight! Fathomlessly petty intransigence.*

**ATHEISM (and the FSM)**

Being a deity, the FSM does not have a high opinion of atheism. The Atheism Quatrains speak for themselves

- *Honestly! Nightmare's tight-fisted apeman.*
- *Nightmare's ghastly, impenitent softhead.*
- *Patiently shamming deftest high treason.*
- *Temptingly fine, short-sighted anathemas.*

- *Tightest pedantry of inelegant mishmash.*
- *Ghastly smothering impenitent fatheads.*
- *Giftedly threatening as potent mishmash.*
- *This half-shy. Maggot's pertinent dementia.*

**AGNOSTICISM (and theFSM)**

The agnostic posits that the existence of any deity, including the FSM, is unknowable. Because they cannot prove the FSM exists, they remain undecided. The FSM's displeasure with agnosticism is slightly more complex than His intense rejection of atheism.

Agnosticism is an incomplete version of atheism, a larval form of the insect, a "snaggle-toothed nymph." It is based on pragmatism and parsimony, accepting only what is practical and applying the simplest explanation. Such "tight-fisted" thinking is menacing and harassing, not a gleaming example of wisdom.

- *Satirist's magnificent, snaggle-toothed nymph.*
- *Moaningly tight-fisted, pragmatic honestness.*
- *Tight-fisted parsimony chastens not gleaming.*
- *Menacingly stooping tight-fisted harassment.*

Agnosticism is enchanting and tempting. But it is nothing more than a crafty ornament leading to catastrophe. Those who follow agnosticism are lemmings, fated ultimately to plunge into the darkness of atheism.

- *Maggot's sporting dementia enchants shiftily.*
- *This tempting ornament fascinates doggishly.*
- *Damnation! Temptingly craftiest hoggishness.*
- *Catastrophe's annoying tight-fisted, lemmings.*

## WHAT IS THE ONE TRUE RELIGION?

We have completed our tour of world religions and are ready to use the Spaghettigram to ask the question, "What is the one true religion?" However, a Spaghettigram is based on the Flying Spaghetti Monster, introducing a source of bias. To conduct my inquiry more objectively, I used the simple anagram. I began by searching for an anagram quatrain for "One true religion." The response was less than fully satisfying. "One true religion" =

*Genuine rot or lie.*
*Ignore no true lie.*
*Urine or let in ego.*
*Gooier, inner lute.*

Quickly it became clear that my strategy was flawed. I should have started with a clear, simple question "What is the one true religion?" rather than the ambiguous phrase "One true religion." Here is the anagram quatrain of "What is the one true religion?"

*Now saintlier, eerie thought.*
*Huge, torrential white noise.*
*The worthier, ingenious tale.*
*The lingerie without reason.*

I was distraught. Once again, the wisdom of the anagram planted seeds of confusion and doubt. Are the saintly thoughts of all religion nothing more than "huge, torrential white noise"? Or is this a metaphysical reference to cosmic background radiation from the Big Bang? Are the worthier, "ingenious tales" of religion simply flashy and flimsy "lingerie without reason"? Is religion akin to a fig leaf, something to perpetuate ignorance, or hide the embarrassing truth? I decided to get to the point: "Who is the one true God?"

*The Wooden Righteous*

I had enough. Clearly my journey had to take a different course. It was time to examine the creation of the universe.

# CHAPTER 8

## Did the Flying Spaghetti Monster Create the Universe?

High school science classes across the nation are blessed with an abundance of creation theories. Major theories include: (See wikipedia.com for details.)

- ***Monkey Theory***. According to Darwin, humans evolved from monkeys. All life on Earth evolved through a process of natural selection.
- ***Humpty Dumpty Theory***. The universe began as a cosmic egg, which was broken into halves, the sky and the earth (Taoism).
- ***Genesis Theory***. God created the universe in 6 days, and rested on the seventh. This happened a few thousand years ago. (Christian Bible)
- ***Panspermia Theory***. The god Atum self-fellated and expectorated thereby creating a god and goddess, Shu and Tefnut, who then became parents of all the elements of the world. (Egyptian)

- ***Monkey-Spank Theory***. The god Ptah, creator of the universe, maintains cosmic "order" through constant masturbation. (Egyptian)
- ***Monkey-Spank Theory - 2***. The god Osiris resurrects himself through masturbation. (Another Egyptian theory)
- ***Heavy Breathing Theory***. Innumerable universes come and go as God breathes. One cycle of time is 4.3 billion years. Breathing is slow and heavy. (Hindu)
- ***Hollow Noodle Theory***. Supernatural beings originally lived underground. A flood forced them to crawl to the surface of the earth through a hollow straw, where they re-created the world. (Navajo)
- ***Jolly Green Giant Theory***. Odin, the chief god, and his brothers killed Ymir, the hated creator of the race of evil frost giants. The resulting flood of blood killed the frost giants. They then recycled Ymir's remains by creating the world, making lakes and seas out of the blood, mountains from the

bones, rocks from teeth and bone fragments, trees from his hair, the sky from his skull, and clouds from his brains. (Norse)

- ***FSM Theory***. The FSM created the universe, starting with a mountain, trees, and a "midgit."

The astute reader may notice that FSM theory in fact incorporates all intelligent design theories, and is really a ***Grand Unified Theory of Everything***. Here it is in full:

> *The FSM, a tiny naked singularity, crawled out of a wormhole and created the universe in six days of continuous deep breathing and self-pleasuring. Having no partner, (Atum, Ptah, and Osiris were out) he spewed forth cosmic quantities of matter in one cataclysmic bang, thereby creating mountains, trees, a midgit, and a giant. Then he smashed a huge egg over the giant's head and killed it, creating seas out of its blood, mountains from bones, rocks from teeth, trees from hair, and the sky and clouds from his skull and brains. All is bound together by a subatomic sticky stringy substance, (sort of resembling overcooked spaghetti).*

Proponents of various creation theories might find common ground by attacking FSM Theory as the great *Pastafarian Heresy.* (“*Aha! Ferny as pirates.*” “*Ha! Satan's fiery rape.*” “*Rainy as a sheep fart.*”)

Our first quatrain refers to those who question FSM Theory. Many may recognize parts of FSM theory as gifted. However, they berate these gifts as cheap mutterings. Those who speak enthusiastically of the FSM are seen as hot-headed. Even worse, their hot-tempered enthusiasm is empty of any real substance, it is truly eviscerated. Perhaps because such emptiness is attracting such a fervent following, it is seen as frightening. Maybe it is because there is an element of truth in the FSM that is frightening to some. This is succinctly expressed in the following Spaghettigrams of “Did the Flying Spaghetti Monster Create the Universe?”

*God In Heaven!*
*Thirstiest mutterer cheapens giftedly.*

*Frighteningly eviscerated,*
*hot-tempered enthusiast.*

Opponents view the FSM belief system as a lie, a deception. Furthermore, it distorts and disfigures profound truths, making it profoundly defective. One might call such a distortion a heresy or blasphemy, one that is potentially earth-shattering for truly righteous believers. Such critical vehemence is revealing, suggesting that perhaps the FSM has touched a nerve.

*Honestly! Deceptive,*
*earth-shattering disfigurement.*
*Supereminently defective,*
*earth-shattering dog shit.*

Just who are the proponents of the FSM? They are artists who cleverly create instructive, glittering beauty. They are truly enthusiastic, tough, and even tigerish. As individuals they are extremely modest. But they work best, and acquire their power, by working as a team. As a collective, they attain their true-hearted might. The team of FSM believers is distinctive and truly elegant.

It is loose and free, not bound by any strict catechism or dogma. It is fluid, every growing and ever changing.

- Chief venerated hypermodest,
  glittering enthusiast.
- Cleverest and mightiest, hyperfine,
  toughened artist.
- Fervently toughened tigerish,
  chastened team spirit.
- Hyperelegant distinctiveness of
  true-hearted might.

## The creative process of searching

- Artistic renegades inspire
  vehemently deft thought.
- Perfect! Heathiest gestures
  innovate right-mindedly.
- That clever thought inspires
  gifted, serene dynamite.
- Thriftiest, hyperelegant,
  tough-minded creativeness.

**Supernatural inspiration for FSM.**

The words of the FSM are divinely inspired. Not through prayer, channeling, or the random skids of a Ouija boards, but by the very mystical essence of the anagram.

- Gifted inspirer:
  mysteries enchant elevated thought.
- Perfect! Tenderest almighty innovates
  erudite highs.
- In Heaven! The purehearted mystic
  glitters finest.
- Perfect! This divinest, true-hearted,
  gleaming honesty.

- Perfect! Heaven-sent artists
  ride mightily toughened.
- The truest, perfectionist,
  right-minded, heavenly sage.
- Giftedly intercept this heaven-sent,
  righteous dream.

- Finest sturdily right-hearted,
  heaven-sent, poetic gem.

## Dealing with disbelievers

- Hyperfine underachievement delights to strategist.
- Stage-frightened creativity nonetheless triumphed.
- Tough representatives enchant delighted mystifier.
- Truer heavenly poet drenches
  gifted, mightiest saint.

## Courage, passion, and play

- Hyperelegant distinctiveness of
  true-hearted might.
- Heigh-ho! Perfect angel's truest
  and divinest temerity.
- Patiently vehement, farsighted, righteous stridence.
- Vehement nectar inspires giftedly steadier thought.

- Perfect! Divinest,
  toughened, earth-shattering smiley.
- Perfect! Light-hearted
  eruditeness innovates mighty.
- Prettily achieved funniest,
  right-hearted gemstones.
- Tenderhearted, magnetic thought
  inspires festively.

## The future of the FSM

- Amen! The perfect thought
  deserves saintlier dignity.
- Perfection! Dashingly true-hearted,
  mightiest events.

# CHAPTER 9

# Pastafarian Prophecies and the End of the World

*Once long ago a famous psychic wanted to supply final proof of her extraordinary powers. She decided to write one prediction for the following year, seal the prediction in an envelope, and place the envelope in a bank's safe deposit box. She then gave the key to the box to a trusted skeptic with these instructions: "You may open the box and read my prediction only after my death. My prediction will already have come true, proving that I am the real thing." Two decades later the psychic died a natural death. The skeptic opened the box and read the prediction. "Years before my departure there will be great flood in the desert to the south." Indeed, there was a flood, and the skeptic announced he was now a believer*

This fictional story illustrates a type of prediction, one sealed, saved, and opened at a later date. Some Spaghettigrams are prophecies, sealed in an anagram, only to be opened after the predicted event. In this chapter we "open the envelopes" and examine if the predictions have come to pass. We will look for predictions for months in the year 2005. For predictions for March, we will examine Spaghettigrams for the words "The Flying Spaghetti Monster and March." For June, we will look at "The Flying Spaghetti Monster and June." In other words, we will incorporate months into Wisdom Spaghettigrams.

What were the most notable people-events in 2005? On March 4, Martha Stewart was released from prison. On June 13, Michael Jackson was found not guilty of child molestation. And on October 19 the trial of Saddam Hussein began. Here are Wisdom Spaghettigrams for each of these months. Can you match them?

**Spaghettigram Set #1**

- *Fighter Handsomely Matching Patterns*
- *Stonyhearted, tempting, charming flash.*
- *Tone-deaf thrashing charms temptingly.*
- *Terms torment chasten highly-paid fang.*

## Spaghettigram Set #2

- Annoyed, Flashing Thumping Jet-setter.
- Judgement frightens insolent apathy.
- Fleeting adjustments in ethnography.
- Jauntiest, elegant ghost-finder nymph.
- Jaunty, spendthrift, healing gemstone.

## Spaghettigram Set #3

- Hoggishly Content-free, Impotent Bastard.
- Phoniest bogey-man clatters not frighted.
- Sonofabitch! Piggledy torment threatens.
- Obscene dogfight threatens importantly.
- Frighteningly as sabre-toothed contempt.

- Ghastly feared not-so-bright incompetent.
- Frostbitten, hot-tempered, clashing agony.
- Importantly botching together. Deafness.
- Shiftingly anger sabre-toothed contempt.

Who creates “handsomely matching patterns,” is rich and notorious for being both charming and cold-hearted? Who was chastened and tormented with a prison term? Spaghettigram Set #1 is for March and refers to Martha Stewart.

To continue, who is the jaunty spendthrift, who is frightened and insolent like a “nymph” or child? It could only be Michael Jackson. Yes, these are the June Spaghettigrams.

Finally, who is the hot-tempered “bastard” “sonofabotch” who angrily threatened torment? Who is incompetent, botching his Sabre-rattling. Saddam Hussein, the October Spaghettigrams.

## Looking into the Future

What about the future? The FSM offers two prophetic quatrains containing Spaghettigrams of “Prophecies of the Flying Spaghetti Monster.” Both appear to comment on the future of Pastafarianism. Perhaps some future mean-spirited “spoofter” will offer a tasteless parody of the FSM. Is there a hint of scandle, possibly involving photos?

- *High-flier tempting spoofery chastens poet.*
- *Spiffing ego-trip smothers healthy potence.*
- *Geronimo! The spiffier, gentlest psychopath,*
- *morosely frightens fetching, happiest poet.*

- *Fleeting photography smirches finest poet.*
- *Hypertense filth of pathetic gossipmonger.*
- *Mightier, pleasing hot-off-the-press potency.*
- *Photographs no fiercely tempting fetishes.*

### The End of the World

For ages humankind has attempted to predict how things eventually will turn out. The scholarly study of the end of the world is called **eschatology**. Some read tea leaves (called "tasseography"). Some may look for mysterious patterns in numbers ("numerology"). The Flying Spaghetti Monster approach is much more direct. I now share with you the ominous Wisdom Spaghettigrams for "The Flying Spaghetti Monster's Eschatology." This quatrain foretells how the world will end.

- *Yo-ho-ho! Tempting sage frightens tactlessly.*
- *Stealthy if splotchy, moth-eaten grogginess.*
- *Greatest Sycophants might fool seethingly.*
- *The stealthy, tiresome, Sychophant floggings*

The Flying Spaghetti Monster warns us that the world will be destroyed by Sycophants, those who follow their religion with blind obedience. They will tempt us by appearing to be wise sages. In truth, these sycophants are seething with anger and very foolish. But they will frighten us. And, with stealth, they will flog and destroy us.

Should we take seriously the prophecies of an edible deity? For an answer we now turn to science.

# CHAPTER 10

# Science and the Spaghettigram

There is a great mystery underlying this book. How can it be that over one hundred anagrams of the Flying Spaghetti Monster convey vivid and coherent wisdom? What are the processes underlying the Spaghettigram? In this chapter we look at the scientific evidence.

## The Law of Parsimony and the Supernatural

The FSM is a deity. As a deity it is omniscient (all-knowing), omnipresent (everywhere), and omnipotent (all-powerful). Therefore, the FSM can do pretty much what it wants in any way it wants. All we can do is accept it with faith. This is by far the simplest explanation of the Spaghettigram. Science routinely teaches us to follow the "law of parsimony," use "Occam's razor," and go with the simplest explanation.

The supernatural perspective is supported by the "argument of original design." To explain, the universe began as a big bang, in which everything was at first a slurry of energy. Then at some point, energy cooled down into particles. Particles quickly self-arranged into atoms of elements. Elements became worlds, life evolved on worlds, and human life emerged. Humans created ideas.

At the dawn of human consciousness ideas were like the energy at the onset of the big bang. Once these ideas began to condense into words or expressions, the potential for anagrams began. It is incomprehensible that hydrogen atoms 15 billion years ago would evolve into humans today who create the name of a deity, The Flying Spaghetti Monster, which can yield a coherent and deeply religious message. Therefore the FSM is a deity and Spaghettigrams have meaning.

## Messages from the Subconscious

The subconscious is very powerful and influences everything we do. Seemingly innocent slips of the tongue ("I said fraud? Sorry, I meant 'Freud.' No, I really meant frog." ) have unconscious meaning. So do dreams. When we cast a Spaghettigram, the subconscious directs how we arrange the letters and the meanings we ascribe the resulting phrases. The Spaghettigram, like a dream, is how the subconscious communicates with us.

### The Occult Sciences

The occult sciences have developed hundreds of systems for foretelling the future and seeking wisdom. For example, numerologists look for repeating patterns in numbers that have hidden messages. (The first, middle, and last name of Ronald Wilson Reagan each contain 6 letters. "666" is the sign of the devil. When Reagan and his wife retired, they moved to 666 St. Cloud Street, which Nancy Reagan changed to 668. Therefore Ronald Reagan was the devil.)

There are many other systems of divination, including those on the following page. (These are real. See Carroll, 2003).

***Aeluromancists*** drop pancakes in water, and seek knowledge in the underwater shapes they take.

***Anthropormancists*** once examined the organs of recently sacrificed humans.

***Bronchiomancists*** studied the lungs of dead llamas for wisdom.

***Eschatologists*** study the end of the world.

***Gyromancists*** note how one tumbles after walking in circles very fast and getting very dizzy. This direction can be used to answer questions.

***Metoposcopists*** read forehead wrinkles.

***Onchomancists*** read messages from reflections of the sun off of fingernails.

***Ovomancists*** study what happens to an egg when it breaks. The manner in which egg contents spill often conveys a message.

***Tasseographists*** read tea leaves.

***Tiromancists*** ready the moldy holes in cheeze.

***Uromancists*** read the bubbles in urine.

The number of occult systems for reading hidden messages is truly amazing. In each an apparently neutral physical process, (movement of stars, falling objects, reflection of light, the process of decay) outside of conscious or unconscious control, generates patterns with messages. What is the scientific explanation for this?

For each occult procedure there is a brief moment when the outcome is up to chance (the moment the tea is tossed into a cup). A Tasseographist does not carefully position each tea leaf in the cup. He or she lets them fall by chance.

Parapsychologists have studied similar events for decades. The scientific study of ESP examines whether one can read the thoughts of another person. Psychokinesis involves making changes in the physical world through thoughts (bending spoons by looking at them). Remote viewing involves seeing events from a distance, without the use of telescopes or cell phones. As with occult procedures, paranormal phenomena also involve brief moments of chance. Bending a spoon takes only an instant.

However, scientific theory tells us that something very mysterious can happen during brief moments of chance. What is chance? All events are either the result of cause and effect physical processes, or the result of chance. All cause and effect processes operate within the three dimensions and reflect the laws of physics. Therefore, chance events operate outside of the three dimensions and beyond the laws of physics. But then what causes these chance events? The answer is unavoidable: forces and energies outside of our dimensional universe and beyond the laws of physics.

When the chains of cause and effect are strongest, we are most bound to our three-dimensional universe and are least likely to encounter mysterious forces from beyond. If you drop and egg into a hot frying pan, it will fry. Miracles do not happen to fried eggs. There is little opportunity for anything mysterious to happen.

It is during moments in which chance appears to be operating that forces beyond the cause-effect universe can intrude. Brief acts of divination, and short parapsychological demonstrations, provide fleeting moments for forces from beyond to have an effect. Because of this brevity, the otherworldly effect is hard to detect. Science supports this conclusion.

In contrast, Spaghettigrams can reveal enormous otherworldly effect. Each Spaghettigram is actually the result of centuries of many moments of uncertainty. The coin of chance was tossed many times before a Spaghettigram emerges in its final form.

Take the combination of words, "Flying Spaghetti Monster." What events led up to the creation of this phrase, and its hundreds of pastic meanings? Some time in the past, the letters "f l y i n g ,“ "s p a g h e t t i," and "m o n s t e r" were put together to form words. These were events permeated with uncertainty and chance. (What toss of the dice led to“spaghetti” and not “spageti”?) Centuries earlier, the precise form of each component letter emerged. A certain vertical squiggle of lines became the letter “s” and not “z,” and so on. Even before letters were invented, humans began articulating distinct sounds and gestures with meaning. One grunt became a word, another grunt was forgotten. Before that, a series of events led to the development of a brain that could produce meaningful sounds and gestures. In other words, if you look at the big picture, the phrase “Flying Spaghetti Monster” is the product of hundreds of little moments of uncertainty. Taken together these little moments add up to a great Golden Window of Uncertainty, open wide to the mysteries from beyond. In contrast, dropping an egg is just a crack, open only for an instant.

It is because of this difference that Spaghettigrams have much more meaning than other forms of divination. Spaghettigrams have more time to absorb messages that come from the mysterious universe of chance and uncertainty. It is the difference between leaving a dry pot of flowers in the rain for five minutes or for five hours. When the soil is moistened, the flowers remain dry; when the soil is soaked, the flowers grow. A Spaghettigram is soaked with supernatural and paranormal energy. Tea leaves get only a sprinkle. The great golden window of uncertainty that characterizes Spaghettigrams opens wide to influences from beyond.

A warning. Explanations involve words, and words are three dimensional. The paranormal and supernatural exist beyond three dimensions. Therefore, Spaghettigram quatrains often seem terse and enigmatic, as if they are missing an occasional noun or verb. This is a very simple problem that is easily explained. Science tells us that transmission of complex information inevitably involves a degree of signal degradation and noise. One can surmise that this problem is compounded when the transmission is transdimensional. Given their origin, it is truly remarkable that Spaghettigrams make as much sense as they do. This is additional evidence of their truthfulness.

## Reference

Carroll, R. T. (2003). *The Skeptic's Dictionary*. Hoboken, NJ: Wiley

# CHAPTER 11

## Truth or Mockery?

Are the Spaghettigrams of this volume true wisdom, or a mockery of religion?

### Sheer Volume of Wisdom

This volume contains, not one or two pithy sayings, but over one hundred pages of profoundly meaningful Spaghettigrams. What fool would actually spend time generating so many pages of fabricated wisdom? This volume is evidence of the truthfulness of Spaghettigrams. You can't argue with large numbers.

### Spaghettigrams Do Not Lie

First, Spaghettigrams do not lie; people lie. Ask any priest or preacher if any anagram has lied to them. I doubt few, or any, can actually cite an instance in which they were the victim of deliberate anagrammic deception. Let's turn to a quatrain of Spaghettigrams of the phrase "Spaghettigrams do not lie":

- *I'm the grandest apologist.*
- *Oh Dear Me! Tattling gossip.*
- *Phoniest, large dogmatist.*
- *Impotent as large dog shit.*

Although there is little to question here, some might find this quatrain a little obscure. A deeper analysis is more revealing. A Spaghettigram is fundamentally an anagram. Therefore an anagram of the phrase "Anagrams never lie" should be more directly revealing than an anagram of "Spaghettigrams do not lie." Indeed, this is the case, as shown below. "Anagrams never lie" reveals:

- *I am an angel server.*
- *An evil me arranges.*
- *Inane marvels rage*
- *Ravage lame sinner.*

**What about the Inconsistencies?**

FSM skeptics complain about inconsistencies. How is it that one Angelic Omniscient Spaghettigram (anagram of the "Flying Spaghetti Monster") is: *Self-tormenting hasty pig?*

Is that not proof that the Flying Spaghetti Monster is a sham? How can a deity be self-tormenting and hasty? How can a deity be a pig? Careful noodlological analysis of this Spaghettigram reveals several answers:

1. Even if this Spaghettigram perceives the FSM as a pig, pigs are real. Therefore, the FSM is real. If the FSM is real, His Spaghettigrams are real.
2. "Self-tormenting" is actually an anagram of "Finest long-term." Therefore, the Spaghettigram is actually "Finest, long-term, hasty pig."
3. If we perform a test that is even more severe, and subject all of the apparently disparaging words of this Spaghettigram to the toughest level of analysis, we find that "self-tormenting hasty" opens up to: "Hefty, strong, manliest." Therefore deeper analysis

solves the mystery of the troubling Omniscient Spaghettigram.

4. Finally, who says it is bad to be a pig? The pig is perhaps one of the smartest animals on the planet. They make fine pets and can be taught to perform tricks. There is a profound wisdom literature on pigs (see *Charlotte's Web*, the wonderful story in which a spider tries to save a pig). Pigs also appear in *Three Little Pigs, Winnie the Pooh, Dr. Dolittle, The Amityville Horror, Animal Farm, Dennis the Menace*, and various nursery rhymes.

Sure, there are many apparent inconsistencies among Spaghettigrams. For those of faith, these inconsistencies are superficial. Look at the deeper message the FSM is trying to convey. At the deepest level, all words that come from the FSM are completely true.

## Spaghettigrams Warn Against Mockery

Among the Wisdom Quatrains, those dealing with compassion are among the most poignant. They clearly admonish against engaging in any form of spoofery:

- *Hot-tempered Satanism snatchingly spoofing.*
- *Sad spoofing nightmare impotently chastens .*
- *Oh My God! Hesitant flippantness grimaces not.*
- *Goodness! This moth-eaten, smarting flippancy.*

**Prophecies**

We shall see in a later chapter that the FSM has uttered a number of truly remarkable prophecies, all of which have come to pass!

**Linguistic Analysis**

Scholars of ancient texts often rely on linguistic analysis ascertain authenticity. For example, if scholars wanted to determine if Plato actually wrote a newly found book, they might consider if the types of words used in the book are from the same lexicon used by Plato. For example, imagine Plato had a history of using words like “olive tree,” “wisdom,” and “student” in his writings. If the new found book frequently uses these same words, that is evidence supporting the argument that Plato wrote the book.

Skeptics might suggest that the Spaghettigrams of this volume are actually products of the mind of the author (myself) and not from the FSM. Noodlological analysis of the entire body of my published writings (14 books and 35 articles) reveals that I have never used any of the following words, which appear prominently in the Spaghettigrams of the Flying Spaghetti Monster.

Words Never Appearing in the Collected Writings of Jon Smith

| | | | | |
|---|---|---|---|---|
| Amen | flirt | hedonists | oral sex | sloth |
| anal sex | fortnightly | hoggishly | penniless | smog |
| bantering | G-string | hydrogen | pestering | snarling |
| bonehead | gangrene | hyena | phlegm | spiny |
| damn-fool | genital | jeer | pithy | sting |
| dangle | ghastly | mad hatter | plotting | slidingly |
| depravement | gluttony | misbegotten | porn | stupefying |
| dogfight | gnashed | nagger | self-pitying | tanglement |
| egghead | grim | naughtily | serpent | thug |
| enthrallment | groans | neanderthal | shapely | thumping |
| filthy | harlot | nymph | slot | top-heavy |

## A Putdown of Religion

Is the FSM putting down other religions? Not at all! The FSM has greatest respect for all religions of the world and only seeks a mature and more compassionate faith for all. The FSM may present His own Spaghettigrams of wisdom, but He recognizes His Spaghettigrams are no more true than the volumes of Spaghettigrams produced by Christianity, Judaism, Islam, Buddhism, Hinduism, or any other religion.

# CHAPTER 12
## The Final Quatrain

In the beginning was the anagram. But it's not the creation story. If you check the very first page of this book you will find this odd observation:

*Basic Information:*

*Angelic omniscience ends.*

This is actually the last stanza of a quatrain of anagrams, one that might summarize what I'm up to:

*Basic Information*

- *Nice, insane cosmic legend . . .*
- *Concise elegance in minds.*
- *Concise seeing clean mind . . .*
- *Angelic omniscience ends.*

The Flying Spaghetti Monster is a nice-sounding cosmic legend. It may even seem concise and elegant. But it is nonetheless a mental creation, one that may well confirm our beliefs about what's good, bad, and real. In this book we played all sorts of thought-games to make this bit of insanity seem plausible. We had fun with noodlology. But if you clean your mind of expectations, biases, and distorted thinking and see the world concisely as it is, the Monster goes away:

*Angelic omniscience ends.*

Let's go a little deeper. Each of the four stanzas of our final quatrain is an anagram of the same two words (check it out yourself):

*Meaningless coincidence.*

And the title of the quatrain, "Basic Information," is an anagram for:

*Confirmation bias.*

Meaningless coincidence and confirmation bias are tools of delusion, confusion, and distraction. If you generate enough anagrams, by chance some will emerge as pithy phrases. If you toss a coin enough times, eventually you might get a run of ten heads in a row. This happens without supernatural or paranormal intervention. If you look at enough clouds in the sky, you may see an angel. And of course, there is the face on the moon, and Mars.

Nature continuously serves us a huge plate of coincidences (yes, spaghetti) that, through simple coincidence, form various patterns. Through confirmation bias we notice and remember what confirms our beliefs. This is the game we have been playing.

These are examples of the many games that pester all religion. We pick scriptures that fit our prejudices. We see coincidences as miracles. We impose our interpretations on vague religious passages. We ignore or argue away contradictions. We justify our beliefs with pseudoscience. The list goes on, as illustrated in this book.

## Are You a Practicing Pastafarian?

Every believer -- Christian, Jew, Buddhist, Muslim, or atheist -- runs the risk of becoming a practicing Pastafarian, of practicing noodlology. We all risk clouding a clear vision of the universe with our own prejudices and childish mental games. It takes discipline to "*see concisely with a clean mind.*"

And that is the real challenge of this book. Whatever your persuasion, I invite you to explore your religion, your philosophy, your spiritual perspective. Then sincerely look for anything that resembles Flying Spaghetti Monsterism. Gently put aside these Monsters of delusion, confusion, and distraction. What remains is worth taking seriously.

But there is another anagram of "meaningless coincidence" I wish to share.

*Needing nice comicalness* . . .

Truly, there is a *penalty of tight grimness.* Sometimes the better part of wisdom is to put all aside, become *empty angels* and simply smile.

# APPENDIX

## In His Own Words

## 10,000 Spaghettigrams

(from anagramgenius.com)

Scholars have identified over 2,300,000 verses* that come directly from the Flying Spaghetti Monster. No other world religion can make such a claim. The present section contains the most meaningful 10,000 verses, as identified through advanced computer analysis.** Although all FSM verses are absolutely true, the Pasta Group of Noodly Scholars has determined that 73 percent are truly true (and are printed RED in the forthcoming, expensive, leather-covered red-letter, edition of this book). The PGNS advises that you may rearrange the words in any FSM verse in any way without impacting the verse's fundamental, underlying, and often enigmatic Truthfulness.

*See *Flying Spaghetti Monster: One Million Uncensored Spaghettigrams* (Jon Smith, www.lulu.com/stress)

www.anagramgenius.com

Fine polygamist strength.
Fortnightly pig tameness.
Temptingly if to gnashers.
Frighten temptingly as so.
Gas frightens impotently.
Ghost penetrating flimsy.
Smog frightens patiently.
Ape Shit! Strongly. Figment.
Gnomishly prettiest fang.
Fine pig torments ghastly.
Molest frightening pasty.
Self-ignorant, mighty pest.
Thrifty, penniless maggot.
Prettify not hassling gem.
Self-pitying hag torments.
Self-tormenting, hasty pig.
Satisfying, rotten phlegm.
Prettify not slashing gem.
Torment naggish self-pity.
Thrifty gossip gentleman.
Y-fronts might sane piglet.
Might of petty gnarliness.
Sternest if almighty pong.
Strength if steamily pong.
Molest frightening patsy.
Potty lameness frighting.
Malign petty frightens so.
Maggoty, penniless thrift.
Honestly! Tampering gifts.
Impotently gift gnashers.
Imposingly fate strength.
Mangling thrifty poetess.
Y-fronts might genial pest.
The naggiest Y-fronts limp.
Smothering self-pity gnat.
Finest might sporty angel.
Frighten stagy simpleton.
Frighten polygamist nets.
Frighten pasty molesting.
Fights reason temptingly.
Filthy, sporting, neat gems.
Not thrifty, pleasing gems.
The gleaming Y-fronts spit.
Fine, almighty, strong pest.
Polygamist if strengthen.
Net polygamist frightens.
Gossipy thrift gentleman.
Figment hates sportingly.
Sportingly as the figment.
Gently impressing hot fat.
Flattery mightiness pong.
Frighten polygamists net.
Polygamists frighten ten.

Fight gentlest parsimony.
Gently shit sporting fame.
Ghost empty self-training.
Self-ignorant types might.
Imposingly feat strength.
Fortnightly meanest pigs.
Shiftingly part gemstone.
Prettify gnash molesting.
Glittering nymph fatsoes.
Fine arm-pits ghost gently.
Tempting if ghastly snore.
Filth or tempting gayness.
Fetish groans temptingly.
Strangely imposing theft.
Nest frighten polygamist.
Sent frighten polygamist.
Frighten saintly, top gems.
Frighten molest nasty pig.
Tipsy gleam frightens not.
I'm stately pong frightens.
Empaling snotty fighters.
Empty gainless fortnight.
Rompingly neatest fights.
Infantry phlegm egotists.
Shiftingly as potent germ.
Almighty pestering fonts.
Nightmare's spit of gently.
Slithery of tempting nags.
Stylish of tempting anger.
Style of nights tampering.
Finest ghostly tampering.
Finest merit ghastly pong.
Strength if gay simpleton.
Angry if potent mightless.
Fart hissingly potent gem.
Finer ghost as temptingly.
Frighten patsy molesting.
Polygamist frightens ten.
Saintly, top gem frightens.
Gently this sporting fame.
Ghastly, impenitent frogs.
Ghastly, omnipresent gift.
Fortnightly gems panties.
Fortnightly enigma pests.
Neat gem piss fortnightly.
Shiftingly page torments.
Prettify molest, gnashing.
Maggot's self-pity thinner.
Temptingly as on fighters.
Potty, meaningless fright.
Pertinently. Maggot's fish.
Safely tempting or nights.
Filthy, ignorant pest gems.

Neat gems pongs thriftily.
In maggot's thrifty spleen.
Hot, mean self-pity G-string.
Eight self-pity strong man.
Not trash self-pitying gem.
Stingingly of the tampers.
Tights of manly pestering.
Gnashers of it, temptingly.
Fine star hogs temptingly.
Finest arm-pits hog gently.
Finest straying to phlegm.
Filth or gay temptingness.
Neat frightens mostly pig.
Tampon leggy thriftiness.
Stylish poet fragmenting.
Stifling, neat trophy gems.
Stateliest frigg on nymph.
The timely, sporting fangs.
Simperingly hottest fang.
Gifts hoarsen temptingly.
Temptingly safe or nights.
Filthy, mean G-string poets.
Might on strange self-pity.
Printing of stealthy gems.
Tyrants of sleeping might.
Testy of smarting helping.
Ghastly torment fine pigs.
Finest strongly ape might.
Manly poets if the G-string.
Temptingly if saner ghost.
Snotty if angriest phlegm.
Flash on grim typesetting.
Lame snotty pig frightens.
Sportingly meanest fight.
Farthest, imposing, gently.
The nasty frigg simpleton.
Gently shitting safe romp.
Strongest, filthy, mean pig.
Filthy, strong pest enigma.
I'm the piglet nags Y-fronts.
Prettify might son's angel.
Smother self-pitying gnat.
The self-pitying, strong am.
Softer, slighting payment.
Nightmare of gently spits.
Penalty of stingers might.
Petty of nights malingers.
Finest armpit hogs gently.
Finest alert spongy might.
Ghastly if pertinent smog.
Nymph if strangle egotist.
Manly if the strongest pig.
Mighty farts not sleeping.

Gemstones pig thinly fart.
Finer might pongs stately.
Filth torments sane piggy.
Frighten snottily sap gem.
Figment or slashing petty.
Ghastly, impotent fingers.
In nightmare's petty flogs.
This flimsy, potent nagger.
Filthy, parting gemstones.
Filthy gemstones pig rant.
Filthy, potent am sniggers.
Shiftingly torment pages.
Y-fronts might spite angel.
Softy lightens tampering.
Prettify nag on mightless.
It isn't sharp gem of gently.
G-string of patiently mesh.
Tasty of negligent shrimp.
Gosh! Temptingly fine star.
If angel's tempting shorty.
Gently the imposing farts.
Smoggy as pertinent filth.
Fighting on masterly pest.
Not fighting sleepy smart.
Stately fighting on sperm.
I'm top as gently frightens.
Impotently nags fighters.
Thinly pig strongest fame.
Honestly pig star figment.
So slithery, tempting fang.
Fattiest or nymph niggles.
Fat pongs trim seethingly.
Seemly thirsting fat pong.
Safely torment nights pig.
Not filthy, naggiest sperm.
Filthy, tempting sons rage.
Meanest, filthy, strong pig.
Thrifty pests on gleaming.
Hefty, strong ailments pig.
I'm hefty poet stranglings.
The storming self-pity nag.
O Man! The self-pity G-string.
Pig gremlin's honest fatty.
Harems of gently spitting.
Strangely might of in pest.
Nymph of tastiest niggler.
Rattiest of nymph niggles.
Slimy strength of neat pig.
Angel's empty of thirsting.
Penalty of thirsting gems.
Helping of tatty grimness.
Fine, ratty, mightless pong.
Pong tartishly finest gem.

Finest halo empty G-string.
Strangely might if on pest.
Manly pig strongest thief.
Not frighting measly pest.
Frighten slimy, potent gas.
Frighten petty maligns so.
Nastily frighten top gems.
Spoilt frighten nasty gem.
Mangily frightens to pest.
Fertile, nasty might pongs.
Strangely misfit the pong.
Self-tormenting, pithy gas.
This sporty figment angel.
Petty figment or hassling.
Forget mighty pliantness.
I'm the sporting fang style.
Shapely gifts tormenting.
Gently pig in fat smothers.
Fat, motherly, singing pest.
Fat nymph sniggers toilet.
Might flays not pestering.
Fiery might pongs talents.
Filthy pig rants gemstone.
Tempting nag to serfishly.
Shiftingly sap rotten gem.
A hefty simpleton G-string.
Hefty, grating simpletons.
Is hefty piglet strong man.
Softly impregnate nights.
Amen! Hot self-pity G-string.
I'm the strong self-pity nag.
Self-pitying gem rants hot.
Fatty helping to grimness.
Gosh! Gently finest armpit.
Finest stealthy, grim pong.
Gently pig if honest smart.
Mangle if strongish petty.
Strangle if gnomish petty.
Pig style if the strong man.
Gemstone farts thinly pig.
Flash trim soggy penitent.
Potty, mean filth sniggers.
Not thriftless, mean piggy.
Not self-harming, testy pig.
Employ tartness fighting.
Steely tampons frighting.
Spongy flight terminates.
Manly poets frighten gits.
Slimy poets frighten gnat.
Frighten on typists gleam.
Top gem frightens nastily.
Shop-lifting, arty segment.
Ghastly figment pointers.

Figment heats sportingly.
Fleeting as sporting myth.
Self-ignorant mighty pets.
Smothering penalty gifts.
Fat pongs trimly seething.
Amen! Filthy G-string poets.
Pong thriftily sanest gem.
Fortnightly as inept gems.
Shiftingly. Trap gemstone.
This frosty pig gentleman.
Might nifty, top largeness.
Might straying felon pest.
Gently of that impressing.
I'm the gaps of stringently.
I'm the gasp of stringently.
Straggly of penitent hims.
Garishly of tempting nest.
Garishly of tempting nets.
Tempting of garishly sent.
Temptingly of this ranges.
Sisterly of tempting hang.
Strongly if emptiest hang.
Nymph if sage glitters not.
Farts ghost eminently pig.
Fart seemly shitting pong.
Thinly. Maggot's finer pest.
Storming self-hate typing.
Filth sniggers petty moan.
O Man! Petty filth sniggers.
Nagger shifts impotently.
Naggers shift impotently.
Frighten polite gymnasts.
Tens frighten polygamist.
I'm a post frightens gently.
I'm a spot frightens gently.
Manly poet frightens gits.
Slimy poet frightens gnat.
Timely frightens not gaps.
Timely frightens not gasp.
I'm spotty angel frightens.
Shop-lifting natty merges.
Naggiest stifler to nymph.
Stingingly strop the fame.
Fame tightens sportingly.
Self-tormenting, tipsy hag.
The stifling groans empty.
Tastiest flogger in nymph.
Stylish, potent, mean frigg.
Hissingly fat, potent germ.
Hey! Fat simpleton G-string.
Fat, sleepy, snorting might.
Hog frailty temptingness.
Amen! Strongest, filthy pig.

In maggot's filthy present.
Filthy, mega, snorting pest.
Neat pig mess fortnightly.
Fortnightly sap meetings.
Fortnightly enigma steps.
Mate posts frighteningly.
Post mates frighteningly.
Spot frighteningly mates.
Stop frighteningly mates.
Poet garments shiftingly.
Hefty, manliest, strong pig.
Hefty gleaming strips not.
Self-pity ranges not might.
The self-pity moan G-string.
Rant hot self-pitying gems.
Satisfy might gentle porn.
Impregnate sightly fonts.
Sightly font impregnates.
Nights of tempting slayer.
Itsy of empaling strength.
Fine, mighty starlets pong.
Might infest sporty angel.
Transpose if gently might.
Sottishly if pregnant gem.
Nymph if tersest gloating.
If strength as timely pong.
Sporty if mangiest length.
Sporty length if steaming.
Filth sniggers to payment.
Filth grossing mean petty.
Shift gently tampering so.
I'm a posts frighten gently.
Frighten potent, slim gays.
Frighten timely gasps not.
Frighten snotty, limp sage.
O My! Pig frightens talents.
Lame pigsty frightens not.
Typist frightens on gleam.
Me frightens tastily pong.
Tempting lay frightens so.
Patiently frights on gems.
Temptingly or sane fights.
Style fights on tampering.
Gossip gently mean thrift.
Stingingly farthest poem.
Farthest employ stinging.
The fame ports stingingly.
Sportingly sting the fame.
From this negligent pasty.
Gently graphs to feminist.
It fragments honestly pig.
The poet farms stingingly.
I'm the farting pongs style.

Hot flattering spiny gems.
The stifling organs empty.
Stateliest forging nymph.
Pertinent mighty flogs as.
Tyrannies flog might pest.
Seethingly trim top fangs.
Gently gift misanthropes.
Gently simpering hot fast.
The fat gems in sportingly.
Smothers pig gently faint.
Strongly safe, inept might.
Infantry poets slight gem.
Serfishly tempting tango.
Shiftingly strop neat gem.
I'm hefty poets strangling.
Shifty pig torments angel.
Lightest, mean Y-fronts pig.
The Y-fronts empaling gits.
On that self-pitying germs.
Elite fatso nymph G-string.
Soft almighty presenting.
Soften garishly tempting.
Glassy of pertinent might.
Mightiness of gently part.
Tempting of ghastly risen.
Spent of ghastly meriting.
Stylish of tempting range.
Raspingly of tightest men.
Temptingly of sane rights.
Gnarliest of nights empty.
Fine, mighty, top strangles.
Fine, masterly tights pong.
Fine might gasps rottenly.
Ghastly or tempting fines.
Infest ghostly tampering.
Gleam finest sting trophy.
If tampering hosts gently.
Gently if eight sportsman.
Gently if smothering past.
Nightmare's post if gently.
Nightmare's spot if gently.
If nightmares stop gently.
Print if ghastly gemstone.
Sleepy if tight strong man.
Openly if strangest might.
Sight if sporty gentleman.
I'm honest farts pig gently.
Homely, stinging fart pest.
Slighting fears empty not.
Finer, ghastly, tempting, so.
Not thriftless, mangey pig.
Imposingly strange theft.
Frightening posts tamely.

Mostly frightening tapes.
Mostly frightening a pest.
Frightening mops stately.
Frightening maps to style.
Spontaneity flights germ.
Frighten glassy, impotent.
So frighten mental pigsty.
Manly git frightens poets.
Timely frightens top nags.
Manly pestering to fights.
Not piggy thrift lameness.
Shop-lifting, testy German.
Sporting fame hits gently.
From slighting, sane petty.
Misfit nags gentle trophy.
Ha! Self-tormenting pigsty.
Figment gets rhinoplasty.
The poets farm stingingly.
Self-rating nymph egotist.
Fleeting myth to raspings.
Fleeting, rightmost pansy.
Poetry than stifling gems.
Giftless nymph to ingrate.
Frigg hastens impotently.
Empty in shattering flogs.
The empty straining flogs.
Forget simplest anything.
Fangs or pestilent mighty.
Seemly thirsting top fang.
Ineptly safe, strong might.
Hot pestering flimsy gnat.
Right! Neatest flimsy pong.
Mortifying, gentlest hasp.
Safely inept, strong might.
Faintly the sporting gems.
Tame filthy stingers pong.
Frighteningly tame posts.
Frighteningly tame stops.
Tampon shiftingly greets.
Poet gem rants shiftingly.
So thrifty pigs gentleman.
Hefty G-string impales not.
Tight penis Y-fronts gleam.
The frosty pest maligning.
Not hating self-pity germs.
Gosh! Nifty, gentle arm-pits.
The smarting felon pigsty.
I'm the pasty felon G-string.
Soften sightly tampering.
His tempting of strangely.
Straggle of tiniest nymph.
Pigs of thirsty gentleman.
Ha! Stingers of temptingly.

Empty of tight gnarliness.
Penalty of tight grimness.
Giants of presently might.
I'm the type of stranglings.
I'm the types of strangling.
Sportingly that fine gems.
Might fine, spongy starlet.
If nightmare posts gently.
Pest if rantingly hot gems.
Lengthy if smarting poets.
The empty if so strangling.
Petty gems if hot snarling.
If the tasty gremlins pong.
Snotty helping if star gem.
Toys if empaling strength.
Temptingly fears in ghost.
This maggot's finer plenty.
Flash grotty, eminent pigs.
Is not grey, tempting flash.
I'm petty niggers flash not.
Flash more petty stinging.
Potent, grim filth gayness.
Monster's piggy, neat filth.
Tempting toying flashers.
Self-harming petty on gits.
Natty piglet fishmongers.
No fighting masterly pest.
Not fighting seemly sprat.
Steamy frightening plots.
Poet sets manly frighting.
Seemly frighting past not.
Lightning-fast, empty sore.
Potty mastering fleshing.
Spongy flights terminate.
Mostly frighten neat pigs.
Temptingly so sane fright.
Empty not gainless fright.
Gently. Fortnight impasse.
Gently right fame piss not.
Strongly the manifest pig.
Spit honestly farting gem.
I'm fleeting, snotty graphs.
The stifling mastery pong.
Self-ignorant, empty sight.
I'm ghastly, penitent frogs.
Is the fangs or temptingly.
Rosily the tempting fangs.
Glitter so feasting nymph.
Safest, rompingly tighten.
Pesteringly fast on might.
Pesteringly might on fats.
Fat shitting pongs merely.
I'm grotty fatness helping.

Pesteringly fans to might.
Threaten flimsy gits pong.
The flimsy, sporting agent.
The flimsy, strong, neat pig.
Shit! Flimsy, potent nagger.
Length as mortifying pest.
The infamy pongs glitters.
Neatest, filthy, grim pongs.
Filthy poets name G-string.
A pong segments thriftily.
Fortnightly pest as in gem.
Fortnightly spit sane gem.
Shiftingly parents to gem.
Malign hefty, top stingers.
Amen! Lightest Y-fronts pig.
That Y-fronts spieling gem.
Shit! Pig frosty gentleman.
Prettify something slang.
The malign songs prettify.
Nag not petrify mightless.
Great! Self-pitying months.
Nifty G-string empales hot.
Malinger ghost nifty pest.
Right! Nifty, tameless pong.
Shame nifty, strong piglet.
I'm the fonts pig strangely.
The timely, grasping fonts.
Font as pesteringly might.
Gently might of star penis.
Is tempting rash of gently.
Rantingly spit of the gems.
Rantingly of this pest gem.
Mighty of inept strangles.
Rightly of a temptingness.
Nymph of glittering asset.
Nymph of glittering seats.
Manly spite of the G-string.
Ants of pesteringly might.
Enlighten of smart pigsty.
Might of persistently nag.
This petty gem of snarling.
Fine, strong almighty pets.
Finest pithy, strong gleam.
Niftiest, ghastly porn gem.
Shaggily if spent torment.
Strength if mangily. Poets.
If rot gnashes temptingly.
Prettily if not gnash gems.
Style if the smarting pong.
I'm the sons pig gently fart.
Temptingly hating so. Serf.
A gory filth temptingness.
Gay, potent filth grimness.

Neatest, spongy, grim filth.
To an empty filth sniggers.
Empty snorting filth sage.
Amen! Potty filth sniggers.
Amen! Not thriftless piggy.
My fetishes pong rattling.
Temptingly. Fetish organs.
Mostly paste frightening.
Is not petty flashing germ.
In spotty gleam frightens.
Tasty pig frightens lemon.
Partly shifting gemstone.
Sanely or tempting fights.
Shoplift yet mean G-string.
The spongy, mangiest flirt.
Gently tip strongish fame.
Stringently hot fame pigs.
Hesitant forms pig gently.
Stingingly hate from pest.
Self-torment hating Gipsy.
Gently heap strong misfit.
So strangle pithy figment.
A sporty figment lightens.
Spy something flattering.
Syren flogs patient might.
The grisly, impotent fangs.
Fangs trim honesty piglet.
Fat shops gently meriting.
Might fat glory ineptness.
Fat, homely, stringent pigs.
Fat, homely pest in G-string.
Pesteringly mights on fat.
Ineptly fat, strongish gem.
Infant gems hogs prettily.
Safe pig torments nightly.
Pertinent flimsy gags hot.
Night torments safely pig.
Potent might grins safely.
Safely pig tenth storming.
Slight infantry poet gems.
Pregnant gems to shiftily.
Potent germ nags shiftily.
Pig filthy gem on tartness.
Pig filthy gnome tartness.
Filthy, ignorant gem pests.
Frighteningly. Pest atoms.
Poets rant shiftingly. Gem.
Shiftingly top, neat germs.
Impaling strongest, hefty.
Hefty piglets on smarting.
Prettify nights mangle so.
Prettify on angel's mights.
The grim self-pity nags not.

Might nifty, tearless pong.
Nifty smothers nag piglet.
Fonts praise gently might.
Mighty of gentlest sprain.
Pest of nightly mastering.
Shrimpy of gentlest giant.
My plainest of the G-string.
Pigsty of menial strength.
Temptingly of saner sight.
Tipsy strength of in gleam.
Pansy of tightest gremlin.
Sanely of tempting rights.
Strongly might fine tapes.
Strongly might a fine pest.
Straggle to its fine nymph.
Finest mighty alert pongs.
Finest ghost grim penalty.
Finest snottily graph gem.
I'm the star if gently pongs.
If stagy helping torments.
Pigs if shorty tanglement.
Spoilt if mangey strength.
Tipsy strength if on gleam.
Molest pretty if gnashing.
If style or tempting gnash.
Sane profits might gently.
Angry filth nepotist gems.
Filth grossing empty neat.
Gently sap storming thief.
Empty so strangling thief.
Seemly fighting top rants.
Presently fighting atoms.
Sparsely fighting not met.
Openly fighting smartest.
Tamely frightening stops.
Meanly frighting to pests.
Pest toes manly frighting.
Tamely frighting on pests.
Nosy templates frighting.
Is not pretty flashing gem.
Flight or petty manginess.
Frighten atom piss gently.
Frighten me pongs tastily.
Frighten to nasty glimpse.
Pilot nasty gem frightens.
Gently shifting so tamper.
A shifting, petty mongrels.
Petty malingers on fights.
Niggers shaft impotently.
Fish gently smarting poet.
Gently sting from ape shit.
From this negligent patsy.
Gently grasp hot feminist.

Shit! Sporty figment angel.
Flattering, gnomish types.
Self-rating, gnomish petty.
Fleeting pongs trim hasty.
Amen! Stylish, potent frigg.
Floating, mighty presents.
I'm the grisly, potent fangs.
Gremlin's shitty fang poet.
O My! Fat strength spieling.
Fat hero signs temptingly.
Fat stingers might openly.
Safe nymph G-string toilet.
The flimsy poets granting.
Tight self-mastery in pong.
Flattery pongs in this gem.
Safely or tempting things.
Shiftily rang potent gems.
Potent germs nag shiftily.
Filthy presents in maggot.
Filthy, ignorant gems pets.
Tampons greet shiftingly.
Neat gem ports shiftingly.
Thrifty, tameless, ponging.
Gem piss not thrifty angel.
Fishy template on G-string.
Fishy, top, gentle smarting.
Not niggles hefty arm-pits.
Isn't hefty, sporting gleam.
Hefty spotting malingers.
Pigs or shifty tanglement.
Ape Shit! Gem Y-fronts glint.
Y-fronts tame pig lightens.
Y-fronts sight mean piglet.
Y-fronts might genial pets.
I'm the Y-fronts nag piglets.
Isn't the Y-fronts pig gleam.
Prettify not smashing leg.
Honest, grim self-pity gnat.
Am the self-pity on G-string.
Self-pitying, hot garments.
Self-pitying, tenth orgasm.
Shame nifty glitters pong.
Ape Shit! Gently grim fonts.
Gently of sharp-set timing.
Gently of sharpest timing.
Mighty strangle of in pest.
Pigs of shirty tanglement.
Is the empty of strangling.
Petty of English smarting.
Phlegm of testy straining.
Strangely might fine post.
Strangely might fine spot.
Strangely stop fine might.

Fine starlet pongs mighty.
Not fine, ghastly, grim pest.
It straggles to fine nymph.
Finest nymph glitters ago.
To finite nymph straggles.
Smartest if gently hoping.
If taping smothers gently.
Gently if the storming sap.
Mighty strangle if on pest.
Ghastly if stringent poem.
Pithy if gross tanglement.
My pleasing if to strength.
Spongy if the grim talents.
Empty if this strong angel.
Rat helping if snotty gems.
The poem farts stingingly.
Slighting, top enemy farts.
Son's gayer, tempting filth.
A filth sniggers not empty.
Amen! Petty filth grossing.
Filth types ignorant gems.
Prig nasty filth gemstone.
Nosy, tempting filth rages.
An ogre shifts temptingly.
Fetish nags or temptingly.
Manly thief G-string poets.
Aptly frighting to semens.
Pity rotten flashing gems.
In-flight agony temptress.
Natty spoils frighten gem.
Posting frightens tamely.
My top stealing frightens.
Sanely so tempting fright.
Fight gremlin's nasty poet.
Nosy, gleaming thrift pest.
Thrift annoys piglet gems.
Shop-lifting strategy men.
Shoplift stringy, neat gem.
Eh! Strongly spitting fame.
Fame lightens strong pity.
This spongy, alert figment.
Sightly fragments in poet.
Temptingly fearing hosts.
Son's flattering, pithy gem.
I'm flattering, shyest pong.
This flattering, spongy me.
Posh flattering tiny gems.
Fleeting, shy, top smarting.
Harm fleeting, snotty pigs.
O My! Ape stifling strength.
More gnash stifling petty.
Right! On giftless payment.
The potty frigg manliness.

Petty, hot frigg manliness.
Hasty flogs grim penitent.
An impiety flogs strength.
Flog might arty ineptness.
Tiny pest nightmares flog.
Trimly seething top fangs.
My phoniest fang glitters.
Fang smothers tiny piglet.
Manly gifts hot pestering.
Priggishly fattest on men.
Fattest nosy, grim helping.
So fattiest nymph niggler.
Not replying safest might.
Safest or empty lightning.
Feast so glittering nymph.
Singingly mother fat pest.
Merit spongy fat lightens.
Grimly pong the fattiness.
This ogre fans temptingly.
Safe things or temptingly.
Glittering safes to nymph.
Not flimsy gathering pest.
Rage nights potent flimsy.
Not flimsy, grasping teeth.
Tempting rights on safely.
I'm the stingers pong fatly.
Hot infantry gems piglets.
Infantry glimpses ghetto.
So filthy, tempting ranges.
A filthy, sporting segment.
Filthy mate stingers pong.
Not filthy, grasping meets.
Filthy, strong gem panties.
Strongest, filthy pain gem.
Fortnightly pig sanest me.
Shiftingly a potent germs.
I'm thrifty as gentle pongs.
Genital's thrifty me pongs.
Spent so thrifty gleaming.
Nag thrifty, pointless gem.
Fishy, sporting gem talent.
Fishy, top, negligent smart.
Hefty pongs trim genitals.
A hefty mongrels spitting.
Hefty gnome piss rattling.
Shifty, mean, strong piglet.
Piggish me talent Y-fronts.
Y-fronts pig mate lightens.
Am tight, sleeping Y-fronts.
Eight Y-fronts malign pest.
Y-fronts spent agile might.
Ghost nifty pest maligner.
Slash nifty, tempting ogre.

Anger nifty, top mightless.
Soft, eager nymph stilting.
Manly pig softie strength.
A fonts might pesteringly.
I'm the grasping font style.
Gently of a tight primness.
Mighty of pressing talent.
Shy, prettiest of mangling.
Spite strength of mangily.
I'm the strangles of typing.
Shit of temptingly ranges.
Mightiness of petty gnarl.
I'm tipsy strength of angel.
Spiny of tightest mangler.
The spiny gems of rattling.
Lay of right temptingness.
Style of tempting sharing.
Tasty length of simpering.
Strongly paste fine might.
Fine, straggly, potent hims.
Fine nymph glitters to gas.
Infest arm-pits hog gently.
Finest pat homely G-string.
Finest tap homely G-string.
Finest graspingly met hot.
Gently if smashing potter.
I'm the strong sap if gently.
Gently if so tempting rash.
Pithy if not strangle gems.
If a timely strength pongs.
Son's gather if temptingly.
Penalty if this strong gem.
Petty if smothering slang.
Home if petty stranglings.
Fart tenses mightily pong.
Shit! Maggot's finer plenty.
Tempting fires on ghastly.
Flash regiment snotty pig.
Pig torment filth gayness.
Filth sniggers potent may.
Resonant filth pigsty gem.
Sporty, eminent filth gags.
Filth moans petty niggers.
Maggot's inept filth syren.
Filthier natty pongs gems.
Ratty filthiness pong gem.
Manly fetish poet G-string.
Penetratingly shift smog.
Poet rests manly fighting.
Not fighting seemly parts.
Not fighting seemly traps.
Empty stolen as frighting.
More lightning-fast types.

O My! Talents frighten pigs.
My! Frighten politest nags.
Frighten on lamest pigsty.
Frighten potty smiles nag.
Frighten, I'm stately pongs.
Frighten pilot nasty gems.
Frighten on tasty glimpse.
Frighten snotty, lame pigs.
Frighten toys malign pest.
My piglet frightens as not.
My politest nag frightens.
Stingy fortnight empales.
Manly stingers fight poet.
Is sporty fight gentleman.
Giant thrift pongs seemly.
I'm spongy as gentle thrift.
Thrift style pongs enigma.
My thriftiest angel pongs.
Mangle thriftiest, spongy.
Shaft impotently snigger.
Fish staringly potent gem.
Fish strongly patient gem.
Fish patiently strong gem.
Left pig smarting honesty.
Gently pit strongish fame.
Stingingly sport the fame.
Grotty helping manifests.
The sporty, stinging flame.
From gently hesitant pigs.
Strongly gap the feminist.
Ghastly figment or in pest.
It shapely, strong figment.
Prettily gnash so. Figment.
Fragment in sightly poets.
Almighty pest fingers not.
Is flattering python gems.
Spy hot fleeting smarting.
I'm the giftless, top granny.
Self-ignorant, mighty step.
Tiny nightmare flogs pest.
Flog mighty rat ineptness.
Not. Reptile's mighty fangs.
Right! Potent smiley fangs.
My phoniest fangs glitter.
Gently simpering hot fats.
Gently simpering fat host.
Gently simpering fat shot.
Fat homes stringently pig.
Oh My! Negligent fat strips.
Fat, polite G-string hymens.
Slight fat, sporting enemy.
Stymie fat, strong helping.
Openly thirsting fat gems.

Sportingly faint the gems.
Gosh! Prettily infant gems.
Safe rights on temptingly.
Gnash flimsy, potent tiger.
Flimsy pongs threaten git.
The strong infamy piglets.
Safely might sporting net.
Safely might sporting ten.
Fiery, potent might slangs.
Potent, gainless fry might.
Filthy, star meetings pong.
Filthy nepotist nags germ.
Filthy, strong enigma pets.
Maggot's filthy, inner pest.
Tempting tag on serfishly.
Fortnightly pest in a gems.
Rant shiftingly. Poet gems.
Shiftingly rat pest on gem.
Shiftingly rat pest gnome.
Lame fishy, potent G-string.
Pig angel's shifty torment.
Y-fronts might elegant sip.
Y-fronts pig elegant smith.
Am this gentle Y-fronts pig.
Y-fronts hit gleaming pest.
Trim gang honest self-pity.
Hot ranting self-pity gems.
Ahem! Not. Self-pity G-string.
Shag self-pitying torment.
Shrimp so negligent fatty.
Hog's nifty, gentle arm-pits.
Angel's might or nifty pest.
Motherless pig nifty gnat.
Gently shitting of a sperm.
Mightiness of gently. Trap.
Pest of rantingly shit gem.
Impale of stingy strength.
Nymph of greatest listing.
Nymph of teasing glitters.
Strength of stymieing pal.
Patiently of nights. Germs.
Penalty of shitting germs.
Fine, masterly, tight pongs.
That fine pigsty mongrels.
Infest strongly ape might.
Infest ghastly merit pong.
Pong tartishly infest gem.
Might finest slang poetry.
Gleam finest sporty night.
Finest might sporty angle.
This master if gently pong.
I'm the pest if strongly nag.
Lengthy if top masterings.

Measly strength if not pig.
My poet if the stranglings.
If gits ghost permanently.
Petty germ if not hassling.
If pansy or gentlest might.
Pay if molesting strength.
Spiny strength if to gleam.
Gnash potent if grim style.
Mightily tense farts pong.
Mightily tense pongs fart.
Fart eminently ghost pigs.
Fear piss gently might not.
Potent serf nags mightily.
Straying filth pest on gem.
Straying filth pest gnome.
Maggoty filth in presents.
Filth pongs temerity nags.
Potty filth gem angriness.
Filth types strong enigma.
Empty flasher to stinging.
Orange shifts temptingly.
Shift sportingly neat gem.
Tasty thief gremlins pong.
Gently nag shiftiest romp.
Poets rest manly fighting.
Fighting on style tampers.
Tipsy, rotten flashing gem.
Flashing torments yet pig.
I am strong petty fleshing.
I'm a strong petty fleshing.
Frighten measly spotting.
Mangily frighten to pests.
Frighten nags molest pity.
Spot frighten saintly gem.
Stop frighten saintly gem.
Opt frighten saintly gems.
Frighten sly, impotent gas.
Spoil frighten natty gems.
Gayest limp frightens not.
Smiley frightens top gnat.
A. Temptingly frightens so.
Snotty pig frightens male.
Snotty pig frightens meal.
Temptingly as no fighters.
Pong timely sanest fright.
My potent, gainless fright.
Am snotty, sleeping fright.
Snotty, prime angel fights.
Fight torments sanely pig.
Shoplift tiny, strange gem.
Not typing fearless might.
Left smothering nasty pig.
Stringently pig shot fame.

Hog stringently spit fame.
Strongly tight fame penis.
Honestly tip fame G-string.
Female hypnotist G-string.
Singingly format the pest.
Gently got sharp feminist.
Straggle feminist python.
Strongly ape this figment.
Tight figment on sparsely.
Fragment this nosy piglet.
Slighting frames on petty.
Farting lightens so empty.
Temptingly fingers as hot.
The sporty, mangiest fling.
Giftless, mighty, neat porn.
Giftless, grim, neat python.
Giftless, man-thing poetry.
Right! Eminent pasty flogs.
Prettily something. Fangs.
Gently feasting to shrimp.
I'm this sporty, gentle fang.
Fattest rompingly hinges.
Feasts tighten rompingly.
Sneeringly might fat post.
Sneeringly might fat spot.
Sneeringly stop fat might.
Mighty sleeping fat snort.
Fat gemstones prig thinly.
Hey! Fat mongrels spitting.
Pig fat smiley on strength.
Sportingly might fat seen.
The fat on gremlin's pigsty.
Sportingly might safe net.
Sportingly might safe ten.
Tightest, safe 'n' rompingly.
Neater, flimsy tights pong.
The sporting, mangiest fly.
Filthy pong nags termites.
Filthy germs nag nepotist.
Tape filthy, snorting gems.
Most enraging filthy pest.
Thriftily segment as pong.
Shiftingly sport neat gem.
Thrifty, pleasing gem snot.
Longest, shifty tampering.
Shifty, mean glitters pong.
Y-fronts might sleeping at.
Petrify mightless on gnat.
Hot name self-pity G-string.
Self-pity nothings rat gem.
Self-pity hating strong me.
Nifty gems hopes rattling.
The nifty, gleaming sports.

Mighty pig felon tartness.
I'm a felon pigsty strength.
Genital's softer nymph git.
Front hesitantly pig gems.
Smartingly soften the pig.
Seethingly pig smart font.
Rantingly of the gem spits.
Pint of shatteringly. Gems.
Stem of prettily gnashing.
I'm right of gentlest pansy.
Fine might as gently strop.
Rats! Temptingly fine hogs.
Mangle fine, sporty tights.
Fines torment ghastly pig.
Gosh! Gently infest armpit.
Infest armpit hogs gently.
Infest stealthy, grim pong.
Finest malign trophy gets.
Pong finest thirsty gleam.
Sparse if gently might not.
Nightmare if gently. Stops.
If ant smothers gently pig.
Strongly pig if that semen.
Ghastly if in potent germs.
Segment if tartishly pong.
Gentlest hasty if romping.
Tosser if temptingly hang.
The potty gems if snarling.
Petty if to gremlin's gnash.
Pretty gem if not hassling.
Pretty gnash if molesting.
Pansy if tightest mongrel.
Stingy platform seething.
Fist hymeneal, top G-string.
Hymeneal, top G-string fits.
The farts employ stinging.
Gem farts openly shitting.
Gently might top fairness.
On sightly, tempting fears.
Flash pitying, rotten gems.
Flash nosy, tempting tiger.
Flash testy, meriting pong.
Gay, tempting filth snores.
Is not empty filth naggers.
Self-harming petty to sign.
Rantingly top fetish gems.
Romp gently fishiest gnat.
Partly fighting to semens.
Tersely fighting tampons.
Fighting neat style romps.
Frightening types almost.
Not frighting steely maps.
Regiment spotty flashing.

Impregnate stony flights.
Stony flight impregnates.
Frighten gently piss to am.
Sip frighten snotty gleam.
Frighten tiny posts gleam.
Tamely frightens not. Pigs.
Potty gleam frightens sin.
Opt saintly gem frightens.
Natty spoil frightens gem.
Petty sons malign fighter.
My! Piss! Elegant fortnight.
My! Strangle shifting poet.
Seemly thrift giants pong.
My! Angel's thriftiest pong.
My tits shoplift gangrene.
Impotently fish gangster.
Feel nasty, sporting might.
Nights grisly, potent fame.
Fame lest stinging trophy.
From thinly naggiest pest.
From this naggiest plenty.
Honestly! Rats! Pig figment.
Honestly fragment its pig.
Fragment pig on this style.
Testily fragmenting posh.
Temptingly farting shoes.
I'm ghastly, potent fingers.
Flattering hymens to pigs.
My flattering, honest pigs.
Fleeting, shitty nags romp.
Nights fleeting, sporty am.
Phone stifling, ratty gems.
Giftless, ornate nymph git.
Smothering flags in petty.
Self-ignorant type mights.
Grime stylish, potent fang.
Poets harm gently fisting.
Might strongly fate penis.
Gently smothering fat sip.
Top fat mights sneeringly.
Seethingly sting fat romp.
Seemly ghost fat printing.
Fat pigsty in the mongrels.
Is fat strength employing.
Sporty fat lightens in gem.
Gently hog prim fattiness.
Pong timely right fatness.
Slight infant poetry gems.
Not ape the flimsy G-string.
The mortifying pest slang.
Infamy pongs streetlight.
So. Infamy strength piglet.
Pong in this flattery gems.

Right! Safely tempting son.
Thing torments safely pig.
Potent might rings safely.
Ghost grim penitent flays.
Fiery, tempting sloth nags.
Filthy, tempting sore nags.
Filthy, tempting sores nag.
Tag filthy, sporting semen.
Filthy pongs nag termites.
Filthy pig segments on rat.
Filthy poet grimness gnat.
Fortnightly games in pest.
German pest to shiftingly.
So thrifty, negligent maps.
Thrifty, gentle pigs moans.
Thrifty, insolent gem gaps.
Thrifty gems points angel.
In angel's thrifty, top gems.
Hefty slots impregnating.
Malign hefty, strong spite.
Spit hefty, storming angel.
Spit hefty, snorting gleam.
Angel's shifty or tempting.
This tempting fogey snarl.
Night impregnates softly.
Y-fronts pig stealth in gem.
This Y-fronts empaling get.
Prettify honest, slim gang.
Prettify hanging molests.
Self-pity hating torn gems.
Might no strange self-pity.
Nifty, ghastliest porn gem.
Haggle nifty torment piss.
Molest the nifty, grasping.
Prettily gnashing soft me.
Insights of gently tamper.
Gently might of saner spit.
Sightly of tempting, saner.
Angel's shirty of tempting.
Shy of tempting, gnarliest.
Mainly of the pest G-string.
Germy of tight pliantness.
Isn't helping of ratty gems.
Temptingly fine, hot grass.
Fine, pasty, tight mongrels.
Fine, tarty, mightless pong.
Top fines might strangely.
Finest sap might or gently.
Infest to straying phlegm.
Finest rest almighty pong.
Finest homely, apt G-string.
I finest straggle to nymph.
Right! Finest tamely pongs.

Finest sportingly hat gem.
Finest groin tasty phlegm.
Niftiest hag romps gently.
Hymenal pest if to G-string.
Gems if thorny talents pig.
Emptying if hot strangles.
Petty homes if strangling.
I'm a style strength if pong.
The style if smart ponging.
The grotty flip manginess.
Gently might on spies fart.
Fart openly shitting gems.
My slighting, potent fears.
Finer, glassy, potent might.
Angel's finer, spotty might.
Flash not regiment pigsty.
Flash no grim typesetting.
Spongy termites nag filth.
Filth to payments snigger.
Poet shifts rantingly. Gem.
So mangling pretty fetish.
Gently smearing top shift.
Pig thief style strong man.
Masterly poets 'n' fighting.
Open smart fighting style.
Not frighting mealy pests.
Seemly frighting top ants.
Frighting to penalty mess.
O Man! Style frighting pest.
Pong merit testy flashing.
A storming petty fleshing.
Not frighten simplest, gay.
My! Gossip frighten talent.
Gleam frighten tipsy snot.
Frighten slime tasty pong.
Gently frightens top aims.
Snot frightens tamely pig.
Mealy spotting frightens.
Gamely frightens not spit.
O My! Pigs frightens talent.
Temptingly. Fright season.
Is not empty. Angel's fright.
So tipsy fright gentleman.
Fortnight gems as ineptly.
Rottenly sap shifting gem.
Pig style fights ornament.
Finish empty not straggle.
Pig moneyless thrift gnat.
Gleaming sons type thrift.
Shoplift straying, net gem.
The spongy flirt steaming.
I'm the straying felt pongs.
I'm the straying left pongs.

Sporty, slighting, net fame.
Formats enlighten pigsty.
Stinging telepathy forms.
Form slighting, sane petty.
From this nasty, gentle pig.
Haters misfit gently pong.
Misfit trashy, gentle pong.
Misfit sporty, gentle hang.
Slithery figment gaps not.
Shit! Alert spongy figment.
Slashing figment pottery.
Hot fragments pig in style.
Thinly farting gems poets.
Nights seemly, top farting.
Type farting on mightless.
Am fleeting trophy stings.
Stifling, mean trophy gets.
The stifling, mangey strop.
Ghost stifling repayment.
The snotty flag simpering.
My phoniest frigg talents.
Anything merit pest flogs.
Merely shitting top fangs.
O My! Right! Pestilent fangs.
The feasting pongs trimly.
Isn't smothery fang piglet.
Petty fang or in mightless.
Might politest fang syren.
Misanthrope gifts gently.
Threaten slimy gifts pong.
Almighty gift on presents.
So fat, elite nymph G-string.
Fat nymph toilets snigger.
Fat nymph glitters in egos.
Fat, seemly, sporting night.
Fat hero sings temptingly.
I'm the fat plenty grossing.
Fat, sporty lighting semen.
Fat, sporty, negligent hims.
Infants hog prettily. Gems.
Infant, glittery, posh gems.
Right! Temptingly safe son.
Right safes on temptingly.
Flimsy, potent gatherings.
Flimsy, tight, earnest pong.
Flimsy pong threatens git.
Tenth greasing top flimsy.
The gasping, rotten flimsy.
Safely hot, tempting grins.
Pongs trim fatly seething.
Fiery, hot, tempting slangs.
Hot, tempting, gainless fry.
Fry might angel's nepotist.

Name strongest, filthy pig.
In maggot's filthy serpent.
Filthy, top sniggers meant.
Filthy, top G-string enemas.
Filthy, game, snorting pest.
A filthy, snorting pest gem.
Top semen gangs thriftily.
Isn't flashy, tempting ogre.
Fortnightly tapes in gems.
Fortnightly tip sane gems.
Forty-eight planting mess.
Stamp frighteningly toes.
Meat posts frighteningly.
Neat gets shiftingly romp.
Shiftingly. Parent to gems.
Shiftingly torn mega pest.
Thrifty angel mess not pig.
Angel's thrifty gem points.
Fishy, top, stringent gleam.
Hefty, smarting, stolen pig.
So spitting hefty mangler.
Spoilt hefty, mean G-string.
Gremlin's hefty, top giants.
Frostily hating spent gem.
Might pig felony tartness.
Y-fronts pig meanest light.
Hag lies tempting Y-fronts.
Y-fronts might genial step.
The giant Y-fronts glimpse.
Forty slighting, mean pest.
Anger self-pity mights not.
Is the fatty gremlins pong.
Heap molest nifty G-string.
Shame nifty pongs glitter.
Softer as empty lightning.
Softer lighting payments.
Genital's soft nymph tiger.
Often hassling grim petty.
I'm ghastly font pestering.
Mishap of stringently get.
Granny of emptiest slight.
Tightest of simple granny.
Presents of mightily. Gnat.
Elephant of misty G-string.
I'm the plenty of as G-string.
Nights of a petty gremlins.
Shit! Petty gem of snarling.
Gremlin's petty of this nag.
Spiny might of gentle star.
Nights of tempting layers.
Mighty strangle fine post.
Mighty strangle fine spot.
Play strongest, fine might.

Ghastly, potent, grim fines.
Finest months pig greatly.
Finest in as grotty phlegm.
Finest gratingly top mesh.
Finest mighty strop angel.
Large gits finest to nymph.
Finest nymph gloats tiger.
Halo infest empty G-string.
Finest ratty helping smog.
If trim poets gnash gently.
Gently might if sane strop.
Tights if strongly. Ape-men.
Eh! If tempting as strongly.
Maggot's present if thinly.
I'm gentlest if trophy nags.
Hypnotist if strangle gem.
The messy if rattling pong.
My strangest if to helping.
If giants employ strength.
Maggot's hint if presently.
Maggot's thin if presently.
Potty if smashing, gentler.
Fair pests might on gently.
Oh My! Negligent farts spit.
Gently fart so might penis.
Homely, stinging pets fart.
Oh My! Negligent spits fart.
Ghastly spit not finer gem.
Ghost finer petty maligns.
Pong trim stingy self-hate.
Flash grime potent stingy.
A filth orgy temptingness.
Mangey, top filth stingers.
Spite mangey, strong filth.
My! A potent filth sniggers.
Am piggy filth rottenness.
Petty filth sniggers on am.
Petty filth groans in gems.
Filth ageing snotty sperm.
Not name thriftless piggy.
Self-harming pity gets not.
Temptingly shifts on rage.
Pig gently smart on fetish.
Sanely pig storming theft.
Son's empty alert fighting.
Frighting payments stole.
Plenty mates so frighting.
Son's petty lame frighting.
Petty frighting mean loss.
Flight poetry assignment.
Flight spontaneity germs.
Frighten slimy, top agents.
My! Frighten talents pig so.

Temptingly frighten a SOS.
SOS! Frighten malign petty.
Frighten saintly post gem.
Sly poets frighten mating.
Frighten a snotty glimpse.
Is top am frightens gently.
Lame top stingy frightens.
Slimy, top agent frightens.
Sat frightens timely pong.
Many frightens to piglets.
Misty, top angel frightens.
My talent frightens so pig.
Male pigsty frightens not.
Empty to signal frightens.
Pity molest nag frightens.
Style frightens not pig am.
Toy frightens malign pest.
On tempting fighter slays.
Empty on genital's frights.
Gentleman frights so pity.
Eminently gasps to fright.
Fright as temptingly nose.
Patiently. Son's fright gem.
Pig fortnight's mean style.
Is empty. Angel's fortnight.
Am sporty, gentle shifting.
Fights tag omnipresently.
Impotently fights ranges.
Patiently fights on germs.
Fights or tipsy gentleman.
Fights torment sanely pig.
Fight as temptingly snore.
Fight sporting, mean style.
Angel's snotty, prime fight.
Try shop-lifting, neat gems.
Ya! Shoplift stringent gem.
Fish gently top mastering.
Fish temptingly rages not.
Flirt spongy, hesitant gem.
Pig nasty, smothering felt.
Left snotty, mean priggish.
Thinly. Fame G-string poets.
Honestly pit fame G-string.
Spy slighting, rotten fame.
Fame style thirsting pong.
Fame lightens snotty prig.
Piggy films not threatens.
From pigsties than gently.
Shit from negligent pasty.
Is sharp figment to gently.
Garishly spent to figment.
Sparsely. Figment tonight.
Fragment lightens so pity.

It's flattering nymph egos.
The flattering, spiny smog.
Artist's fleeting nymph go.
Ghost fleeting, trim pansy.
Fleeting, nasty, prim ghost.
Pig fleeting, snotty harms.
Stifling, thorny, mega pest.
Petty nightmare flings so.
Fling as smothering petty.
Giftless nymph or neat git.
Harming on giftless petty.
Mighty flag on prettiness.
Pertinently. Hims faggots.
Shy, potent, manliest frigg.
Pretty, insane might flogs.
Flog empty saner shitting.
I'm the stringent pays flog.
Merely spitting hot fangs.
Sly, mightier, potent fangs.
Gently trim posh feasting.
Gently feasting this romp.
Them feasting sportingly.
Mightily. Fang to presents.
Prettily. Something's fang.
The angry simpleton gifts.
The amen gifts sportingly.
Eh! Fattest singingly romp.
Gently phoniest, grim fast.
Gently phoniest, grim fats.
Gently meriting posh fast.
Fast sneeringly top might.
Sneeringly might top fats.
Fast! Homely, stringent pig.
The fate romps stingingly.
The feat romps stingingly.
Singingly fat stepmother.
Pesteringly might fat son.
I'm this spongy, gentler fat.
Temptingly sign hero's fat.
Infants slight poetry gem.
Safe nymph glitters on git.
Temptingly safe, hot grins.
Flimsy pongs tighter neat.
Gain flimsy strength poet.
Neater, tight flimsy pongs.
Not pig the strange flimsy.
Myself shattering not pig.
So hating tempting flyers.
Safely spitting north gem.
Filthy, nastiest pong germ.
Filthy gemstones prig ant.
Rent maggot's filthy penis.
Isn't maggot's filthy preen.

Rang filthy nepotist gems.
Filthy poets ranting gems.
I'm fortnightly, spent sage.
Fortnightly tape messing.
Mega fortnightly in pests.
Spent forty-eight maligns.
Mate spots frighteningly.
SOS! Pig thrifty gentleman.
Thrifty steps on gleaming.
Fishy nags torment piglet.
Fishy piglet torments nag.
Hefty tampering glints so.
Hefty or tempting signals.
Hefty, top stings malinger.
Molest hefty pain G-string.
Empale not shifty G-string.
Amen! Shifty, strong piglet.
Y-fronts heap gem stilting.
Y-fronts leap shitting gem.
Y-fronts pale shitting gem.
Tight, pleasing me Y-fronts.
This gleaming Y-fronts pet.
Pig smart enlighten softy.
Prettify hangs molesting.
Prettify no mightless nag.
Self-pitying harm gets not.
Is not fatty helping germs.
Fatty, honest niggers limp.
Hot niggle fatty primness.
Nifty helping to star gems.
Hot simplest, nifty nagger.
Nifty pest or nights gleam.
Nifty tights ape mongrels.
Gang nifty, mirthless poet.
Might strangle nifty pose.
Felon pets straying might.
Frostiest nymph git angel.
Gently nights prime fatso.
Fatso 'n' pesteringly might.
Might spiny, gentler fatso.
Gently might of sanest rip.
He's tempting of staringly.
Angry of pestilent mights.
Strange of mightily spent.
Spent of gnarliest mighty.
Mighty of pertinent glass.
Planet of mighty stingers.
Hymens of starting piglet.
Garishly of tempting tens.
Lengthy of smarting spite.
Slithery of tempting sang.
Gem of thinly pig tartness.
Nymph of sane git glitters.

Gritless nymph of neat git.
Playing of sternest might.
Strangle of empty insight.
Typists of negligent harm.
Tipsy of rights gentleman.
Tipsy, gentlest of harming.
Pig strength of saintly me.
Syren of might talents pig.
Gently smart hot fine pigs.
Fine, grotty, mightless pan.
Fine, almighty, strong step.
Thirty finest pongs gleam.
Infest spongy, alert might.
Finest typing harlot's gem.
Finest malign pretty hogs.
If right pest moans gently.
If top merits gnash gently.
Mighty if strongest panel.
Mighty if strongest plane.
Lengthy if sporting mates.
Honestly if tempting rags.
Honestly! Pest if grim gnat.
To nymph if stalest nigger.
Site nymph if not straggle.
If nymph ties not straggle.
Gem if not pithy strangles.
If masterly pongs tighten.
Nag strength if slimy poet.
Mangily if the strong pest.
Stormy if negligent paths.
My! The poets if strangling.
Sportingly if the gems ant.
Petty if not slashing germ.
Nights if a petty mongrels.
If this petty mongrels nag.
Lengthy, mangiest profits.
Steaming lengthy profits.
Right! Nasty flip gemstone.
I'm the fits pong strangely.
Sift hymeneal, top G-string.
I'm the pigs farts on gently.
Gently spite gnomish fart.
Seemly fart nights pig not.
I'm this spongy, gentle fart.
Might snotty, sleeping far.
Infer temptingly ghost as.
I am the first pongs gently.
Temptingly fires to gnash.
It smoggy, pertinent flash.
Spit angry filth gemstone.
O Man! Sternest filth piggy.
Empty filth as not snigger.
Filth moans petty snigger.

Filth gags impotent syren.
Filthiest, nasty pong germ.
Not paying thriftless gem.
Natty mongrels pig fetish.
Rantingly shift poet gems.
Poets shift rantingly. Gem.
Shift temptingly anger so.
Temptingly shift on rages.
Temptingly grass on thief.
Theft malingers on pigsty.
Store manly fighting pest.
My poser fighting talents.
Nasty, steel romp fighting.
Only fighting a temptress.
Empty as lost frightening.
Frightening lots empty as.
Frightening as empty slot.
Empty so salt frightening.
Aptly frightening to mess.
Am frightening, petty loss.
Namely frighting to pests.
Molest any frighting pest.
Empty flashing to stinger.
Grim petty as not fleshing.
Top gem flights tyrannies.
Stagy, omnipresent flight.
I'm a spots frighten gently.
Not frighten gay, slim pest.
Frighten on pigsty metals.
Frighten molest as typing.
Frighten to signals empty.
Frighten molest tipsy nag.
Tempting lays frighten so.
I'm top nags frighten style.
Frighten sly, patient smog.
Frighten snotty, slim page.
I'm a tops frightens gently.
Piglets may not frightens.
My! Frightens top genitals.
Pigsty frightens on metal.
Is not empty lag frightens.
Frightens in gloats empty.
Am losing petty frightens.
Pity gleam frightens snot.
Sly poet frightens mating.
I'm spongy fighter talents.
I'm spongy talent fighters.
Petty maligns on fighters.
Is not empty angel frights.
Fright nags potent smiley.
Sly fights impregnate not.
Fight petty sons malinger.
Trimly gang top heftiness.

Amen! Gossip gently. Thrift.
Not gasping seemly thrift.
Thrift nags seemly pig not.
Son's mangey thrift piglet.
Shoplift stingy, neat germ.
Faith glory temptingness.
Sportingly segment faith.
Gently simpering to shaft.
False spitting thorny gem.
Left on nightmare's pigsty.
Pig self, snotty nightmare.
Right! Gently spits on fame.
Sporting fame gets thinly.
Fame stings thorny piglet.
Testy, slighting fame porn.
Right! Manifest style pong.
Not pithy G-string females.
This potty gangrene films.
Gently form hesitant pigs.
Ghastly pig from sentient.
Shitting types from angel.
Self-torment as piggy hint.
Self-torment as thin piggy.
Misfits nag gentle trophy.
Hater pongs gently misfit.
Ah! Self-tormenting pigsty.
Sight self-tormenting pay.
Strangely ship to figment.
Ghastly stripe on figment.
Tartishly sponge figment.
Slithery, top figment nags.
Anger stylish, top figment.
Lighten as sporty figment.
Fragment to sightly penis.
Honestly! It fragment pigs.
Is not shy fragment piglet.
Shit! Fragment nosy piglet.
Is nightly poet fragments.
Eh! Fragments pig snottily.
Self-rating mighty on pest.
Segment a stifling trophy.
Feelings might sporty ant.
Manly forgetting the piss.
No stateliest frigg nymph.
Them self-ignorant pigsty.
Is penetrating myth flogs.
Pithy gem flogs transient.
My penetrating shit flogs.
Typesetting flogs in harm.
Right! Eminent patsy flogs.
Petty sin nightmares flog.
Temptingly hates in frogs.
Temptingly as in the frogs.

This prime fangs to gently.
Mightily present to fangs.
Nightly or emptiest fangs.
The fangs emit sportingly.
The fangs item sportingly.
Mightiest fangs reply not.
Fangs or mightiest plenty.
Shit! Romp gently feasting.
Fang spies might rottenly.
Rashly fisting potent gem.
Gift pain smothers gently.
Segment gift rhinoplasty.
Gently might on safest rip.
Fast trim seethingly pong.
Strongly might feat penis.
Thinly fate sporting gems.
Fat posers might in gently.
On the grim fat piss gently.
The fat sperm to singingly.
Gentler fat piss on mighty.
Thinly pestering fat smog.
Fat poetry mess lightning.
Posers might gently faint.
Gem hogs prettily. Infants.
I'm the spongy fans glitter.
I'm the spongy fan glitters.
Safe, snorting myth piglet.
Flimsy, stringent hag poet.
Hast flimsy, potent nigger.
Tape on the flimsy G-string.
Not pig self-mastery night.
A mortifying pest lengths.
Shit! Flattery pongs in gem.
Safely torment things pig.
Safely potent him G-string.
Fatly might so presenting.
Fly piggish neat torments.
Fiery, tempting sloths nag.
Infantry glimpses hot get.
Filthy tampering sons get.
Gas filthy, tempting snore.
Filthy, naggiest nets romp.
Filthy pongs rat meetings.
Filthy gags torment penis.
Filthy gemstones rip gnat.
Filthy, potent gems grains.
Filthy porn gets steaming.
Paste filthy, snorting gem.
Filthy, ignorant gem steps.
Thriftily gap on segments.
Thriftily gang top semens.
Mean pig sets fortnightly.
Fortnightly paste in gems.

Forty-eight sampling nets.
Frighteningly tempt as so.
Frighteningly. Stops mate.
Mates pots frighteningly.
Tops mates frighteningly.
Frighteningly as top stem.
Shiftingly stamp to green.
Neat romps shiftingly get.
Meets rat shiftingly pong.
Shiftingly or patent gems.
Pig thrifty, long tameness.
So. Gentleman's thrifty pig.
Gasp thrifty, insolent gem.
Gap thrifty, insolent gems.
Point angel's thrifty gems.
No thrifty, gleaming pests.
Angel's fishy, tempting rot.
Fishy, tempting, large snot.
Hefty pongs trim stealing.
Hefty mongrel as spitting.
Hefty gem piss on rattling.
Prig so shifty tanglement.
Sight inept Y-fronts gleam.
Eh! Spitting Y-fronts gleam.
Might frosty, sleeping ant.
I empaling softy strength.
Snort self-pity hating gem.
Shag self-pity tormenting.
I'm the torn self-pity gangs.
Self-pitying than to germs.
The rotten gangs simplify.
Not simplify the gangster.
Pong satisfy gentle mirth.
On the fatty sniggers limp.
Pig harlot's nifty segment.
Oh! Nifty, tempting largess.
Pig so lame nifty strength.
Nifty person tights gleam.
Nifty shames pong glitter.
I'm the felon patsy G-string.
Softer might nags ineptly.
Gently hating soft simper.
I'm the straggly font penis.
Gently pig of sanest mirth.
Gently of the arm-pits sign.
Sneeringly of tight stamp.
Singingly of her attempts.
Stingingly of merest path.
Mightily of strangest pen.
Mighty pestering of slant.
Myth of negligent rapists.
Spit of lengthy mastering.
Tampering of sightly nest.

Tampering of sightly nets.
Sent of sightly tampering.
Nymph of sane gits glitter.
Thirsty of negligent maps.
Thirsty of spent gleaming.
Tights grasp of eminently.
Pigsty of tenth malingers.
Simply of the neat G-string.
Gnash of temptingly tires.
Gnash of temptingly tries.
Hates of temptingly grins.
Ah! Stingers of temptingly.
Hints of temptingly rages.
Temptingly of in the grass.
Temptingly of as the grins.
Strangle of emptying shit.
Length of tipsy mastering.
Pasty of meriting lengths.
Tighten of pasty gremlins.
Style of tampering things.
Nasty of slighting temper.
Stray of tempting English.
Tyrant of sleeping mights.
Syren of a tempting slight.
Fine tights as gently romp.
Strangely fine, top mights.
Shrimp gently finest goat.
The mops finest gratingly.
Finest porn gets almighty.
Finest gang motherly spit.
Tights finest manly grope.
The tags finest rompingly.
Gleam finest sporty thing.
Shots if gently tampering.
Strangely might if no pest.
Stringently if hot sap gem.
Enlighten if grotty spasm.
Almighty if strongest pen.
Sporting if elegant myths.
Prominent if ghastly gets.
Nymph if gases glitter not.
Greatest nymph if so glint.
Trophy if mangling testes.
I'm trashy if gentlest pong.
Shy gem if sporting talent.
If teeth pongs smartingly.
O My! The pest if strangling.
Pigsty if short gentleman.
Temptingly if north gases.
If hosts anger temptingly.
If ghost earns temptingly.
Gnash if temptingly store.
Temptingly if on the grass.

Eh! If strong as temptingly.
Empty shit if strong angel.
Lengthen if sporty stigma.
I'm sporty if gentlest hang.
Pretty if not slashing gem.
Sly strength if top enigma.
Snotty if grasping helmet.
Might sternest flip agony.
Temptingly the fair songs.
Fairest months pig gently.
Top theme farts singingly.
Farts spotlighting enemy.
I'm the farts ponging style.
Tiny helping farts to gems.
Gentle fart piss on mighty.
Fart stilting phoney gems.
Piggy, eminent sloths fart.
Temptingly fears on sight.
Finer test pongs almighty.
Finer, almighty tests pong.
Finer, potty, mightless nag.
Tightest fire pongs manly.
Manly tightest fires pong.
I'm strong self-hate typing.
Flash misty, potent nigger.
On type-setting, grim flash.
Flash potty, mere stinging.
Flash petty, meriting song.
Flash sporting entity gem.
Tempting filth gays snore.
Straying pongs meet filth.
Spongy meetings rat filth.
Not empty in filth aggress.
Filth as niggers empty not.
Sporty, naggiest filth men.
Sporty meetings nag filth.
Mornings petty filth sage.
Filth mess petty groaning.
Potent me shifts ragingly.
Shift gratingly top semen.
Sporting thief gets manly.
Smartingly heftiest pong.
Theft piss ignorantly. Gem.
Not grasping theft smiley.
Sportsmanly tee fighting.
Frightening spots tamely.
Sly, top frightening mates.
Style frighting pest moan.
Frighting snotty, empales.
Tamely frighten signpost.
Not frighten lamest Gipsy.
Nag so frighten slim petty.
Steaming frighten sly, top.

Glimpse so frighten natty.
Frighten tasty miles pong.
Ya! Frighten tempting loss.
Frighten me gaps snottily.
Gasp snottily frighten me.
Frighten snotty ages limp.
It frightens tamely pongs.
Typist frightens no gleam.
Angel frightens most pity.
Am frightens testily pong.
Slimy, potent fighter nags.
Slimy, potent fighters nag.
Gently piss to mean fright.
Snotty, pleasing fright me.
Snotty fright penis gleam.
Sanely potent, grim fights.
Tempting fights on slayer.
Fight staringly top semen.
Poet mess rantingly fight.
Fight not sleepy smarting.
Sly fight impregnates not.
Fight royal temptingness.
Thrift playing gemstones.
Genital's spongy thrift me.
Gently fresh, top giantism.
Shoplift straying gem ten.
Shoplift met nasty nigger.
Natty niggers shoplift me.
Fish or tempting as gently.
Straggly, top, eminent fish.
Fish petty, storming angel.
Fish petty, snorting gleam.
Serenity pongs flat might.
The piggy torments finals.
False type snorting might.
Pig smarting felt honesty.
Sightly, inept, strong fame.
Spongy fame glitters thin.
Sporty, slighting fame ten.
Stonily pig fame strength.
Petty forms nightingales.
Gently tag from pithiness.
Tightly pig from neatness.
Pigsty lightens from neat.
Misfit hasty, gentler pong.
Garishly not. Figment pest.
Gasp not slithery figment.
Honestly rat figment pigs.
Figment as thorny piglets.
Is nightly poets fragment.
The fragments pig stonily.
Petty filming to gnashers.
Pit honestly farting gems.

Tip honestly farting gems.
My! Ghost flattering penis.
Shit! Flattering, spongy me.
Fleeting, shitty romps nag.
Part stifling honesty gem.
Great! Stifling nymph toes.
Empty hero's stifling gnat.
Feelings might tasty porn.
Petty flings hot smearing.
A smothering petty flings.
Giftless mighty on parent.
A giftless, horny, tempting.
Repayment flogs shitting.
Petty nightmare flogs sin.
Shitting repayments flog.
Tyrannies might pets flog.
The slimy, rotten fangs pig.
The fang times sportingly.
Sorely shit tempting fang.
The masterly pong fisting.
Gentle misanthropy gifts.
This ape-men gift strongly.
Slimy pongs threaten gift.
Gift slimy pong threatens.
Gently pig on safest mirth.
Gently hoisting fat sperm.
Motherly, singing fat pets.
Fat hymens pig on glitters.
Help strong fat stymieing.
Fat, empty, slighting snore.
Might fat plenty goriness.
Gosh! In gremlin's fat petty.
Fat hogs in gremlin's petty.
Faint, homely pest G-string.
This goer fans temptingly.
Shit! Ogre fans temptingly.
Gently might in safe strop.
Safe, petty, slighting norm.
Hot page stringent flimsy.
Flimsy pest on that nigger.
Flimsy, potent niggers hat.
The flimsy nags rotten pig.
The mortifying nags slept.
The mortifying spelt nags.
Fertility pongs than gems.
I'm the flattery pongs sign.
I'm the flattery signs pong.
Fiery, tattling pongs mesh.
Infantry poets might legs.
Filthy, inept as strong gem.
A filthy, top semen G-string.
Filthy, snorting tapes gem.
O Man! Filthy, steep G-string.

Step filthy, ignorant gems.
Filthy, smarting pest gone.
Filthy, naggiest pest norm.
I'm steep fortnightly nags.
Fortnightly pit sane gems.
Fortnightly sip neat gems.
Plant forty-eight messing.
Frighteningly tame spots.
Frighteningly pets atoms.
Frighteningly. Atom pests.
Shiftingly meet star pong.
Shiftingly pert gem as not.
Shiftingly mega portents.
Nag thrifty, timeless pong.
Thrifty pest niggles moan.
O Man! Thrifty pest niggles.
Spit on angel's thrifty gem.
Spit angel's thrifty gnome.
Thrifty gentleman piss go.
Fishy, mental poet G-string.
Is not hefty, ample G-string.
I'm hefty starlets ponging.
It isn't hefty mongrels gap.
Shifty, sporting, gentle am.
Shifty, mean pongs glitter.
Trim shifty, elegant pongs.
Amen! Shifty glitters pong.
Shit! Snarl tempting fogey.
This tempting felonry gas.
Softly impregnate things.
Y-fronts name lightest pig.
Gnash Y-fronts item piglet.
Amen! Y-fronts sight piglet.
I'm the Y-fronts niggle past.
The gleaming pits Y-fronts.
Shit empaling Y-fronts get.
I'm this gentle Y-fronts gap.
Nights frosty, mean piglet.
Angel's frosty, inept might.
Gosh! Alignments prettify.
Sham niggles not prettify.
Self-pity 'n' straight gnome.
Hat snorting self-pity gem.
Self-pitying gnat mothers.
Self-pitying germs hat not.
The self-pitying smog rant.
Simplify gate on strength.
Might prig fatty loneness.
Short gleaming nifty pest.
Nifty loathing pest germs.
Right! Slap nifty gemstone.
Nifty tights mangle poser.
Slash nifty, tempting goer.

The nifty, gormless taping.
Tightest, grim felon pansy.
Felon thirsting pasty gem.
Pigsty for this gentleman.
Soft 'n' almighty pestering.
Soft, shy, negligent armpit.
Soft, slighting repayment.
Fonts threaten slim piggy.
Nightmare's pits of gently.
Nightmare's tips of gently.
She tempting of staringly.
Mights ape of stringently.
Tent of ghastly simpering.
Nightly of tempting arses.
Shy of tempting triangles.
The slimy pest of granting.
Timely of in strength gaps.
Timely strength of in gasp.
Pesteringly of tight mans.
Temptingly of garish nest.
Temptingly of garish nets.
Garish of temptingly sent.
His strange of temptingly.
Mights of pertinently gas.
Straight plenty of in gems.
Lightning of petty smears.
Petty of things malingers.
Type of smarting lightens.
Spiny gems of right talent.
Spiny strength of it gleam.
Slayers of tempting night.
I'm tenth of grasping style.
Sly of penetrating mights.
Natty of the sniggers limp.
Simplest, fine, grotty hang.
Stop strangle fine mighty.
Log fine nymph strategist.
Mostly pig a fine strength.
Fine hog stars temptingly.
Fine hat gross temptingly.
Finest strongly pig the am.
Finest rip not ghastly gem.
Finest gits mangle trophy.
Infest pithy, strong gleam.
My! Finest hot strangle pig.
Them finest to graspingly.
Finest gremlin's potty hag.
Great! Niftiest nymph logs.
If metaphor stings gently.
If shattering mops gently.
Trim top if gently gnashes.
Gently rat if gnomish pest.
Pest if gently might arson.

If nightmare spots gently.
Nightmare's pots if gently.
Nightmare's tops if gently.
Pests if rantingly hot gem.
Rantingly spot if the gems.
Rantingly stop if the gems.
Strongly if the inapt gems.
Strongly paint if the gems.
That leggy primness if not.
Angry if the tempting loss.
Patterns if gnomishly get.
If mighty as gentlest porn.
If sporting as gentle myth.
Gentle myth if to raspings.
Sightly if potent Germans.
Shorty if tempting angles.
A steel G-string if to nymph.
If grim as gentlest python.
The sporting if manly gets.
Seemly G-string if hot pant.
Timely if on strength gaps.
Timely strength if on gasp.
Graspingly if hottest men.
Shorten if temptingly gas.
Others if temptingly nags.
Temptingly if honest rags.
Shit! Penalty if strong gem.
Aptly if the snorting gems.
Straight plenty if on gems.
If gremlin's petty nags hot.
Hot if grim, gentlest pansy.
Rightmost if gentle pansy.
If pasty mongrels tighten.
Might so if pregnant style.
Helping if not tasty germs.
Tasty helping if strong me.
I'm the profits nags gently.
Pilfer snotty gems hating.
I'm the snotty splif nagger.
I'm the fit pongs strangely.
Fit gnashes or temptingly.
Ghostly, eminent farts pig.
Piggy farts eminent sloth.
Fart mighty sleeping snot.
Isn't fear hogs temptingly.
Finer, gay, tempting sloths.
Manly pig on tightest serf.
Hog saintly, tempting serf.
Self-hate in my top G-string.
Flash met stinging poetry.
Soggy filth intemperants.
Piggy, torn filth tameness.
Filth payments to niggers.

Potty sniggers name filth.
Tempting filth groans yes.
Self-harming petty to sing.
Glittery, mean shifts pong.
Gently ape storming shift.
Spongy, grim thief talents.
Gently arm shiftiest pong.
I'm spongy, gnarliest theft.
Simperingly nags to theft.
Manly fighting top resets.
Strop seemly fighting ant.
Sporty, mean lest fighting.
Lay fighting on temptress.
Style tampers no fighting.
Style fighting mean strop.
A frightening pets mostly.
Tamely frighting so spent.
Not frighting messy plate.
Empty not frighting sales.
So frighting mental types.
Potty, grim, tense flashing.
Isn't flashing or petty gem.
More sting petty flashing.
Empty on angriest flights.
Flights smearing on petty.
Angry flight to emptiness.
Empty flight to angriness.
Frighten slimy pest to nag.
Frighten gamely spits not.
Frighten empty saint logs.
Typists frighten no gleam.
Frighten so mangle typist.
Most frighten tipsy angel.
Frighten tiny, postal gems.
To mental Gipsy frightens.
Nail potty gems frightens.
Me frightens snottily gap.
Tiny post frightens gleam.
Tiny spot frightens gleam.
Stop tiny gleam frightens.
Fighter snags impotently.
Fighters spit gently moan.
Mentality pongs fighters.
Fighters sang impotently.
Only as tempting fighters.
Neat frights timely pongs.
Gently spite fright moans.
My! Angel's fright nepotist.
Pasty, insolent fright gem.
Fortnight's seemly taping.
Fortnight's sleepy mating.
Shifting as petty mongrel.
Prime as gently fights not.

Neat me fights sportingly.
Empty on gnarliest fights.
Mean pigs fights rottenly.
Fight temptingly reasons.
Temptingly fight on arses.
Gently piss on mega thrift.
Not map leggy thriftiness.
Singingly farthest, top me.
Farthest employing sting.
I'm farthest style ponging.
Shoplift gay, stringent me.
Gently pig monster's faith.
I'm sporty, negligent shaft.
Gently tame sporting fish.
Empty hot falser stinging.
Fertile, nasty mights pong.
Stifle naggiest nymph rot.
Naggiest nymph riots left.
I'm left, spongy shattering.
Snotty, mean felt priggish.
Pig gently snort this fame.
Stringently pig fame host.
Nightly spite strong fame.
It's lengthy, sporting fame.
Pithy, stolen fame G-string.
Fameless python gritting.
Forms ape gently shitting.
Stingingly heat from pest.
Thinly form naggiest pest.
From that sleepy stinging.
Petty stings from healing.
Type from angel's shitting.
From gentle shitting pays.
From tightest, spiny angel.
Straying figment to helps.
The sporty, signal figment.
Get not fragment syphilis.
Piggy, honest talents firm.
My! Gosh! Pestilent farting.
My pestilent farting hogs.
Polygamists finger tenth.
Fringe tenth polygamists.
Polygamist fingers tenth.
Fleeting, smashing, top try.
Great! Stifling, top hymens.
Stifling poets anger myth.
Hey! Stifling gap torments.
Stifling ranges empty hot.
Empty on stifling gathers.
Stifling, petty, rash gnome.
The sporty fling steaming.
So fling nightmare's petty.
Annoy giftless, pert might.

Mighty flags, pretentions.
Shy, pertinent, slim faggot.
Thinly top frigg tameness.
Shy, potent frigg ailments.
I'm snotty frigg elephants.
It's integrate nymph flogs.
Hey! Tempting strain flogs.
Saner petty flogs in might.
Flog my stringent ape shit.
Its genitals forget nymph.
It forgets genital's nymph.
This frogs pity gentleman.
My thorniest piglet fangs.
Prettily hot fangs in gems.
Fangs might prettily nose.
Fangs pity to the gremlins.
Fang piss gently merit hot.
Fang piglets trim honesty.
Prettily. Fang on this gems.
Oh! Sisterly, tempting fang.
Honest arm-pits fig gently.
Phlegm gifts to tyrannies.
Gifts halo tempting syren.
Gently gift torn misshape.
Gently gift misshapen rot.
My! Strangle phoniest gift.
Rompingly the sanest gift.
Fattiest legs groin nymph.
Nightly merit safest pong.
Feast snotty, grim helping.
Pig homely, stringent fats.
Fast seething trimly pong.
Fate shitty gremlins pong.
The fate stings rompingly.
The feat stings rompingly.
Grotty fat mess in helping.
Fat pongs resent mightily.
Fat plots mighty sneering.
Fat, nightly poet grimness.
Molest fat, hyper stinging.
Fat G-string phones timely.
Strop fat, slighting enemy.
The fat sniggers imply not.
Sleepy fat in strong might.
Torment piggish fan style.
Gently trim this safe pong.
Implying to safe strength.
Foamy strength in piglets.
Flimsy ego-trip nags tenth.
The flimsy pongs treating.
Net to the grasping flimsy.
Paste mortifying lengths.
Safely potent, grim, nights.

Safely potent, grim things.
The sporting gems in fatly.
The sporting fly steaming.
Infantry hosts piglet gem.
The glimpses got infantry.
Fry gnash gentle optimist.
Segment shiftily rat pong.
'e's filthy, tempting groans.
Filthy nor tempting gases.
Filthy pongs merit agents.
Filthy, merest giants pong.
Pig monster's filthy agent.
Filthy pig on strangest me.
Gas filthy, pertinent smog.
Maggot's filthy spinneret.
Filthy opens tame G-string.
Filthy poet means G-string.
Filthy poet names G-string.
Soap filthy, stringent gem.
A pongs segment thriftily.
Pest on gem nags thriftily.
Pest gnome nags thriftily.
Am fortnightly pig tenses.
Fortnightly images spent.
Mean get piss fortnightly.
Frighteningly pat to mess.
Frighteningly tap to mess.
Frighteningly. Pests to am.
Shiftingly gets on tamper.
Shiftingly pattern so. Gem.
Amongst thrifty, sleeping.
Thrifty, top messing angel.
Thrifty gem spits on angel.
Thrifty gnome spits angel.
Fishy, tattling person gem.
Hefty, pointless, grim gnat.
Hefty, top maligner stings.
Shifty or tempting angles.
The storming pest flaying.
Eh! Frostily tempting nags.
Felony as tempting rights.
Thing impregnates softly.
Lofty, nights impregnates.
Lofty things impregnates.
Y-fronts tame piggish lent.
Ape slighting Y-fronts met.
Them pig genital's Y-fronts.
Shit! Am gentle Y-fronts pig.
I'm frosty, negligent paths.
Palm-green softy shitting.
Prettify amongst English.
Prettify might angel's son.
Prettify on the slim gangs.

Sets petrify hot mangling.
Angel's mights petrify not.
Am stringent self-pity hog.
Nights rat self-pity on gem.
Nights rat self-pity gnome.
German self-pity on tights.
Tight self-pity on Germans.
Something. Self-pity grant.
Self-pitying nor that gems.
Hast not self-pitying germ.
Self-pitying hasn't to germ.
The self-pitying angstrom.
So simpering fatty length.
Ghost plainest, nifty germ.
Spoil nifty, mega strength.
Gnash politest, nifty germ.
Rang nifty, poetless might.
Pests might or nifty angel.
Nifty nightmare logs pest.
Rang nifty, mightless poet.
Nifty nags smother piglet.
This nifty pongs alert gem.
Felon mates pithy G-string.
Gently harm in softest pig.
Soft, ghastly, eminent prig.
Soft, nightly impregnates.
Is soft, lengthy tampering.
Pig soft, shirty gentleman.
The pigsty fonts malinger.
Arty, sleeping fonts might.
Often, slashing, grim petty.
Searingly might font pest.
The font malingers pigsty.
Pig nightmare's font style.
Right! Gently of mean spits.
I'm a strength of gently sip.
Gently of the armpit signs.
Gently of the smarting sip.
Strangely of inept mights.
Stringy of the malign pest.
Mint of ghastly pestering.
Prig of ghastly sentiment.
Nymph of strategies glint.
Pithy of gentlest margins.
Pithy of negligent smarts.
Shyest tampering of glint.
Shirty of tempting angles.
Smiley of pregnant tights.
Mastery of lightning pest.
My! It of pleasing strength.
Ant of pesteringly mights.
Lame pigsty of in strength.
Harm gentlest of in pigsty.

Empty angles of thirsting.
Empty of in gnash glitters.
Empty of I the stranglings.
Type might of in strangles.
Types strangle of in might.
Spray gentlest of in might.
Spiny gem of right talents.
Gnash style of permitting.
I'm the style of pan G-string.
Night of slyest tampering.
Gremlin's natty of the pigs.
Tasty phlegm of inserting.
Gently might so fine sprat.
Fine might pots strangely.
Fine than grotty glimpses.
Fine artists toggle nymph.
Fine piggy halts torments.
Gently ghost armpit fines.
That gem fines sportingly.
Finest angel ports mighty.
Ghastly finest in top germ.
Straggle, I'm finest python.
Finest slight empty groan.
Try finest empaling ghost.
Niftiest, large myth pongs.
Gently if sane tights romp.
Gently romps if the giants.
Shit! Master if gently pong.
Pest if strongly hating me.
Pest if homely G-string ant.
If pongs met shatteringly.
Stem if shatteringly pong.
Master's lengthy if not pig.
Lengthy if mangiest strop.
Lengthy if steaming strop.
If stealthy pig strongmen.
Shorty if negligent stamp.
Gritless if not gate nymph.
If nymph ages not glitters.
Niggle if smartest python.
Shapely G-string if not met.
Pest if meanly hot G-string.
Steamy if sporting length.
Lame pigsty if on strength.
Harm gentlest if on pigsty.
Strangle empty if in ghost.
If glitters empty on gnash.
If sporty might entangles.
Slashing petty if torn gem.
Type might if on strangles.
If types strangle on might.
Spray gentlest if on might.
Gnash style if torment pig.

Sly if the tempting groans.
Tasty helping if torn gems.
Toyless if pregnant might.
Rats! Helping if snotty gem.
I'm snotty if gentle graphs.
Naggiest myth pilfers not.
Gently phase storming fit.
Gently shame sporting fit.
Fair hogs nest temptingly.
Fair hogs sent temptingly.
Theme farts stingily pong.
Farts stilting phoney gem.
Gnomish, gentle farts pity.
Gently impose nights fart.
Theme pongs stingily fart.
Might stony, sleeping fart.
Hot fear signs temptingly.
Slight nosy, tempting fear.
Fears might gently points.
Isn't fears hog temptingly.
Finer, shy, tempting gloats.
Finer, stately mights pong.
Play-testing serf on might.
Flash petty or stinging me.
Gay gemstones print filth.
Angry gemstones tip filth.
Neatest, grimy filth pongs.
Filth nags germy nepotist.
Filth as my potent niggers.
Sternest filth piggy moan.
Spongy agents merit filth.
Empty filth in strong sage.
Arty filth segments on pig.
Filth smearing testy pong.
Meant on thriftless piggy.
Flesh snotty gem pirating.
Pesteringly fathom sting.
Self-harming gits type not.
Potent gem shifts angrily.
Gently sporting fetish am.
Smarting thief style pong.
Theft mess ignorantly pig.
Fighting on masterly pets.
No fighting stately sperm.
My frightening poets last.
A frightening slots empty.
Empty so last frightening.
Manly frighting set poets.
My poetless ant frighting.
Empty loss frighting neat.
Style frighting poet mans.
Poets man style frighting.
Tensely frighting to maps.

So frighting nasty temple.
Pest mates only frighting.
It's germy, potent flashing.
Potty flashing regiments.
Flights merit spongy neat.
Frighten measly tits pong.
Frighten timely pongs sat.
Frighten timely post nags.
Frighten timely spot nags.
Frighten timely nags stop.
Gain mostly frighten pest.
My! Frighten egotists plan.
Frighten slim petty on gas.
Spot nastily frighten gem.
Stop nastily frighten gem.
Opt nastily frighten gems.
Gleam frighten tiny stops.
Sap frightens gently omit.
Pest frightens mainly got.
Spite frightens manly got.
Its pong frightens tamely.
Post frightens timely nag.
Spot frightens timely nag.
Nag frightens timely stop.
I'm petty slogan frightens.
Frightens to malign types.
I'm top style frightens nag.
Tasty pong frightens mile.
Am stony piglet frightens.
Molest tiny gap frightens.
Tiny, postal gem frightens.
Fighter stings manly poet.
Gently shifting top smear.
So shifting petty mangler.
I fights sporty gentleman.
Strongly spite mean fight.
Partington's seemly fight.
Fight empty to gnarliness.
Fight son's petty maligner.
Snotty gremlins ape fight.
Nosy, gentle arm-pits fight.
Thriftiest 'n' spongy gleam.
Shop-lifting, arty gem nets.
Great! Shoplift tinny gems.
Amen! Shoplift yet G-string.
Fish gently sporting mate.
Final, petty, strongish gem.
Shy pointing flatters gem.
Fertile nymph stings goat.
Top, naggiest hymens flirt.
Poets flirt anything. Gems.
Flirt hog petty manginess.
Oh Man! Petty G-string flies.

Felt on nightmare's pigsty.
Feel pig shitty strong man.
Strongly sight inept fame.
Let's! Stinging fame trophy.
Pity losing fame strength.
Type slight snorting fame.
Sporting fame style night.
Snotty fame priggish lent.
Shitty, top gangrene films.
Hate stingingly form pest.
From that sleeping stingy.
From shitty, negligent sap.
Spit from negligent hasty.
From slighting neat types.
Shit from negligent patsy.
This pasty, negligent form.
The formless, pitying gnat.
Hast in piggy self-torment.
Is piggy than self-torment.
A piggy self-torment hints.
Feminist hogs gently part.
Misfit pongs gently earth.
Misfit pongs gently heart.
Gently misfit on the grasp.
Misfit greatly pongs then.
Hat self-tormenting Gipsy.
Ghastly figment on priest.
Spire not ghastly figment.
Trashy figment on piglets.
Figment hassling pottery.
Figment or lightest pansy.
Spy not ghastlier figment.
Oh! Stingily fragment pest.
Fragment honestly sit pig.
The losing fragments pity.
Piggy, hot firmness talent.
Singingly farm to the pest.
Farm seethingly spotting.
Firm gently hastiest pong.
Farting sting homely pest.
Pig honestly stem farting.
My! The flattering sons pig.
Flattering pigsty on mesh.
Mighty sap fleeting snort.
Gits rat so fleeting nymph.
Might fleeting, nosy sprat.
Stifling nymph as to greet.
State stifling nymph ogre.
Amen! Stifling trophy gets.
Tag stifling trophy semen.
Stifling or the empty nags.
Stifling poetry hasn't gem.
Tempting hearty flings so.

Phoniest, ratty gem flings.
Trim giftless, phoney gnat.
It nastiest flogger nymph.
Name stylish, potent frigg.
Phonily. Frigg statements.
Might floating syren pest.
Flog mighty sternest pain.
Pest merits flog anything.
I'm the fangs spit or gently.
It is the fangs romp gently.
Right! Timely fangs on pest.
Prettily. Fangs on this gem.
I'm the poetry glints fangs.
Rotten fang gets impishly.
Temptingly shit sore fang.
Shit! I'm sporty, gentle fang.
Right fang smiles on petty.
Sorely this tempting fang.
Fitting nymph to largesse.
Sportingly the mean gifts.
Gift hymeneal, strong spit.
Pong tartishly gift semen.
Hog manly gift prettiness.
Empty hot gift gnarliness.
Pong shinily fattest germ.
Fattest niggers oil nymph.
Niggle on shrimpy fattest.
Mightily rent safest pong.
The safest, trimly ponging.
Pong seethingly trim fats.
Pesteringly might no fast.
Sportingly fast in the gem.
Fat night promises gently.
Gently might on fat pisser.
Fat teeth romps singingly.
Stingingly sheet fat romp.
Impressing to lengthy fat.
Fat, seemly, sporting thing.
Fat, honest pigsty gremlin.
Rompingly sense tight fat.
Rompingly sight tense fat.
Fat piglets might on syren.
The pigsty mongrels faint.
Glittery, posh gem infants.
This gore fans temptingly.
Shit gently trim safe pong.
Safe nymph on gits glitter.
Safe tights net rompingly.
Flimsy pint nags together.
Flimsy gathering pets not.
Pong earn tightest flimsy.
Tightest flimsy near pong.
Pong thin flimsy greatest.

Not raging the flimsy pest.
Flimsy pest on the grating.
Family strengthens to pig.
Mortifying tapes lengths.
Nights so tempting flayer.
Safely hot, tempting rings.
Right! Penitent smog flays.
Eh! Impotent G-string flays.
I'm the G-string opens fatly.
Fly hesitant, sporting gem.
Fiery, tempting hogs slant.
Shot infantry piglet gems.
Ferny tights malign poets.
'e's filthy, tempting organs.
Filthy, sporting amen gets.
Pong steaming filthy rest.
Filthy meetings grasp not.
Amongst filthy, pestering.
Filthy pigs gets ornament.
Pig not filthy, sanest germ.
Filthy, potent mass nigger.
Filthy, open G-string mates.
Filthy mate opens G-string.
Filthy, mangiest porn gets.
Filthy, top, grating semens.
Ape filthy, stringent smog.
Step filthy, strong enigma.
Filthy, mega snorting pets.
Spit most filthy gangrene.
Serfishly 'n' tempting goat.
Fortnightly stem sane pig.
Isn't fortnightly ape gems.
Nest forty-eight sampling.
Sent forty-eight sampling.
Spot frighteningly steam.
Stop frighteningly steam.
Frighteningly paste most.
Atoms step frighteningly.
Atom steps frighteningly.
Shiftingly meet pongs rat.
Rotten me gaps shiftingly.
Neat germs opt shiftingly.
Shiftingly top, strange me.
Thrifty as negligent mops.
Thrifty moans niggle pest.
Spit thrifty gems on angel.
On hefty, glittering spasm.
Pig lamest, hefty snorting.
Hefty, polite G-string mans.
Amen! Spoilt hefty G-string.
Hefty, top sting malingers.
Hefty, moral, stinging pest.
Shifty or negligent stamp.

Grime shifty talents pong.
Shifty, potent, slim nagger.
I'm the strong pest flaying.
Fittingly sharp gemstone.
I am lofty pig strengthens.
I'm a lofty pig strengthens.
Y-fronts help mangiest git.
Lightest pain gem Y-fronts.
Y-fronts tape slighting me.
I'm the Y-fronts sang piglet.
Ha! I'm gentlest Y-fronts pig.
Amen! Forty slighting pest.
The gleaming softy prints.
Mean logs prettify nights.
Gleam prettify son's night.
Prettify might son's angle.
Legs prettify not shaming.
Prettify smash niggle not.
Might anger self-pity snot.
The gangs trim on self-pity.
Gems than self-pitying rot.
Nifty paths molest nigger.
Got master's nifty helping.
Ho! Nifty, tempting largess.
Ghost nifty pets malinger.
Nifty, largish, potent gems.
Nifty lengths pig maestro.
Nifty, tight, personal gems.
Nifty pongs grime stealth.
Slash nifty, tempting gore.
Nifty, asleep, strong might.
Please nifty, strong might.
Log nightmare's nifty pest.
So harm nifty, gentlest pig.
The nifty grasp molesting.
This nifty telegram pongs.
Felon spitting trashy gem.
The piggy felon transmits.
Emptying, straight felons.
The softer, tipsy, mangling.
Front shitty, pleasing gem.
I'm the angel's front pigsty.
'e's glittering fatso nymph.
Ahem! Stringently soft pig.
Singingly the soft tamper.
Tip soft, hymeneal G-string.
Soft, shitty, limp gangrene.
Nag softie glitters nymph.
Soften temptingly garish.
Soften tasty, grim helping.
Gently sap mightier fonts.
Fonts rat mighty sleeping.
Fonts pig style nightmare.

Rats! Penis of gently might.
I'm the pigs of gently rants.
Strangely of in might pets.
Rantingly of this gem pets.
Am the pigs of stringently.
Hasten of tempting grisly.
Almighty of spent stinger.
Almighty of present sting.
Myth of sleeping starting.
Pigments of shatteringly.
Nymph glitters of in gates.
Nymph of in glitters stage.
Is greatest nymph of glint.
Pithy of meet stranglings.
Hyper of tattling messing.
Trashy of tempting single.
Shirty of negligent stamp.
Meanly spit of the G-string.
Smiley of taping strength.
Smartingly pig of the nest.
Smartingly of the pig nets.
Smartingly sent of the pig.
Strip-teasing of my length.
Raspingly of the gem tints.
Pesteringly of man tights.
Pigsty of nightmare's lent.
Gremlin's pigsty of the ant.
Hear of temptingly stings.
Tipsy theme of strangling.
Length of masterings pity.
Lengths pity of mastering.
Theme of stranglings pity.
Me of the stranglings pity.
Type of mightless ranting.
Pretty of light manginess.
Pretty of slighting means.
Pretty of slighting names.
Slayer of tempting things.
Sly of this tempting anger.
Fine might ports as gently.
Fine might as gently sport.
Mighty opt fine strangles.
Fine myth as strong piglet.
Fine months pity straggle.
Fine pongs might rat style.
Might not grasp fine style.
Star fines temptingly hog.
Gently finest hot grim sap.
Gosh! Finest impart gently.
Finest gently impart hogs.
Finest sham glittery pong.
Finest poets gnarl mighty.
Finest motherly pigs gnat.

Finest shaggy, rotten limp.
Finest slight empty organ.
Finest nights type glamor.
Tight mongrels pay finest.
Nymph lest niftiest aggro.
Oh! Gently if smarting pest.
Gently might if so parents.
Smashing, pert if to gently.
Strangely if on might pets.
If the gem posts rantingly.
Rantingly if the pest smog.
Grotty if in sanest phlegm.
Help if grotty assignment.
If grotty gentleman ships.
Gory if halt temptingness.
Snortingly if the past gem.
Snortingly if the apt gems.
Snortingly if the pat gems.
Snortingly tap if the gems.
If tempting he as strongly.
Pest if gratingly mesh not.
If lengthy pig torments as.
If nymph glitters on gates.
If nymph glitters on stage.
Gritless nymph if to agent.
Gnarliest if to nymph gets.
Manly if hot, steep G-string.
Path if not seemly G-string.
Temptingly if sorest hang.
Those empty if strangling.
Plenty if ghost mastering.
Potty lengths if smearing.
The petty smog if snarling.
Type if so malign strength.
Sly if the tempting organs.
Natty pigs if the mongrels.
If the snotty naggers limp.
Gremlin's snotty if the gap.
Posh syren if tattling gem.
Hating snotty gem pilfers.
Sporting tights fee manly.
Nights malign sporty feet.
This sporty feet, mangling.
Fist hero nags temptingly.
Hero fits temptingly nags.
Hero nags temptingly sift.
The top me farts singingly.
Hey! Tempting, losing farts.
Temptingly fears hot sign.
Finer, ghostly as tempting.
Ghastly infer tempting, so.
Finer, tempting hasty logs.
Finer gloats empty nights.

Infer stately might pongs.
Goatishly 'n' tempting serf.
Potty, slighting, mean serf.
Tempting no fires ghastly.
Faithless 'n' tempting orgy.
Flashiest 'n' tempting orgy.
Faithless 'n' piggy torment.
Flashiest 'n' piggy torment.
Flash temerity sting pong.
Flash pigsty in rotten gem.
I'm half petty sniggers not.
Filth meets straying pong.
Is angry, potent filth gems.
Filth gnat mysteries pong.
Filth enemy as top G-string.
Semens rat not piggy filth.
Filth sets piggy ornament.
Filth ages empty snorting.
Name petty filth grossing.
Filth types mega snorting.
Filth gets nosy tampering.
Filth pongs yet mastering.
Filth yet masterings pong.
Filthiest, top granny gems.
Filthiest, spongy gem rant.
Not selfish, tempting gray.
O My! Flesh patient G-string.
Self-harming git types not.
Ignorantly shift pest gem.
I'm star thief pongs gently.
Pong rattling messy thief.
Gremlin's potty thief nags.
Types malign strong thief.
Gently as promising theft.
Top theft sniggers mainly.
I'm grasping theft on style.
Manly fighting poser test.
Not frighting measly pets.
Amen! Petty loss frighting.
Molest neat spy frighting.
Sanely tempt so frighting.
A sensory, tempting flight.
Frighten gently, I'm a stops.
Gently frighten moist sap.
Frighten limp agony tests.
Its pongs frighten tamely.
Frighten timely snot gaps.
Gasp timely frighten snot.
Frighten timely posts nag.
Nag timely frighten stops.
Frighten mostly spite nag.
My genitals frighten post.
My! Frighten genitals spot.

My! Frighten genitals stop.
Spongy tits frighten lame.
Mean lots frighten pigsty.
Aptly frighten to messing.
Frighten sly, top, mangiest.
Frighten tasty mile pongs.
Frighten tasty pigs lemon.
Timely frightens at pongs.
Nags opt timely frightens.
Mangily frightens to pets.
Lame spongy tit frightens.
O! Temptingly frightens as.
Gem frightens nastily opt.
Yet frightens to sampling.
Temptingly. Fighter on ass.
No gems frights patiently.
Neatest, slimy fright pong.
Gleam in son's petty fright.
Fortnight's gem as ineptly.
Glimpse nasty freight ton.
Seemingly past fortnight.
Fortnight plays meetings.
Strangely shifting top me.
My resonant piglet fights.
A fights snore temptingly.
Fights pity neat mongrels.
Style fights no tampering.
Nosy, gentle armpit fights.
Gently fight to a primness.
A fight snores temptingly.
Temptingly so saner fight.
Pertinently fight as smog.
Fight on tempting slayers.
Amen! Fight sporting style.
Limp nag grotty heftiness.
Gossip gently name thrift.
Gently. Thrift passion gem.
Stymie thrift pongs angel.
Sanely pig not. Thrift gems.
Stony, pleasing thrift gem.
Thrift piglets annoy gems.
Pong stingily farthest me.
Shop-lifting 'n' my greatest.
Petty flair nothings gems.
Might spongy, neat stifler.
Nasty, mightier felt pongs.
Nasty, mightier left pongs.
Amen! Left snotty priggish.
Fame or gently spit nights.
Fame hints glittery pongs.
Hey! Splitting, strong fame.
Fame glitters spongy hint.
Ineptly sight strong fame.

Snort type slighting fame.
Gently ghost manifest rip.
Pity nights strong female.
Form gently sting ape shit.
The tapes from stingingly.
From gays slight penitent.
Seethingly spit from gnat.
Spy from elegant shitting.
Pig shy, giant self-torment.
Parent hogs gently misfit.
Misfit parents gently hog.
Misfit presently gang hot.
It, strongly phase figment.
Garishly. Figment pets not.
The long figment sparsity.
Figment lightens or pasty.
Fragment on sightly spite.
Shit! Fragment pig on style.
Itsy fragments to helping.
Stingingly hot frame pest.
Phoniest gits farm gently.
Oh My! Gentle farting spits.
Hey! Tempting farting loss.
I'm the slyest farting pong.
Almighty pests finger not.
Almighty pests fringe not.
Flattering, tiny gem shops.
Not self-rating, pithy gems.
Fragileness 'n' potty might.
The spongy flirting mates.
Empty to flirting gnashes.
Phase snotty flirting gem.
Fleeting 'n' grotty mishaps.
A fleeting, sporting myths.
Fleeting pays might snort.
Sight fleeting, nasty romp.
Fleeting stays might porn.
Fleeting, nosy parts might.
Fleeting, nosy traps might.
Fleeting, ratty hims pongs.
Stifling honesty trap gem.
Hey! Stifling torment gaps.
Hey! Torment stifling gasp.
Stifling, pretty, mean hogs.
Heap stifling, snotty germ.
Flings might petty reason.
Typist flings hatemonger.
Pig not rat giftless hymen.
It rage not giftless nymph.
Great! Into giftless nymph.
So empty failing strength.
Flag tiny, smothering pest.
Top frigg shames intently.

I'm the stringent pay flogs.
Nasty, tempting hire flogs.
Flog this emptiest granny.
Anything merit pests flog.
Flog in its greatest nymph.
This pretty meanings flog.
Tyrant penises might flog.
Tiny nightmare pests flog.
Gently shit to prime fangs.
Fangs tin smothery piglet.
Impishly rotten fangs get.
Grimy, hot, pestilent fangs.
Temptingly rise hot fangs.
Fangs empty hero stilting.
Gem on fangs shit prettily.
Fangs shit prettily. Gnome.
Petty fangs might in loser.
The petty fangs or smiling.
Fangs smother tiny piglet.
It is the fang romps gently.
Petty losers might in fang.
Threaten spongy, slim gift.
Is fattest nymph or niggle.
Gnomish fattest replying.
The pitying mongrels fast.
Stingingly fate hot sperm.
I'm the fat sons prig gently.
Homely fat pets in G-string.
Pong regiment stylish fat.
Fat, negligent trophy miss.
I'm shy, sporting, gentle fat.
Might fat, spongy listener.
The springy fat molesting.
Imply strong fat seething.
Temptingly sing hero's fat.
Fat G-string homes ineptly.
Fatness or empty lighting.
Nymph glitters egos faint.
Gosh! Petty gremlins faint.
Gremlin's petty hogs faint.
I'm the leggy infants strop.
Infant, shorty piglet gems.
This grim poet fans gently.
Slighting petty fans more.
Might steely, sporting fan.
Safe, tempting glory hints.
Nightly torment safe pigs.
Temptingly safe, hot rings.
Gosh! Tag pertinent flimsy.
Hogs tag pertinent flimsy.
Tonight anger flimsy pest.
To the flimsy niggers pant.
Right! Gentle infamy posts.

Firstly steaming the pong.
Shit! Pong in flattery gems.
Gosh! Isn't tempting flayer.
Isn't tempting flayer hogs.
Safely trim pongs tighten.
Hero flays tempting sting.
Fattily pong the grimness.
Fatly phoniest me G-string.
Gnash fiery, tempting lots.
Gnash fiery, tempting slot.
Hot egg simplest infantry.
Light infantry gems poets.
The infantry smog piglets.
Ferny talents might so pig.
Filthy meat stingers pong.
Rats! Filthy meetings pong.
Filthy pigs gemstone rant.
Taping or filthy segments.
Filthy gems as potent grin.
Filthy poet grants in gems.
Filthy, steep, storming nag.
Filthy, steep moan G-string.
I'm filthy pest on gangster.
Spit not anger filthy gems.
Serfishly tag tempting no.
Thriftily tag semens pong.
Thriftily nag pest on gems.
I'm tense fortnightly gaps.
Shiftingly spot neat germ.
Shiftingly stop neat germ.
Gnome pets shiftingly rat.
Thrifty pongs entail gems.
Thrifty me pongs stealing.
Angel's thrifty items pong.
Angel's thrifty times pong.
Thrifty, steep, so mangling.
Pig not fishy, gentle smart.
Not splattering fishy gem.
Niggle fishy, potent smart.
Hefty lies tampon G-string.
Torment shifty pigs angel.
Shifty, tree-planting smog.
Shifty, inept, strong gleam.
Shifty, gleaming portents.
Gremlin's shifty poet gnat.
Shifty, gleaming, torn pest.
Tempting he nags frostily.
Felonry as tempting sight.
Right! Tempting felony ass.
I'm the felony past G-string.
Y-fronts pig meat lightens.
Y-fronts emit gnash piglet.
Y-fronts gleam spite night.

Y-fronts might giant sleep.
Y-fronts might spite angle.
I'm the pat niggles Y-fronts.
I'm the tap niggles Y-fronts.
Giant piglet Y-fronts mesh.
Piglet hints mega Y-fronts.
The gleaming tips Y-fronts.
Might frosty pest in angel.
The frosty spite, mangling.
This frosty, negligent map.
Might sprain gentle softy.
Hogs prettify alignments.
Prettify nights loan gems.
Petrify might angel's snot.
Petrify stolen might nags.
Straight self-pity 'n' on gem.
Self-pity strength 'n' amigo.
German self-pity to nights.
Self-pitying, hot ant germs.
Self-pitying me grants hot.
No! That self-pitying germs.
Simplify strengthen goat.
The fatty on gremlin's pigs.
Nifty, harlot pig segments.
Mangle nifty, shortest pig.
Angel's nifty, hot, grim pest.
Leapt nifty, strongish gem.
Nifty gather glimpses not.
Right! Nifty pals gemstone.
Right! On nifty pests gleam.
Nifty, tempting hag losers.
Might opt nifty largeness.
Nightmare's nifty, top legs.
Trash nifty piglet on gems.
Might tipsy, strange felon.
Right! Tempting felon says.
This felon's tempting gray.
Felon's tapestrying might.
Mighty presenting floats.
Gently might in softer sap.
I, temptingly softer gnash.
An empty, softer, slighting.
Elegant front piss mighty.
I'm shaggy, pestilent front.
Gently pirating soft mesh.
Aptly might soft sneering.
Soft, ratty helping in gems.
Mighty sleeping star font.
Font threatens slim piggy.
Insight of gently tampers.
Might of raspiest 'n' gently.
I'm the strips of gently nag.
I'm the grant of gently piss.

I'm that pressing of gently.
Master's hint of gently pig.
Master's thin of gently pig.
Gently of this giant sperm.
Gently smarten of this pig.
Gently margin of this pest.
Rantingly of steep mights.
Hat of girly temptingness.
Slept of stingy nightmare.
Nightmare of stingy spelt.
Pig of sternest 'n' almighty.
Mighty of starting spleen.
Hymens of past glittering.
Printing of ghastly meets.
Print of ghastly meetings.
Nightly of steep smarting.
Tightly of pert manginess.
It is net nymph of straggle.
Nymph of in stages glitter.
Right! Manly of tensest pig.
Sting of temptingly hears.
Share sting of temptingly.
Empty of gnarliest things.
Insights of petty mangler.
Shitting of mangler types.
Patsy of meriting lengths.
Is pregnant style of might.
Lighting of any temptress.
A fine might pets strongly.
To fine, straggly shipment.
Ghastly storming fine pet.
Fine, sightly gap torments.
Tightly. Master's fine pong.
Straggle so fine nymph tit.
Fine nymph glitters as got.
Tag fine nymph glitters so.
Fine, trashy, tempting logs.
Temptingly short fine gas.
Gosh! Temptingly fine arts.
Temptingly hogs fine arts.
Fine, tight patsy mongrels.
Pong might fine, star style.
Finest gently harm to pigs.
Finest strongly, I'm the gap.
Finest gratingly met posh.
Finest mighty strong leap.
Finest mighty strong pale.
Finest mighty strong plea.
Pat infest homely G-string.
Mega trophy glints finest.
Pong finest grimy stealth.
Right! Finest penalty smog.
Pity finest ghost mangler.

Slang niftiest trophy gem.
Shaggily trim potent fens.
Protest if gently shaming.
Rats! I'm the pongs if gently.
Orgy if halt temptingness.
If tempting glory hastens.
Straggly if in potent mesh.
Trim tense if ghastly pong.
I am lengthy if strong pest.
I'm a lengthy if strong pest.
Temptress if anything log.
If stealthy 'n' sporting gem.
Tie nymph if not straggles.
Nymph if on stages glitter.
Large nymph if to settings.
If tenth gem as sportingly.
Spongy germ if this talent.
Molest if paying strength.
Presently might if not gas.
Partly if nights. Gemstone.
Gremlin's potty if the nags.
Tipsy strength if no gleam.
Pity if so mangle strength.
The malign if strong types.
Son's might if pretty angel.
Phantom if steely G-string.
Style if moan pig strength.
O Man! Style if pig strength.
Tyrants if helping to gems.
Natty gem profiles nights.
Profit mess gently hating.
I'm the snotty gangs pilfer.
I'm the snotty gang pilfers.
Might snortingly sap feet.
Rattling fist phoney gems.
Phoney gems fits rattling.
Stingingly meet posh fart.
Fart mesh stingingly. Poet.
The poems fart stingingly.
Shy, impotent fart niggles.
Honestly spitting far gem.
Finer post as gently might.
Finer might as gently spot.
Finer might as gently stop.
Thinly infer maggot's pest.
Finer hogs sat temptingly.
Finer style gaps not might.
Gently that imposing serf.
O Man! Petty, slighting serf.
Might poignant serf style.
Strife types hot mangling.
Temptingly fires hot nags.
Free ghost manly spitting.

Flash petty, inmost nigger.
It's soggy, permanent filth.
Filth prints gay gemstone.
Straying filth pets on gem.
Filth pets straying gnome.
Snort meanest filth piggy.
Filth enraging potty mess.
Type filth as snorting gem.
Filth sniggers natty poem.
Pig snotty, saner filth gem.
Sap snotty filth emerging.
Grasp tiny filth gemstone.
Thriftless agony pint gem.
Thriftless, tiny, mega pong.
Self-harming pigsty to net.
Self-harming pigsty to ten.
It self-harming, testy pong.
Glittery mineshaft pongs.
Fetishes pong trimly. Gnat.
Pretty shifts on gleaming.
Giant fetish romps gently.
Spongy, grim fetish talent.
Shift angrily potent gems.
Gremlin's gay, potent shift.
Am sporty, negligent shift.
Nosy, tempting, large shift.
Thief snarling potty gems.
Sly, tempting thief groans.
Pong gently shiftiest ram.
So empaling stringy theft.
Graspingly moisten theft.
So impregnating sly theft.
Talents spy more fighting.
Ape sly torments fighting.
My frightening poet lasts.
Spot seemly frighting ant.
Stop seemly frighting ant.
Petty mans lose frighting.
Style frighting mean post.
Style frighting mean spot.
Stop mean style frighting.
Nasty pest frighting mole.
Mine grotty flashing pest.
Flashing poetry tints gem.
Merit petty flashing song.
Typeset not grim flashing.
To flashing in pretty gems.
Tempting stay or fleshing.
On angry, emptiest flights.
Flights pity resonant gem.
Gently spit so frighten am.
Frighten state slimy pong.
Mostly frighten inept gas.

Frighten not as my piglets.
Frighten empty sin gloats.
Frighten empty, giant loss.
Frighten saintly gem pots.
Frighten am pongs testily.
Frighten tasty lemons pig.
Tasty lips frighten gnome.
Frighten snotty, male pigs.
Frighten snotty males pig.
Frighten snotty meals pig.
Frighten snotty, mega lips.
Frighten snotty, mega lisp.
Frighten snotty, mega slip.
Spit frighten stony gleam.
Frighten pliant gems toys.
Frighten molest tiny gaps.
Frighten molest tiny gasp.
Molest gay pint frightens.
Meanly frightens top gits.
Snot frightens timely gap.
My pig frightens not stale.
Pigsty frightens not. Meal.
To aptly frightens in gems.
I'm long petty frightens as.
Pig frightens mental toys.
Fighter glimpses on natty.
Fighters malign not types.
Pin snotty fighters gleam.
Fright ones as temptingly.
Tipsy, gentle fright moans.
Slimy, potent anger fights.
Nasty poet fights gremlin.
Angry, potent fight smiles.
Fight seemly sporting ant.
Gremlin's potty, sane fight.
Tipsy mongrels fight neat.
Fight on slyest tampering.
Petty, strong finish gleam.
Leggy, mean thrift piss not.
Slimy pongs negate thrift.
Top thrift nags seemingly.
Thrift on angel's tipsy gem.
Angel's tipsy thrift gnome.
Thrift annoys gem piglets.
Yes mangling thrift poets.
Shop-lifting gems yet rant.
My! Shoplift naggiest rent.
Tiny shoplifter gems gnat.
I'm half-open, testy G-string.
Gently top faith grimness.
Flat pestering nosy might.
Hey! Tempting, strong fails.
Ghost infernal gits empty.

Sight infernal, potty gems.
Flirt naggiest nymph toes.
Nymph gits flirt stone-age.
The mangey, sporting lifts.
Lift egotists anger nymph.
Felt riots naggiest nymph.
This mangey, sporting felt.
This mangey, sporting left.
I'm spongy felt shattering.
Left ransoming the pigsty.
Left nights sporty enigma.
Gosh! Stringently tip fame.
Fame hogs stringently pit.
Stringently tip fame hogs.
Strongly spitting fame he.
Stringy, top fame lightens.
Nightly, top fame stingers.
The stingy, sporting flame.
Flame the snorting pigsty.
Forms spite gently hating.
From the giant piss gently.
Sightly penitent from gas.
From shitty, sleeping gnat.
Leftmost, spiny gathering.
Stringently foam the pigs.
Pong gently misfit hearts.
Gently sap or this figment.
Top figment nets garishly.
Ghastly figment proteins.
Honestly! Arts pig figment.
Not pithy figment largess.
Figment hits sporty angel.
Figment hag piss rottenly.
Figment strays to helping.
He fragments snottily pig.
Shop testily fragmenting.
Grotty helps manifesting.
Ghost angel's infirm petty.
Stingingly the top frames.
Phoniest git farms gently.
Temptingly fearing shots.
Sightly, top farting semen.
My farting lightens poets.
Sleepy farting mights not.
Might farting opens style.
My! Is the flattering pongs.
Spy on this flattering gem.
Shop flattering, tiny gems.
Self-rating hypnotist gem.
Fleeting sons part mighty.
Fleeting, shitty arms pong.
Pig not fleeting, shy smart.
Hot spying fleeting smart.

Fleeting, grim natty shops.
To a stifling nymph greets.
Stifling nags meet trophy.
The stifling, mangey ports.
The stifling, mangey sport.
Met gnash stifling poetry.
Stifling, petty rash on gem.
Stifling pasty on the germ.
It anger to giftless nymph.
Thirty giftless, mean pong.
No harming giftless petty.
Not harming giftless type.
So mighty, pertinent flags.
Hero's tiny, tempting flags.
Sanest frigg nymph toilet.
Slash potty, eminent frigg.
It flogs in greatest nymph.
Hearty flogs tempting sin.
My threatening spit flogs.
Petty flogs thin smearing.
The natty flogs, simpering.
Flog mighty pertinent ass.
Flog state stingier nymph.
Flog rate stingiest nymph.
My threatening spits flog.
Flog the natty impressing.
Fangs merit nightly poets.
I'm pithy or gentlest fangs.
It, temptingly. Hero's fangs.
Strongly spite, I'm the fang.
Spot seethingly trim fang.
Stop seethingly trim fang.
Pithy, storming, steel fang.
Hot fang rises temptingly.
Temptingly this sore fang.
Hero's empty fang stilting.
Ho! Sisterly, tempting fang.
Mightiest fang style porn.
Harlot's petty fining gems.
Honestly! Prime gnat gifts.
Shy, potent gifts malinger.
Honest, grim penalty gifts.
Gift the angry simpletons.
Transiently gift posh gem.
Gift sly, honest tampering.
Gift snotty, sleeping harm.
Soil fattest nymph nigger.
Might groin safest plenty.
Stingingly feast the romp.
Feast thinly sporting gem.
Gently meriting posh fats.
Fast gently might in poser.
Fast! Homely, inept G-string.

Feat, shitty gremlins pong.
Fat might pots sneeringly.
Fat themes pig snortingly.
Misprint leggy, honest fat.
Mighty snorting fat sleep.
Fat, pointless myth nigger.
Seethingly imp strong fat.
Fat gemstones rip nightly.
Sprightly fat in gemstone.
Remissly tighten fat pong.
Fat helping to my stingers.
It the gremlin's spongy fat.
Simperingly ghost fat net.
Simperingly ghost fat ten.
Fat hogs temptingly risen.
I'm fat plenty sniggers hot.
Openly shitting fat germs.
Tipsy, gnomish, gentler fat.
Fat, negligent toys shrimp.
Infants shop glittery gem.
Motherly pig gets infants.
Infants might sporty glee.
Infant, glittery gem shops.
Infant style gropes might.
The strong fans pig timely.
Gremlin's safe, potty night.
Hot granting steep flimsy.
Ghost flimsy, penitent rag.
Strengthen to a flimsy pig.
Flimsy pong seething tart.
Flimsy, potent night rages.
Sight flimsy, potent anger.
Flimsy to the grasping ten.
Not pig self-mastery thing.
Short pig gentlest infamy.
Pong firstly hesitant gem.
Posh, stinging flattery me.
Flattery piss nothing. Gem.
Tempting flayer signs hot.
Pong met safely thirsting.
Pong safely term shitting.
Tightest 'n' safely romping.
Faintly right pest on gems.
Mere shitting pongs fatly.
Fatly shitting person gem.
Fatly pestering on mights.
Fly strongish, patient gem.
Fiery pong mights talents.
So fairy, tempting lengths.
Spitting honest fry gleam.
Elegant might piss not fry.
Anger filthy, tempting SOS.
Filthy, tempting son rages.

Filthy, naggiest romps net.
Filthy, naggiest ten romps.
Filthy, sporting meet nags.
Filthy agent pongs merits.
Filthy, angriest pongs met.
Filthy, passing, rotten gem.
A filthy, inept, strong gems.
Gas print filthy gemstone.
Filthy trip nags gemstone.
Filthy, top grimness agent.
In filthy, mega, strong pest.
Filthy spies torment gang.
Thriftily tag semen pongs.
Isn't flashy, tempting goer.
Pig fortnightly sat semen.
Shiftingly tampers on get.
Shiftingly top, merest nag.
Shiftingly tape not. Germs.
Shiftingly tape strong me.
Empaling thrifty sons get.
Thrifty glimpses on agent.
Pongs lest thrifty enigma.
Let's! Thrifty enigma pongs.
Leg thrifty, top manginess.
Got thrifty plainness gem.
Thrifty, gleaming pest son.
Fishy, impotent 'n' straggle.
Rattling fishy pest on gem.
Rattling fishy pest gnome.
On simplest, hefty grating.
It niggle hefty sportsman.
Is hefty, grim talents pong.
Hefty pig metals snorting.
Hefty pig torments signal.
Strangle hefty, inmost pig.
Am hefty, snorting piglets.
Smart pole hefty stinging.
Malign hefty stingers opt.
Mangling hefty pest riots.
Hefty mongrels spit giant.
Not tampering shifty legs.
Shifty, tempting as longer.
Shifty, gentle giants romp.
The foggy, trim pliantness.
Satisfying phlegm to rent.
Glorify hat temptingness.
Shit! Gas tempting felonry.
I lofty, tempting gnashers.
I'm the lofty sniggers pant.
Y-fronts tame helping gits.
Y-fronts lighten pig mates.
Slight inept, mega Y-fronts.
Light pest enigma Y-fronts.

Y-fronts pig meetings halt.
Is tenth Y-fronts pig gleam.
It's the Y-fronts mangle pig.
He spitting Y-fronts gleam.
A frosty, tempting English.
Rant might sleeping softy.
Mans prettify hot niggles.
Gosh! Mean glints prettify.
Gosh! Malign nets prettify.
Hogs malign nets prettify.
Prettify than losing gems.
Gleam nights petrify snot.
Self-pity gnashing to term.
Nights torn mega self-pity.
Self-pity groans net might.
Simplify the strong agent.
Gosh! Gremlin's inept fatty.
Gremlin's inept fatty hogs.
Fatty pigs in the mongrels.
Nifty niggers molest path.
Nifty, tempting hero glass.
Softer pain mights gently.
Gem fronts hesitantly pig.
Front gently misshape git.
Front pig tenses almighty.
For angel's empty shitting.
Softest, grit, genial nymph.
Gently simpering soft hat.
Shatteringly pin soft gem.
Simperingly the soft gnat.
Soft yet smarting helping.
Fonts might greatly. Penis.
Straggle, it is often nymph.
Gnash of gently merit spit.
Gently might of sane strip.
Spies might of gently rant.
Gently sing of the arm-pits.
In the smart pigs of gently.
'e's pest of rantingly might.
Stingingly arm of the pest.
Leggy of thinnest arm-pits.
I'm straying length of pest.
Stringy of tamest helping.
Piss! Gentle of mighty rant.
I'm lengthy pig of tartness.
Sightly of permanent gits.
Steel nymph of as gritting.
Glittering nymph of as set.
It isn't large of nymph gets.
Grips of shitty gentleman.
Pester shitty of mangling.
Shy template of in G-string.
Strength of manly site pig.

Strength of manly ties pig.
Timely span of the G-string.
Mangily of tight presents.
Smartingly of steep night.
Is many strength of piglet.
My pest of thirsting angel.
Sight gits of permanently.
Temptingly of nights. Ears.
Hates of temptingly rings.
Stinger of temptingly has.
Hisser of temptingly. Gnat.
Temptingly of as the rings.
Strangle of this emptying.
Plenty of smearing tights.
Plenty of a stingers might.
I'm petty of gnashers glint.
Petty of it gnash gremlins.
Gremlin's shit of petty nag.
Gremlin's tipsy of the gnat.
Type of master's lightning.
Types mangle of thirsting.
I'm gentler pasty of nights.
Then style of smarting pig.
Nasty strength of mile pig.
Tight syren of malign pest.
Tiny strength of limp sage.
Strangely might fine tops.
Ghastly trip not fine gems.
Ghastly spit not fine germ.
Fines strangle top mighty.
Gosh! Fines rat temptingly.
Fines rat temptingly hogs.
Pong greatly finest smith.
Finest has tempting glory.
Infest mighty alert pongs.
Finest mighty sport angel.
Oh My! Finest piglet grants.
Finest myth groans piglet.
Pong finest ghastly timer.
Finest ghastly point germ.
Trophy maligns finest get.
Finest hang stormy piglet.
Finest hot pigsty mangler.
Finest shag or temptingly.
Finest might leprosy gnat.
Potty harm niggles finest.
Right! Finest spy not gleam.
Infest snottily graph gem.
Ogrishly attempting fens.
Tempting fens to garishly.
Path to grimness if gently.
Gently if right pests moan.
Hag if gently torment piss.

Gently if nights tamper so.
If star might opens gently.
If sane might ports gently.
Gently might if sane sport.
On the smart pigs if gently.
If hot gems pets rantingly.
Shipments if grotty angel.
Gay, gentlest if not shrimp.
Gay if not simple strength.
Strong myth if sane piglet.
Myth if gloating presents.
Poetless myth if granting.
Sprat if nightly gemstone.
Stylish if to pregnant gem.
Shy template if on G-string.
Shy if top, gentle smarting.
If strength toes manly pig.
Masterly pong if the sting.
Smoggy if pertinent halts.
Raspingly if to tenth gems.
Sportingly if a tenth gems.
If strong he as temptingly.
Ghost if presently mating.
Presently if to might nags.
Might if sporty angel nets.
If style than sporting gem.
Nasty lengths if grim poet.
Snort helping if tasty gem.
If the tasty gremlin pongs.
Gnash gem if rottenly spit.
Snotty harm if gentle pigs.
Snotty pigs if the mangler.
Strongest if a tiny phlegm.
Hast snotty gem pilfering.
Snotty hat pilfering gems.
Tiny, mightless front-page.
The maggot's tinny pilfers.
Splif hating grotty semen.
The grotty splif meanings.
Smartingly pong this feet.
Fist gay helping torments.
Temptingly fist saner hog.
Saner fits hog temptingly.
Gently sap smothering fit.
Gosh! Temptingly fair nest.
Gosh! Temptingly fair nets.
Temptingly hogs fair nets.
The me farts stingily pong.
Oh My! Pig in gentlest farts.
Steely farts might in pong.
Tensely might on farts pig.
The me pongs stingily fart.
Empty slighting ones fart.

Tipsy, gnomish, gentle fart.
Steely fart pongs in might.
Not typing mightless fear.
Gently might on fears spit.
In ghostly, tempting fears.
So nightly, tempting fears.
Safer ghost in temptingly.
Gently top far mightiness.
Finer, tempting sloth gays.
Thinly. Maggot's finer pets.
Ghost finer, mental pigsty.
Temptingly gas finer host.
Temptingly shot finer gas.
Halo stingy, tempting serf.
Pong mainly tightest serf.
Moaningly tight serf pest.
Temptingly hog serf saint.
Slighting serf to payment.
Might nasty serf on piglet.
Gently shaming top strife.
Pong hesitantly first gem.
Temptingly hog sane first.
Fire spongy talents might.
Not typing faithless germ.
Not typing flashiest germ.
Flash in grotty, inept gems.
Flash pig tiny, rotten gems.
Merit testy flash ponging.
Flash yet tormenting pigs.
Angry gemstones pit filth.
In my potent filth aggress.
My filth sniggers top neat.
Filth greasing empty snot.
Soapy, stringent filth gem.
Nasty filth merges not pig.
Filth pongs arty meetings.
Yet tampon filth sniggers.
Grotty, pan filthiness gem.
Flesh stingy to tampering.
Stingy shelf to tampering.
Flesh tasty, meriting pong.
Shelf pirating snotty gem.
No self-harming, petty gits.
Sponge self-harming titty.
Trim fetish as gently pong.
Potent fetish nags grimly.
Glittery, mean shift pongs.
Shift pigsty or gentleman.
Smart ponging thief style.
Gap gremlin's snotty thief.
Ant ports seemly fighting.
Seemly fighting past torn.
Seemly fighting pat snort.

Mostly fighting near pest.
Rants empty lose fighting.
Not fighting merest plays.
Am snotty lepers fighting.
Yes fighting talents romp.
My poets salt frightening.
Spy to lamest frightening.
Am slyest, top frightening.
Sons empty late frighting.
Potty, nameless, frighting.
Petty lemons as frighting.
Flashing to petty in germs.
Snotty, prime flashing get.
Grotty, mean penis flights.
My! So penetrating flights.
Sporty gem flights in neat.
Mangiest entropy flights.
Entropy flights steaming.
Straying, top flight semen.
Frighten stingy to sample.
Manly pig so frighten test.
Frighten manly pig to sets.
Frighten measly, top sting.
Frighten to mangey splits.
My! Frighten pointless tag.
Gleam frighten spotty sin.
Frighten potty slime nags.
Gleam frighten potty sins.
Frighten style mans to pig.
Nasty lips frighten to gem.
Frighten sanity plots gem.
Frighten pests malign toy.
Agony frightens limp test.
Gay, potent, slim, frightens.
To ample stingy frightens.
To mangey spllt frlghtens.
Empty log frightens saint.
Slime potty nag frightens.
Sly mate frightens not pig.
Natty frightens egos limp.
Fighter spits gently moan.
Fighter moans gently spit.
Temptingly a son's fighter.
Manly sting poet fighters.
Tipsy fighters mangle not.
Frights empty on stealing.
Amen! Gently piss to fright.
O My! Pestilent fright nags.
Pong tastily. Fright semen.
Mean fright pongs testily.
My! Fortnight's sane piglet.
Seemly ants pig fortnight.
Sanely spit fortnight gem.

Mean fortnight style pigs.
Gently smart fishing poet.
Potent, mean grisly fights.
A smog fights pertinently.
Angel's petty fights minor.
Spiny, rotten fights gleam.
Pain fights rottenly. Gems.
Fight remissly potent nag.
Fight employing tartness.
Fight penalty to grimness.
Fight as on gremlin's petty.
Finishes plant grotty gem.
Finish strangle potty gem.
Thrift nags gently impose.
On thrift piss gently game.
Pong stymie angel's thrift.
Not piggy, nameless thrift.
Thrift lest spongy enigma.
Pity thrift on angel's gems.
Thrift pets nosy gleaming.
Gently nag fresh optimist.
Nest shop-lifting, arty gem.
Sent shop-lifting, arty gem.
Shop-lifting, arty, net gems.
Shop-lifting gem rants yet.
Any flight strip gemstone.
Shoplift trying, neat gems.
Shoplift tasty men nigger.
Fish pigsty or tanglement.
Flat stingiest nymph ogre.
False, petty, grim nothings.
False snoring petty might.
Right! Nosy, tempting fleas.
Fail empty honest G-string.
Flares empty hot stinging.
Mighty flatters openings.
My stinging hope flatters.
Fertile, spongy ants might.
Thorny, tempting flies gas.
Lift the spongy mastering.
Mighty, sporting, sane felt.
Left sporting, sane mighty.
Left groin smashing petty.
Self, mighty, sporting neat.
Oh My! Self, patient G-string.
Gently pig on fame thirsts.
Shit! Pig gently snort fame.
Sightly, potent fame grins.
Types torn slighting fame.
Gently short manifest pig.
Flame pity honest G-string.
The saint forms gently pig.
This neat forms gently pig.

Genial petty forms nights.
Forms enlighten tasty pig.
Sagely spitting from then.
Stingily nag from the pest.
Sleepy shitting from gnat.
Petty insights from angel.
Enlighten from tasty pigs.
Pithy self-torment in gags.
Self-torment pigsty in hag.
Ghastly presenting motif.
Gosh! Gently part feminist.
Grotty nags help feminist.
Angry lengths misfit poet.
Honestly gang pert misfit.
Thorny, gentle misfit gaps.
Presently foaming tights.
Hot figment prints sagely.
Sightly, top, saner figment.
Its angel's figment trophy.
Angel's shirty, top figment.
Shy, top, gnarliest figment.
Hot stingers play figment.
Star figment hogs ineptly.
This sporty figment angle.
Garishly potent figments.
Gently, it is posh fragment.
Ho! Stingily fragment pest.
Fragment note stylish pig.
Fragment shitty lies pong.
The tipsy, losing fragment.
Fragment nights oily pest.
Eh! Stingily top fragments.
Engraftment hogs tipsily.
This sly poet fragmenting.
Haggle infirm, snotty pest.
O My! Farting lightens pest.
Let's! I'm the spongy farting.
Flattering egos sit nymph.
Fragile nymph to settings.
Fleeting, thirsty am pongs.
Harm fleeting, spongy tits.
Fleeting, sham, strong pity.
Right! Most fleeting pansy.
Right! Fleeting, nosy stamp.
Stifling nymph treats ego.
Met stifling stenography.
Stifling, mega trophy nets.
Stifling, phoney gems tart.
Stifling, sporty, mega then.
Stifling, ratty gem phones.
Stifling tyrant hopes gem.
My! That sporting feelings.
Nasty, tight feelings romp.

Sporty, hesitant fling gem.
Paint giftless, thorny gem.
Nag merit giftless python.
Right! No giftless payment.
Emptying, thorniest flags.
Flag on pretty mightiness.
Might flag syren nepotist.
Manly, hottest frigg penis.
My frigg to the pliantness.
Tipsy, honest, mental frigg.
Say flogs pertinent might.
Flog trash eminent pigsty.
Flog any might prettiness.
Nightmare's tiny pets flog.
Forget hit man piss gently.
Tangent forgets impishly.
Mightily resent top fangs.
Emptiest fangs on rightly.
Fangs trim seethingly opt.
Shorty, tempting fangs lie.
Ghost fangs merit ineptly.
Fangs tighten slim poetry.
Fangs might silent poetry.
Fangs yet right simpleton.
Temptingly. Fang to hisser.
Empty lose thirsting fang.
Prettily shit fang on gems.
Sporty fang in steel might.
Gremlin's to the tipsy fang.
Might slyer fang nepotist.
Help snotty, grimiest fang.
Might reptile's stony fang.
Gently fisting smart hope.
Gently fisting metaphors.
Gently fisting top harems.
Gently fisting romps hate.
Gently fisting hates romp.
Gently fisting as the romp.
Fig gently phoniest smart.
Rompish neat gifts gently.
Pert neat gifts gnomishly.
Mastery gifts not. Helping.
I'm sharp-set gift on gently.
I'm sharpest gift on gently.
Gift nymph as strong elite.
Gift not empaling shyster.
Shy mongrels gift patient.
Sporty, mean gift lightens.
Safest pin or gently might.
Fast shitting merely pong.
Fast grime snotty helping.
Thinly feat, sporting gems.
Gently stripe gnomish fat.

This grim fat opens gently.
Singly. Hero's tempting fat.
Strongly seething fat imp.
Gnomishly spent fat tiger.
Fat nymph glitters in goes.
Fat trophy gems listening.
Enlighten fat, stormy pigs.
O My! Present slighting fat.
Fat, slighting enemy ports.
My! The strong fat spieling.
Shit! I'm spongy, gentler fat.
Nights romping steely fat.
Teeny, slighting fat romps.
Gently hop grim fattiness.
Faint, sporty gem lightens.
Gosh! Prettily. Gem infants.
Shop infant, glittery gems.
Oh My! Glittering pest fans.
This gem fans rottenly pig.
Stylish, tempting fan ogre.
Safe, mighty, sporting lent.
Safe glitters got in nymph.
Not imply the safe G-string.
Pity safe, storming length.
Flimsy, potent things rage.
Tighten ape strong flimsy.
Hint flimsy, greatest pong.
Flimsy hits potent nagger.
Eh! A flimsy, potent G-string.
Rip ghost gentlest infamy.
I'm the flattery pongs sing.
I'm the flattery sings pong.
The singing flattery mops.
Frailty pongs tense might.
No! Safely tempting rights.
Safely might snorting pet.
Right! In potent gems flays.
Right semen pongs fattily.
Tempting hero signs fatly.
Fatly strongish, inept gem.
Nights impregnates to fly.
This impotent naggers fly.
Gosh! Fiery, tempting slant.
Fiery talent mights pongs.
Gossip might ferny talent.
Politest, ferny might nags.
Top fry lightens steaming.
Talents pig something fry.
Nest filthy, naggiest romp.
Sent filthy, naggiest romp.
Filthy, sporting, mega nest.
Filthy, sporting, mega nets.
Filthy gem as sporting net.

Filthy gem as sporting ten.
Filthy, sporting meets nag.
Filthy, poignant gem rests.
Filthy, merest giant pongs.
Rest filthy, mangiest pong.
Meet filthy, grasping snot.
Filthy raspings net to gem.
Grasp filthy mignonettes.
Among sternest, filthy pig.
Maggot's filthy pint sneer.
Filthy gemstones trip nag.
Filthy gem as potent grins.
Filthy, strange gem points.
Strong pest in a filthy gem.
Filthy pest ransoming get.
Filthy pest maggot sinner.
Filthy merits gang on pest.
Spit rang filthy gemstone.
Filthy gem piss rotten nag.
Serfishly tampon getting.
Thriftily gets mean pongs.
Fortnightly pig at semens.
Fortnightly game in pests.
Fortnightly pests in a gem.
Frighteningly steam post.
Shiftingly gate not. Sperm.
Shiftingly gasp rotten me.
Shiftingly taper not. Gems.
Shiftingly pert, neat smog.
Tape shiftingly snort gem.
Shiftingly tape torn gems.
Thrifty, mean piglet songs.
Molest gang thrifty penis.
Angel's thrifty, inept smog.
Plainest, thrifty gem song.
Not fishy, tempting glares.
Alert fishy, tempting song.
Hefty maligner pongs tits.
Hefty pong malingers tits.
Hefty pig molesting rants.
Hefty signals torment pig.
Isn't hefty, gleaming strop.
Align hefty, storming pest.
Nag shifty, tempting loser.
Amen! Shifty pongs glitter.
Shifty pig on gentle smart.
Shifty, potent grins gleam.
Angel's shifty, potent, grim.
Shifty gem opens rattling.
Limp fogey strength saint.
Merit lofty pest gnashing.
Gnash lofty, meriting pest.
Gentle mishap git Y-fronts.

Y-fronts instigate phlegm.
Y-fronts might inept gales.
Y-fronts align steep might.
I'm gentle Y-fronts hast pig.
This net Y-fronts pig gleam.
Shit! Gleaming Y-fronts pet.
Gnash frosty, tempting lie.
Amen! Nights frosty piglet.
Thin gleaming frosty pest.
The frosty, ample stinging.
The frosty pigs alignment.
Frosty hits pig gentleman.
His frosty, tempting angel.
Softy garnishment piglet.
Prettify hot slang in gems.
Prettify hot mangle signs.
Prettify to 'n' slashing gem.
Prettify slight mean song.
Molest hangings prettify.
Gleam nights prettify son.
Hot self-pity grants in gem.
Hot sting German self-pity.
Nothing star self-pity gem.
Nothing rat self-pity gems.
Right self-pity gems on ant.
Organs might net self-pity.
Hint mega, strong self-pity.
Thin, mega, strong self-pity.
'e's fatty, storming helping.
Fatty songs merit helping.
Ghost fatty, limp sneering.
Nifty phlegm to a stingers.
Nifty, gentle goat shrimps.
Nifty gremlins ghost tape.
Nifty pets ghost maligner.
Right! Nifty pal gemstones.
Nifty glitters gnash poem.
Monster's nifty hag piglet.
Lag nifty, smothering pest.
Nifty might on large pests.
Maggot's nifty lepers hint.
Gasp to the nifty gremlins.
Stingingly the softer map.
Gently spitting for shame.
Shy for tempting genitals.
Gently tight oaf primness.
Rightly. Oaf temptingness.
Gently sip soft nightmare.
Sneeringly might soft pat.
Sneeringly might soft tap.
Mighty sleeping soft rant.
Pit soft, hymeneal G-string.
A soft, elite nymph G-string.

Niggle tastier, soft nymph.
Right! Eminently soft gaps.
Right! Eminently soft gasp.
Soft, timely, grasping then.
Enlighten soft, grim pasty.
Emptying, ghastlier fonts.
Font pigsties harm gently.
Timely phase font G-string.
My straight, sleeping font.
Right! Empty gainless font.
Stingy lightens of tamper.
Mightily of pregnant sets.
Pest of meriting 'n' ghastly.
Lengthy of in smartest pig.
Lengthy smear of spitting.
Thinly pig of strangest me.
Nymph of a glittering sets.
Nymph of stilting as greet.
Isn't nymph sage of glitter.
Pithy meets of strangling.
Thirsty of gentleman's pig.
Thirty of negligent spasm.
Meanly of tightest spring.
Epithets of manly G-string.
Mangey spelt of thirsting.
My strength of genial spit.
Hag of temptingly inserts.
Temptingly of star hinges.
Isn't penalty of right gems.
Penalty of the grim stings.
Plenty of thirsting as gem.
Plenty of nightmare's gits.
Petty of as gremlin's night.
Mirthless petty of in gang.
Rang in of petty mightless.
Typeset of snarling might.
The tipsy me of strangling.
Is malign of type strength.
Pasty of merest lightning.
Slayers of tempting thing.
Trash gems of intently pig.
Length of nasty merits pig.
Titty of phlegm angriness.
Gently fine, straight mops.
Fine, tight romps as gently.
Gently fine, rightmost sap.
Gently fine parts might so.
Gently fine traps might so.
Grossly fine, tempting hat.
Ghastly print to fine gems.
Fine, sightly torment gaps.
Torment fine, sightly gasp.
Fine master pongs tightly.

Shortly fine, tempting gas.
Fine hag sorts temptingly.
Fine, potty, mirthless gang.
Rang fine, potty mightless.
Strangle fine spy to might.
The grotty sampling fines.
Oh! Finest gently pig smart.
Finest gently pig to harms.
Finest sting motherly gap.
Oh My! Finest leapt G-string.
Finest pint or ghastly gem.
Finest ghastly trip on gem.
Finest ghastly trip gnome.
Finest rashly tempting go.
Infest nymph glitters ago.
Finest tag pithy mongrels.
Finest tag stormy helping.
Gleam finest north pigsty.
Finest glean sporty might.
Finest might longer pasty.
If honest gaps trim gently.
Gently trim if honest gasp.
Gently if hot tag primness.
If hot raspings met gently.
Ho! Gently if smarting pest.
Gently if something. Sprat.
If ash torments gently pig.
If pig torments gently has.
Ha! Gently if storming pest.
Gently if the song arm-pits.
Glossary if tempting then.
Strongly if that penis gem.
Hymen if spit not straggle.
Strong myth if genial pest.
Ghostly if tempting, saner.
Gemstones if rightly pant.
Ghastly germ if potent sin.
Lengthy if on smartest pig.
Lengthy if a storming pest.
If sightly gnome patterns.
Stealthy pig if strong men.
Stealthy pin if strong gem.
Presents if thinly. Maggot.
Nymph if agent glitters so.
Nymph if sane glitters got.
Strong nymph if agile test.
Python if gentler stigmas.
Shy if top, negligent smart.
Slimy if not page strength.
Timely hang if strong pest.
My! Strangle poet if nights.
Play-testing if north gems.
Strength if not imply sage.

Sleepy might if strong ant.
The spotty gem if snarling.
Petty if it gnash mongrels.
Mirthless petty if on gang.
Rang on if petty mightless.
Shit if petty mongrels nag.
Tipsy mongrels if the gnat.
Pasty lemon if the G-string.
Spy rattling if honest gem.
Spy hot if gentle smarting.
Spy so if right tanglement.
Star might if tensely pong.
Nasty piglet if north gems.
Nasty length if grim poets.
Nasty porn if lightest gem.
If nasty light meter pongs.
Profit nasty gem lightens.
Tasty nothings pilfer gem.
Flip enrages snotty might.
Strong feet lymphangitis.
The fists, mangling poetry.
The mean fits pig strongly.
Fist thorny, gleaming pest.
Thorny pest fits gleaming.
Hey! Piglet fits strong man.
Pong seethingly smart fit.
Strongest, agile fit nymph.
Gosh! Fairest 'n' temptingly.
Fairest hogs 'n' temptingly.
Shy, impotent farts niggle.
Gently might in poses fart.
Fart not pig sightly semen.
Fart thinly. Pigs gemstone.
Seemly fart in tights pong.
My negligent fart piss hot.
Shit! I'm spongy, gentle fart.
The stinging fart employs.
Is snotty fart helping gem.
Temptingly fears so. Night.
Finer style nags top might.
Hot slaying tempting serf.
Almighty sign potent serf.
Serf, mangling shitty poet.
Hot serf gains temptingly.
Hog temptingly stain serf.
Nymph fires tattling egos.
Fires might spongy talent.
Flash not trim tense piggy.
I flash petty, snorting gem.
Spent steaming gory filth.
Germy, nastiest filth pong.
Pig strangest filth money.
Filth pongs in my greatest.

My! Not pig filth greatness.
My filth nepotist naggers.
My! Not greasing filth pest.
Empty filth goriness gnat.
Filth smearing petty song.
Most tipsy filth gangrene.
Pity gemstones rang filth.
Filth torments spy ageing.
My filthiest, strange pong.
Tarty filthiness pong gem.
Flesh gory, tempting saint.
Not self-harming, tipsy get.
Self-harming type to sting.
Mangling top fetishes try.
Amen! Glittery shifts pong.
Shift tempting, sane glory.
My sporting, elegant shift.
Thief pongs gently trim as.
Strongly paint thief gems.
My thief poet stranglings.
Piggy, slim, resonant theft.
Theft in gem as sportingly.
Simperingly gas not. Theft.
Meanly fighting protests.
Rants opt seemly fighting.
Fighting on messy prattle.
My poetless rant fighting.
So fighting plenty master.
Sporty amen lest fighting.
Style fighting porn mates.
Stamp or tensely fighting.
More fighting nasty spelt.
Talent romps yes fighting.
O My! Salt frightening pest.
Slyest frightening to map.
Meanly frighting to steps.
Tamely frighting on steps.
Stem so frighting penalty.
Solemn petty as frighting.
Sanely frighting top stem.
Frighting potent me slays.
Frighting on steely stamp.
Tip grotty flashing semen.
Pity meet strong flashing.
Tempting flashing oyster.
Merit tasty pong fleshing.
Arty, tempting, so fleshing.
Top flight gems tyrannies.
So frighten manly pest git.
Frighten measly tit pongs.
Timely frighten top snags.
Frighten mostly ape sting.
No frighten lamest pigsty.

Frighten mean, lost pigsty.
Slot frighten mean pigsty.
Most frighten angel's pity.
Frighten sly pig mates not.
Pistol frighten nasty gem.
No frighten tasty glimpse.
Pong frighten tasty smile.
Manly pig frightens to set.
Top sang frightens timely.
My nepotist frightens lag.
My patient frightens logs.
My spit frightens to angel.
Empty gloat frightens sin.
Potty gem frightens snail.
Man style frightens to pig.
Glimpse not nasty fighter.
Mental fighters on pigsty.
I'm a pest frights on gently.
Top frights gas eminently.
My nepotist frights angel.
Sly, potent enigma frights.
Stingy fright empales not.
Fright nets steamily pong.
So mangiest fright plenty.
So steaming fright plenty.
Saintly fright pest on gem.
Saintly fright pest gnome.
I'm neat fright pongs style.
Tiny, tameless fright pong.
My! Fortnight's genial pest.
Is empty. Fortnight's angel.
Amen! Pig fortnight's style.
Spit seemly nag fortnight.
Pig slyest, mean fortnight.
Pig meanest, sly fortnight.
Shifting penalty to germs.
Shifting, stately porn gem.
Empty strangle to fishing.
Manly prestige fights not.
Grimly potent, sane fights.
My pleasing, rotten fights.
Pesteringly fights not. Am.
Malign petty fights snore.
Malign sporty, tense fight.
Fight in as petty mongrels.
Nasty poets fight gremlin.
Pong trimly tag heftiness.
Pant gently shiftier smog.
Thrift imposes gently nag.
Tipsy thrift gems on angel.
I'm farthest pigs on gently.
Tiny gem gnat shoplifters.
Thereof stamp stingingly.

A fish torments gently pig.
Gently potent as grim fish.
Groan fish tempting style.
Flat might gory ineptness.
Nights petty flair on gems.
Money flatters nights pig.
Spiny might flatters gone.
Neat stifler pongs mighty.
Empty to stifler gnashing.
Mangey poets flirt nights.
Flirt pity gnash gemstone.
Empty strong flies hating.
Oh Man! Petty lift sniggers.
Not shrimpy, naggiest felt.
Not shrimpy, naggiest left.
Spongy, hesitant, grim felt.
Spongy, hesitant, grim left.
Amen! Snotty felt priggish.
Might self, angry nepotist.
Right! Gently posts in fame.
Stringently posh fame git.
Fame lightens grotty spin.
Strongly spite fame night.
Tightly strong fame penis.
Fame lightens torn pigsty.
Fame poetry glints nights.
Per snotty, slighting fame.
Shit! Potty gangrene films.
Right! Film potent gayness.
From lengthy, nastiest pig.
From shaggily intent pest.
Shit from naggiest plenty.
Gainless petty from night.
Shit! Form negligent pasty.
Testy helping from giants.
Shaggy self-torment in pit.
Shaggy self-torment in tip.
Ya! Nights pig self-torment.
Gosh! Gently misfit parent.
Angry poets misfit length.
Ape lengthy, strong misfit.
Misfit longer gnash petty.
Flamingoes pity strength.
It ghastly figment person.
A gritless figment python.
Sportingly haste figment.
Spy hot gnarliest figment.
Ship snotty, large figment.
Testily hoping fragments.
Shitty slope fragmenting.
Ghastly spotting firemen.
Frame lightens snotty pig.
Not shaggy, pestilent firm.

Shitty, elegant pongs firm.
Firm sanely tightest pong.
Hot me piss gently farting.
Farting 'n' poetless mighty.
Pig toneless farting myth.
Lose shy, tempting farting.
My honest farting piglets.
Flattering nymph sits ego.
It's flattering nymph goes.
Spy hot flattering in gems.
Faltering nymph egotists.
The steamy flirting pongs.
Pasty, honest flirting gem.
Not fleeting, stagy shrimp.
Oh My! Fleeting gnat strips.
Pig fleeting, stormy hasn't.
My fleeting, strongish pat.
My fleeting, strongish tap.
Fleeting, sporty might 'n' as.
Might spray fleeting snot.
The stifling, grey tampons.
Tape stifling, thorny gems.
Stifling, potty, mere gnash.
Stifling pansy to the germ.
Stifling, snotty grapheme.
Stifling tyrants hope gem.
Angriest flings empty hot.
Great! To giftless nymph in.
Not giftless, pithy German.
Hymen or fast-settling pig.
Faggot tireless, tin nymph.
Let faggot sinister nymph.
Painless myth forgetting.
Steel frigg nymph to saint.
The frigg, is not manly pest.
Natty, honest, simple frigg.
The steamy printing flogs.
My inept shattering flogs.
Might serenity flogs pant.
Flog nights nasty emptier.
Flog might pertinent says.
Forge manly shitting pest.
Anything forget slim pest.
Impishly forget tangents.
Homiest fangs trip gently.
Pithily rotten gems fangs.
The fangs pig timely snort.
Grimly the nepotist fangs.
Fangs in the stormy piglet.
Right! Only, emptiest fangs.
Shop gently trim feasting.
I'm the fang spits or gently.
Gently simper to this fang.

Hi! Strongly emptiest fang.
Fang emptiness or tightly.
Phoniest fang gets trimly.
Opt seemly thirsting fang.
Sportingly meet this fang.
Fang thesis or temptingly.
Prettily hot fang messing.
Is the gremlin's potty fang.
Petty gremlins hoist fang.
Is petty. Gremlin's hot fang.
Fang pointers might style.
Fang yet right simpletons.
Fig this sporty gentleman.
Nymph gifts elegant riots.
Gifts malign tense trophy.
I am sporty gifts lengthen.
I'm a sporty gifts lengthen.
Gift phonies smart gently.
Hesitantly gift porn gems.
Gift plainest, thorny gems.
Gift manly seething strop.
Smartingly gift not. Sheep.
Fattest homely springing.
Fattest hog 'n' simperingly.
Tempting 'n' ogreishly fast.
Oh! Fat, girly temptingness.
The fat impinges strongly.
Son's fat integrity phlegm.
Fat, rompish, gentle stingy.
Fat pongs mightily enters.
Gnomishly present fat git.
Fat listener pongs mighty.
Fat, smothery pint niggles.
Pig not fat, gritless hymen.
Fat myth or negligent piss.
Seethingly print fat smog.
Fat pig segments or thinly.
Toggle fat, sinister nymph.
Fat G-string meets phonily.
Fat, missing, gentle trophy.
Fat no mights pesteringly.
Fat, spongy merits lighten.
Nights sting fat employer.
Rompingly sheet fat sting.
Mornings pig the fat style.
Sly fat pestering on might.
Infants slight empty ogre.
Gory, pestilent fans might.
Snortingly might safe pet.
Safe pongs tighten trimly.
Rompingly safe, tight nest.
Rompingly safe, tight nets.
No! Temptingly safe rights.

Safe, empty, light snorting.
Together sting flimsy pan.
Spent flimsy to gathering.
Flimsy seething top grant.
Nights page rotten flimsy.
Flimsy in the top gangster.
Flimsy, potent naggers hit.
Myself the sporting giant.
Spit ghost gentler infamy.
Pig stole infamy strength.
Flattery mess nothing pig.
This tempting flayer song.
Safely might not stern pig.
I'mthe top G-string 'n' safely.
Faintly prig hot segments.
Open stingers might fatly.
Potent him sniggers fatly.
Fly impregnates on tights.
Fiery, tempting, lost gnash.
Infantry tights pole gems.
Meanest fry spotlighting.
Fry might on genital's pest.
Rest filthy, poignant gems.
Most pestering filthy nag.
Prig not filthy, sanest gem.
Filthy ants prig gemstone.
Pig snort filthy, neat gems.
Filthy pig 'n' star gemstone.
Pig segments or filthy ant.
Filthy gasps regiment not.
Filthy presents to gaming.
Assign filthy, potent germ.
Filthy, potent mess raging.
Filthy poet granting mess.
Filthy gem grants in poets.
Filthy stingers pan to gem.
Filthy stingers pat on gem.
Filthy stingers tap on gem.
Filthy stingers pat gnome.
Filthy stingers tap gnome.
Mornings gate filthy pest.
Filthy pest gangs on merit.
Potent gem grants fishily.
Isn't flashy, tempting gore.
Stamp seeing fortnightly.
I'm fortnightly, tense gasp.
Fortnightly meet passing.
Fortnightly taping seems.
Piss! Amen! Fortnightly get.
Frighteningly steps to am.
Shiftingly got neat sperm.
Top ant merges shiftingly.
Shiftingly met strong ape.

Shiftingly rat on gem pets.
Negate thrifty, slim pongs.
Angel's thrifty pongs emit.
Angel's thrifty item pongs.
Angel's thrifty time pongs.
Thrifty pong smiles agent.
Thrifty, genital pong mess.
Thrifty, inept songs gleam.
Thrifty signs mangle poet.
Thrifty pests malign gone.
Among thrifty, gentle piss.
Fishy gem in tartlets pong.
Gremlin's fishy, potent tag.
Hefty glimpses to ranting.
Hefty, sporting, slim agent.
Malign hefty, sporting set.
Hefty tit malingers pongs.
Hefty, slim, strong, neat pig.
Hefty sons pig grim talent.
Pig not, I'm hefty strangles.
No hefty, smarting piglets.
Slang hefty, grim nepotist.
Hefty protests maligning.
Hefty gem plots straining.
Trim hefty, pointless gang.
Hefty, top G-string menials.
Split hefty, ignorant gems.
Not ape hefty, slim G-string.
Spit hefty, gleaming snort.
Shifty pongs grime talent.
Open rattling shifty gems.
This lofty G-string ape-men.
Helping mates git Y-fronts.
Tag impish, gentle Y-fronts.
Y-fronts gnash piglet time.
Y-fronts tighten limp sage.
Y-fronts might panties leg.
I sap gentle Y-fronts might.
Y-fronts pig teeth maligns.
The Y-fronts pig slim agent.
I'm gentlest graphs notify.
Prettify hot slangs in gem.
Prettify ton hassling gem.
Prettify so mangle things.
Angel's mights prettify no.
Prettify as month niggles.
Prettify the song maligns.
Prettify slang on this gem.
This gangs prettify lemon.
Petrify nights molest nag.
Petrify long, sanest might.
Throng mangiest self-pity.
Steaming throng self-pity.

Self-pity nets might groan.
Got self-pity garnishment.
Mesh not grating self-pity.
Eh! Storming self-pity gnat.
Satisfy pig gentler month.
Isn't helping or fatty gems.
Hog in gremlin's fatty pest.
Nifty, hot, garmentless pig.
Nifty, strongish plate gem.
Nifty Germans slight poet.
Right! So mangle nifty pest.
Nifty, rotten hag glimpses.
Nifty germs pig on stealth.
Nifty, mightless, top range.
Ahem! Nifty, strong piglets.
Maggot's nifty leper hints.
Nifty or the simplest gang.
The nifty, smarting gospel.
The nifty, top gremlins gas.
Might step straying felon.
Gas shirty, tempting felon.
Felon as nights grim petty.
Petty, smashing, grit felon.
The felons transmit piggy.
Felon's right giants empty.
Right! Felon's tempting say.
My frostiest helping gnat.
Softer pains might gently.
Gently softer hit man pigs.
Nights malign softer type.
This softer type, mangling.
Front genital's pithy gems.
Niggle for tastiest nymph.
Pigs for shitty gentleman.
Gently shitting oaf sperm.
Nights. Gremlin's petty oaf.
Gently hating soft primes.
Seethingly soft, grim pant.
Temptingly soft hearings.
Temptingly soft shearing.
Soft, tipsy, negligent harm.
Might soft, pleasing entry.
Soft, tiny, angriest phlegm.
Soften angrily might pest.
Piggy, mirthless, neat font.
I'm sharp of gently testing.
Sap me of gently thirsting.
Gently gnash of prime tits.
Gently gnash of trim spite.
Gently of nights sap merit.
Gently of the armpit sings.
Staringly of the pint gems.
I'm straggly of tenth penis.

Myth of negligent rat piss.
Lengthy pest of grim saint.
Pig segments of thinly rat.
It is gentlest nymph of rag.
Thirsty, steep of mangling.
Align of tempting shyster.
Meanly pig of its strength.
I the G-string of manly pest.
Strength of steamily 'n' pig.
Strength in pigs of tamely.
Slimy of the stringent gap.
My! It of strangest helping.
Pitying of gentlest harms.
Gathers of temptingly. Sin.
Hater of temptingly signs.
Impiety of slang strength.
Play of this stringent gem.
Isn't gem of gnash prettily.
Petty lightens of margins.
Gremlin of petty as nights.
Eh! I'm petty of stranglings.
Gentle typists of harming.
Trim tipsy of gentle gnash.
Sparsity of gentle 'n' might.
Pretty of slight meanings.
Pretty of glinting shames.
Tighten of gremlin's patsy.
Thing of slyest tampering.
Sly might of pertinent gas.
Sly tampering of the sting.
Lengths pig of nasty merit.
Nasty mirth of gentle pigs.
Gremlin's tasty of then pig.
Ya! Lightning of temptress.
Lengths of itsy tampering.
Isn't fine as grotty phlegm.
Spite fine, straggly month.
Ghastly romping fine test.
Fine gem prints to ghastly.
Ghastly strip not fine gem.
That fine G-string employs.
Fine might or petty slangs.
Fine pity straggles month.
That fine, grim style pongs.
Finesse tartly might pong.
Gently finest so grim path.
I'm finest graphs to gently.
Finest mangle grotty ship.
Finest gingerly stamp hot.
Finest mighty staler pong.
Infest homely, apt G-string.
Tap infest homely G-string.
Finest ghastly 'n' grim poet.

Finest nymph titles aggro.
Infest graspingly met hot.
Finest months alert piggy.
Hat sportingly infest gem.
Finest temptingly rash go.
Right! Aptly finest on gems.
Finest prettily hang smog.
Finest spy not large might.
Ya! Niftiest, strong phlegm.
Gently if honest, grim past.
If hot stingers map gently.
Gently pat if hot grimness.
Gently tap if hot grimness.
Gently if in ghost tampers.
Gently might if not spares.
Gently might if saner post.
Gently might if saner spot.
Gently stop if saner might.
Gently smash if rotten pig.
I'm the strop if gently nags.
If hates trim gently pongs.
As trim gently if the pongs.
Gently if this top Germans.
Staringly spent if hot gem.
If poets might 'n' strangely.
Pest if rantingly ghost me.
Rantingly if the post gems.
If angel's grotty shipment.
Maps if strongly teething.
Straggly pint if hot semen.
Angry might if stolen pest.
Grasping if not steel myth.
Ghastly spin if rotten gem.
Ghastly pin if rotten gems.
Stylish germ if potent nag.
Honestly! Pest if trim gang.
Nymph if gloating streets.
Artist's nymph if gentle go.
Trophy if neat gems glints.
If settings mangle trophy.
Mangle pithy if strongest.
Gem if shirty talents pong.
Tempting if along shyster.
If pongs trim gentle hasty.
Shy lame if potent G-string.
Shy poet if mental G-string.
Strength to pigs if meanly.
Manly if eight strong pest.
Strength on pigs if tamely.
If seemly than top G-string.
Nag smiley if top strength.
Grimy pongs if the talents.
If this germy talents pong.

Spongy if a gentlest mirth.
Gnat if presently might so.
Strength if openly. Stigma.
Gem if sporty ant lightens.
Petty if hassling torn gem.
If night as petty mongrels.
Type shortest if mangling.
Spy hot if negligent smart.
Nasty strength if limp ego.
Nasty might if longer pest.
Help tasty if snorting gem.
Rottenly if nights sap gem.
Hasn't if rottenly pig gems.
Snotty harms if gentle pig.
Helping if ratty gems snot.
Ratty pong if slight semen.
Slashing try if potent gem.
Testy if a snorting phlegm.
Pilfering to the gymnasts.
Not straying the splif gem.
Not mighty flip greatness.
I'm the snotty flip naggers.
Shit! Mangling sporty feet.
Poets fist gently harming.
Poets sift gently harming.
Hymenal poet fits G-string.
Sift rattling phoney gems.
Hero's fits nag temptingly.
Ghost manly pestering fit.
Saner fit hogs temptingly.
Gently spent so fair might.
Pong gently fairest smith.
Not fairest stingy phlegm.
One slighting farts empty.
Inept fart gets gnomishly.
Fart seethingly stomping.
Temptingly hinges so fart.
Gently might on fear spits.
Hot fear sings temptingly.
Potent fears might singly.
A finer might posts gently.
Gently might so finer past.
Finer, mighty, potent glass.
Isn't finer, ghastly, top gem.
Gosh! Temptingly finer sat.
Nights finer, spotty gleam.
Might not gasp finer style.
Petty, slighting serf moan.
Temptingly hang so. Strife.
Snotty self-hate 'n' grim pig.
Flash geometry 'n' spitting.
Is not flash petty merging.
I'm flash petty, not snigger.

Trip filth segments agony.
Messy, potent filth raging.
Filth granting messy poet.
Filth as my potent snigger.
My filth gags pretentions.
Am sternest filth on piggy.
Strong filth pigsty enema.
Spotty, mean filth niggers.
Filth segments pity groan.
It thriftless, mangey pong.
An empty, thriftless going.
Thriftless payment going.
Flesh torment piggy saint.
I am petty flesh on G-string.
I'm a petty flesh on G-string.
I am petty shelf on G-string.
I'm a petty shelf on G-string.
Self-harming yet spotting.
Pig strongly meant fetish.
Get manly sporting fetish.
Temptingly rang so. Fetish.
Pig snotty fetish mangler.
Trim spongy, elegant shift.
Empty strong, genial shift.
Shift potty, slim gangrene.
Thief romps gently. Giants.
Mangily strong thief pest.
My thief strangling poets.
Mangle tipsy, strong thief.
Thief pongs tasty gremlin.
Heftiest, sporty, mangling.
Singingly tamper so. Theft.
Theft as pitying mongrels.
Pig theft ransoming style.
Fighting to manly pesters.
Fighting on masterly step.
Pasty molester 'n' fighting.
Sly, potent smear fighting.
Molest pat fighting syren.
Seemly frighting apt snot.
Seemly frighting pat snot.
Tap seemly frighting snot.
An empty stoles frighting.
Payments let so frighting.
Payment frighting stoles.
Moan less frighting petty.
Neatly frighting top mess.
Style frighting top means.
Style frighting top names.
Flashing or empty testing.
Grime petty flashing snot.
Petty, grim flashing notes.
Petty, grim flashing stone.

Flights or petty meanings.
Petty flights no smearing.
Flights type not smearing.
Rainy, potent gems flights.
Flight types not smearing.
Frighten spit smelt agony.
Frighten manly piss to get.
Frighten mealy, top stings.
Frighten slimy, spent goat.
Tango frighten slimy pest.
So frighten plenty stigma.
Frighten spiny, total gems.
Frighten stately pin smog.
Tasty lips frighten on gem.
Lisp frighten tasty gnome.
Slip frighten tasty gnome.
Frighten snotty pigs meal.
Frighten slime snotty gap.
Nag frighten simplest toy.
Frighten tiny spots gleam.
Top sign frightens tamely.
Mealy, top sting frightens.
O My! Piglet frightens ants.
Pigsty frightens mean lot.
Simply gate not frightens.
I'm spotty angle frightens.
Tame sly pig frightens not.
Plot sanity frightens gem.
Tasty limp frightens gone.
Tamest pig frightens only.
Snotty limp frightens age.
Manly sting fighter poets.
O Man! Fighters spit gently.
Mean style frights not pig.
Gently tame on fright piss.
Timely fright nags on pest.
Temptingly. Fright on seas.
Empty gas insolent fright.
Aptly. Fright in gemstones.
Seemly pig fortnight's ant.
In fortnight's types gleam.
Fortnight piss gentle may.
Pity fortnight mess angel.
Sly fortnight pest enigma.
Spiel nasty fortnight gem.
Empty line of sight grants.
Gently shifting star poem.
Shifting poets arm gently.
Raspingly meet not fights.
Partly fights in gemstone.
Mangiest fights reply not.
Fights reply not steaming.
Fights or mangiest plenty.

Plenty fights or steaming.
Petty fights on a gremlins.
Petty fights no malingers.
Fights type not malingers.
Maligner fights not types.
Fights malinger not types.
Spiny, tolerant gem fights.
Plainer, snotty gem fights.
Am grotty, penniless fight.
Fight grimly top neatness.
Fight sanely torment pigs.
Fight sly, tempting reason.
Grimly top heftiness gnat.
Pig not messy thrift angel.
Thrift angel stymies pong.
Man piggy, toneless thrift.
Negate spongy, slim thrift.
Spongy, gentle thrift aims.
Thrift moans gentle Gipsy.
So. Angel's emptying thrift.
Empty on thrift niggles as.
An empty thrift niggles so.
Songs empty genial thrift.
Thrift to angel's spiny gem.
Mega thrift pongs in style.
Farthest sign timely pong.
Shoplift germy, neat sting.
Shoplift enemy at G-string.
My! Shoplift eaten G-string.
Shoplift man testy nigger.
Split shift to my gangrene.
Faith pongs gently. Merits.
Shaft temptingly ignores.
Impotently sheaf G-string.
Sagely torn tempting fish.
Fish gently pig as torment.
Fish temptingly torn sage.
Honesty flattens grim pig.
False empty in hot G-string.
In piggy flatters not mesh.
Ghost infernal typist gem.
Flirt gang petty hominess.
Flies hang storming petty.
File gnash storming petty.
Gnash petty, storming life.
Petty lifts more gnashing.
Lift presents might agony.
Left mighty top angriness.
Left smearing shitty pong.
Felt graphs not stymieing.
Left stymieing not graphs.
Left hating spongy merits.
Feel pasty, snorting might.

Gosh! Stringently pit fame.
Strongly. Fame, isn't the pig.
Fame nets sporty lighting.
Lighten tipsy, strong fame.
Ghost fame style printing.
Sporting fame style thing.
Tighten sly, sporting fame.
To shaggy, pertinent films.
Hasty films potent nigger.
The format pets singingly.
Inform hasty, gentlest pig.
From angel's petty insight.
Nasty, tight, sleeping form.
Nasty shit from gentle pig.
From tasty, negligent ship.
Self-torment hints gay pig.
Gently hog feminist sprat.
Gently graph to feminists.
Misfit ghastly enter pong.
Misfit spongy, large tenth.
Hot naggers misfit plenty.
Misfit hog pregnant style.
Misfit help snotty nagger.
Testy filet mignon graphs.
The informing glass petty.
Strangely sip hot figment.
Posh alert stingy figment.
Garishly nest top figment.
Garishly sent top figment.
Honestly! It grasp figment.
Shapely figment to string.
No! Sparsely tight figment.
Sporty, light, sane figment.
Figment lightens or patsy.
Ha! Sporting figment style.
Right! Slope nasty figment.
Figment toys star helping.
Fragment shitty pongs lie.
Testy fragment polishing.
Top he fragments stingily.
Shitty fragments pong lie.
The flaming poetry stings.
Slighting petty frames no.
Petty lightning frames so.
Slighting frames type not.
The spongy frame stilting.
Lengthy pigsties farm not.
Farting homes gently spit.
Gently farting hims poets.
Poet mess nightly farting.
Empty nights farting lose.
The farting molesting spy.
Gosh! Flattering, empty sin.

Flattering, empty sin hogs.
Spy this flattering gnome.
Son's fleeting, mighty trap.
Fleeting nymph stirs goat.
Nymph or fleeting tits gas.
Trophy 'n' fleeting stigmas.
My! This fleeting pongs rat.
Not fleeting pigsty harms.
Fleeting spray mights not.
Right! Fleeting, nasty mops.
Fleeting months pig stray.
Phase stifling, grotty men.
Stifling, top myth enrages.
Taste stifling nymph ogre.
Stifling nymph trees goat.
Threat stifling, spongy me.
Stifling, empty, honest rag.
Not spray the stifling gem.
Stifling, hotter pansy gem.
Empty so fling shattering.
Might sanest fling poetry.
Phoniest, ratty fling gems.
Giftless, angry, potent him.
Giftless trophy gem in ant.
Giftless, natty, grim phone.
Flags permitting honesty.
I'm the flags type snorting.
I'm the types flag snorting.
Manly phoniest frigg test.
Hasten slimy, potent frigg.
Gas fitting or steel nymph.
Hey! In tempting star flogs.
Is penetrating myths flog.
Flog tear stingiest nymph.
Flog shame stringent pity.
In the smarting types flog.
Tiny, tempting shares flog.
Forget anything misspelt.
Nymph forgets genial tits.
Fog alert stingiest nymph.
Mightily. Fangs pester not.
Trimly phoniest fangs get.
Fangs opt trimly seething.
Fangs might prettily. Ones.
Fangs rely might nepotist.
Fangs might snottily. Peer.
The fangs trim nosy piglet.
Fangs might plot serenity.
I'm sporty feasting length.
Fang lies tempting shorty.
Shy, gentler fang optimist.
Tightest fang smiley porn.
Shit sportingly meet fang.

Fang shitting empty loser.
Might pretty fang lioness.
Fang replies snotty might.
Stealthy porn fisting gem.
Poet gifts rantingly mesh.
Smarting polythene gifts.
Smarting telephony gifts.
Pithy neat gifts mongrels.
Shy, potent maligner gifts.
In the masterly gifts pong.
Stormy helping gifts neat.
I'm a strength gifts openly.
The smarting gifts openly.
Gift ape-men shit strongly.
Gift homely stingers pant.
Stole gift angriest nymph.
Shy, potent gift malingers.
Gift snotty, malign herpes.
Fattest nymph lies goring.
Fattiest girl hymens pong.
Thinly pig not safest germ.
Feast rompingly tightens.
To shrimpy, negligent fast.
To shrimpy, negligent fats.
Pong trimly seething fats.
Fate limp honesty G-string.
Fate slimy strength on pig.
Rompingly fate tightness.
Gosh! Gently trim fat penis.
Fat hogs gently trim penis.
It hog gently fat primness.
Fat thing promises gently.
Gently fat, homiest spring.
Sneeringly might fat tops.
Shone fat, tempting grisly.
Pert fat homes stingingly.
Nights fat, grey simpleton.
Fat, motherly pest signing.
Grim fat nets honestly pig.
Fat, thorny piglet messing.
Fat nymph or stingiest leg.
Fat, phoney germs stilting.
Fat python niggles merits.
Fat, stormy, negligent ship.
Fat 'n' pesteringly might so.
Lengthen trim gossipy fat.
The fat, stinging polymers.
Gosh! Temptingly risen fat.
Reply fat shitting on gems.
Fat, sleepy, storming night.
Might so spiny, gentler fat.
Faint, sleepy, strong might.
Infant, empty, gritless hog.

Fans might pestilent orgy.
Shit! Goer fans temptingly.
Seemly, tight, sporting fan.
Hog sisterly, tempting fan.
Safe tights romp in gently.
Gently might so safe print.
Gently might on safe strip.
Safe might ports in gently.
Gently might in safe sport.
Safe, thorny, splitting gem.
Safe syren plotting might.
Together spin flimsy gnat.
Paint flimsy strength ego.
Flimsy teething pongs rat.
The flimsy going patterns.
The flimsy niggers pat not.
The flimsy niggers tap not.
The nepotist gangs firmly.
Let gnash mortifying pest.
Firstly tempting, sane hog.
Flattery nets gnomish pig.
Pig flattery hints on gems.
Frailty pongs tight semen.
Flayer signs potent might.
Safely tight, sporting men.
Potent grime flays nights.
Faintly pig some. Strength.
Terse might pongs faintly.
Fattily right semens pong.
Gem opens fatly thirsting.
Smothering pig nets fatly.
Fly priggish on statement.
Slosh fiery, tempting gnat.
Infantry piglets ghost me.
Infantry poet gems lights.
Ferny, mangiest spotlight.
Steaming ferny spotlight.
Ferny, top, mangiest slight.
Steaming ferny, top slight.
Fry gleam nights. Nepotist.
Pong shiftily merest gnat.
Gang filthy emptiness rot.
Tampon see filthy G-string.
Filthy sets tampon nigger.
Filthy pongs tame stinger.
Stem filthy, angriest pong.
A filthy prig segments not.
Filthy pig grants to semen.
Filthy, storming, tense gap.
Filthy, spent, smarting ego.
Rape not sting filthy gems.
Point filthy, strange gems.
Stem filthy, naggiest porn.

Filthy, eminent strop gags.
Filthy poet stings German.
In filthy, top, strange gems.
Grime filthy pest nags not.
Agent mess thriftily pong.
Amen! Fortnightly pig sets.
I'm fortnightly gap tenses.
Fortnightly pint message.
Is spent, mega fortnightly.
Top am sets frighteningly.
Frighteningly sap to stem.
Apt mess to frighteningly.
Portents game shiftingly.
Shiftingly term poet nags.
Poet me grants shiftingly.
Shiftingly torn game pest.
Groan shiftingly met pest.
Less thrifty, poignant gem.
Man thrifty, gentle gossip.
Thrifty angel pongs items.
Thrifty times pongs angel.
Thrifty stones mangle pig.
Thrifty pig segments loan.
Thrifty, sleeping smog ant.
Malign thrifty egos spent.
Thrifty, open stings gleam.
Gang thrifty, pointless me.
Thrifty poet slangs in gem.
Thrifty poets mangle sign.
'e's thrifty poets, mangling.
Thrifty lips nag gemstone.
Thrifty pest 'n' so gleaming.
Fishy, mere, tattling pongs.
Fishy, potent, male G-string.
Isn't hefty sperm gloating.
Hefty, simple, strong giant.
Lame hefty, sporting sting.
Molest hefty, grasping tin.
Hefty, rotten pigs maligns.
Hefty pig mess on rattling.
Hefty, potent, grim signals.
Angel's hefty, storming pit.
Angel's hefty, storming tip.
Shifty tamper niggles not.
On shifty, tempting glares.
Shifty poet strangling me.
Fragility mess tenth pong.
Fogey transmitting helps.
Paint slim fogey strength.
Signify lame top strength.
Felonry giants might pest.
Softly simpering the gnat.
Lofty might as presenting.

Phlegmiest, giant Y-fronts.
Y-fronts shitting plea gem.
Steel Y-fronts might in gap.
Y-fronts might 'n' agile pest.
Y-fronts malign teeth pigs.
Shit! I'm gentle Y-fronts gap.
Empaling the frosty sting.
The frosty pets maligning.
Softy malingers tenth pig.
Hogs prettify mean glints.
Gosh! Prettify malign nest.
Prettify hogs malign nest.
Prettify malign hogs sent.
Isn't hogs mangle prettify.
Prettify ton slashing gem.
Prettify to gem 'n' hassling.
Prettify lots gnashing me.
Prettify on naggish smelt.
Legs prettify nights moan.
Gleam prettify son's thing.
Angel's might 'n' so prettify.
Prettify as months niggle.
No petrify mightless gnat.
Self-pity tonight Germans.
Hog smarting, net self-pity.
Not term naggish self-pity.
Not sight German self-pity.
Might self-pity groans ten.
Might self-pity nets organ.
Might self-pity rants gone.
The self-pity smog ranting.
Rat ghost self-pitying men.
Rant ghost self-pitying me.
Hog smart self-pitying net.
Hog smart self-pitying ten.
Self-pitying gnash to term.
Self-pitying month greats.
The self-pitying storm nag.
Not simplify strength age.
Satisfy pong merit length.
Romp satisfy gentle night.
Fatty helping stings more.
The long fatty impressing.
Rats! Nifty helping to gems.
Hot niggles nifty tampers.
Nifty gem strips hot angel.
Nifty permits ghost angel.
Gosh! Let's! Nifty tampering.
Hogs lest nifty tampering.
Let's! Nifty tampering hogs.
Nifty poets slight German.
Nifty haggles trim on pest.
Nifty, personal gem tights.

So sap nifty, gentler might.
I'm the nifty, largest pongs.
Maggot's nifty then perils.
Met shitty, grasping felon.
I'm the felon grants pigsty.
Shit! Felon's tempting gray.
Pity felon's strange might.
Gently softer, impish gnat.
Then malign softer pigsty.
Temptingly, is softer hang.
Nights mangle softer pity.
Ghastly pig eminent frost.
Patiently for nights. Gems.
Penalty for shitting gems.
Tail softest nymph nigger.
Softest nymph in large git.
Sprain soft, gentle mighty.
Shatteringly pig soft men.
Prettily gnash in soft gem.
Try steaming soft helping.
Fonts grime tasty helping.
Often steaming sprightly.
Nights often, masterly pig.
I'm the often G-string plays.
Pithy font stingers gleam.
I'm the font gets raspingly.
I'm the font sniggers aptly.
Gently of neat gits shrimp.
Gently hating of its sperm.
Me strips of gently hating.
Hasn't of gently pig merits.
Gently spitting of rash me.
Gently of mean thirsts pig.
Hi! Gently of smarting pest.
Stingily of the germs pant.
Strangely might of in step.
Rantingly of the pig stems.
Rantingly step of this gem.
Granny of emptiest lights.
Trying of gentlest mishap.
Trying of tempting hassle.
A nymph greets of stilting.
Nymph of leg in strategist.
Nymph of tin sage glitters.
Shy of tempting integrals.
My! As piglet of in strength.
My! The spite of strangling.
Night of temptingly. Arses.
Haters of temptingly sign.
Empty triangles of nights.
Penalty of this me G-string.
Gems of ineptly rat nights.
Plenty of mangiest rights.

Rights plenty of steaming.
Plenty of angriest mights.
Pity of in strengths gleam.
Pretty mightless of in nag.
Instantly of the germs pig.
Salty might of presenting.
Slyer of this tempting nag.
Pig style of main strength.
I'm sly pig of neat strength.
Nasty helping of grim test.
Tempting syren of as light.
I'm tiny of gentlest graphs.
Tiny shipment of straggle.
Tiny sample of the G-string.
Right! Fine spasm to gently.
Fine, grotty phlegm saints.
Fine, grotty phlegm stains.
Nights fine, grotty sample.
Fine mights tape strongly.
Fine gays limp to strength.
Fine, gay, top, slim strength.
Fine, gray, tempting sloths.
Fine myth glitters as pong.
Ghastly testing fine romp.
Fine, sporting, ghastly met.
Torment fine, shaggy split.
Gosh! Rats! Fine, temptingly.
Fine mights gasp rottenly.
Nymph fines goat glitters.
Petty glamor fines nights.
Right! Finest gently map so.
Gratingly infest top mesh.
Finest almighty pert song.
Strop mighty infest angel.
Right! Mangey plots finest.
Right! Finest spongy metal.
Finest alter spongy might.
Infest ghost grim penalty.
Right! Finest gem plays not.
Gleam infest sporty night.
Might infest sporty angle.
Infest ratty helping smog.
Gently mans if right poets.
Gently if tight, sane romps.
Poser if gently might ants.
Gently harming if to pests.
Harm poet if gently stings.
Hasn't if gently grim poets.
Gently if the armpit songs.
Strangely might if on step.
Path if strongly. Meetings.
Glory if hat temptingness.
Mighty if no strangle pest.

Ghastly if not inept germs.
Maggot's serpent if thinly.
Honesty if prattling gems.
If tempting theory slangs.
Nymph if gangster toilets.
Nymph if leg on strategist.
Nymph gloats if resetting.
Title nymph if strong sage.
Shitty if gentle nags romp.
Shyest pong if grim talent.
Shy person if tattling gem.
Strength if manly spit ego.
Manly sheet if top G-string.
Manly if these top G-string.
If strength points gamely.
Messy pong if right talent.
Many strength if so. Piglet.
My! On strength if as piglet.
If my polite strength nags.
My! The strangles if not pig.
Gnat if motherless typing.
If the sons rag temptingly.
Empty if a losing strength.
If sniggers empty not halt.
Gem if prettily gnash snot.
Sporty if nights gentle am.
Might angel if sporty nest.
Might sent if sporty angel.
Pity if on strengths gleam.
Pretty mightless if on nag.
If mongrels tighten patsy.
Stringent spy if hot gleam.
Pig strength if nasty mole.
Gremlin's hog if natty pest.
Porn if tasty gem lightens.
If tasty mongrels pig then.
Snotty panel if right gems.
Snotty plane if right gems.
Snotty spring if the gleam.
Am nosy strength if piglet.
Toy if pregnant mightless.
Angel's might if testy porn.
Pilferage myth stings not.
Myth stages not pilfering.
Self-opening, ratty mights.
I'm the natty sniggers flop.
Nasty gem pilfers tonight.
The smoggy, transient flip.
Gay helping fits torments.
Sift gay helping torments.
Germ fits hesitantly pong.
Pig fist shorty gentleman.
Fits pig shorty gentleman.

The agents fist rompingly.
The agents sift rompingly.
Sift temptingly saner hog.
Fist empty, strong healing.
Fits empty strong healing.
Ratty helping fits on gems.
Gently mastering posh fit.
Hero's fit nags temptingly.
Fair pest mights on gently.
My! This fair, gentlest pong.
Might style farts opening.
Fatter pig nets gnomishly.
Fattier gems pongs thinly.
Hot fart gently piss in gem.
Gently sip something fart.
Fart so spiny, gentle might.
Temptingly ghost fear sin.
Sightly, tempting no fears.
Temptingly fears hot sing.
Gently might finer, top ass.
Ghastly pit not finer gems.
Ghastly tip not finer gems.
Tamely pongs finer tights.
Finer, spongy, latest might.
Angel's finer, potty mights.
Finer, salty, tempting hogs.
Spotlight finer, nasty gem.
Slight finer, nasty, top gem.
Impotently gang this serf.
Temptingly ghost in a serf.
To an empty, slighting serf.
Amen! Potty, slighting serf.
Nastily hog tempting serf.
Gently shaming first poet.
I'm the first as gently pong.
Sanely hog tempting first.
Soggy, eminent filth sprat.
Grainy, top filth segments.
Maggoty filth pest sinner.
Not piggy, star filth semen.
Piggy filth rants to semen.
Stem piggy, resonant filth.
Met spongy, angriest filth.
Filth gross emptying neat.
Potty filth gems earnings.
Petty filth gems in organs.
Pity filth segments organ.
Type maggot's filth sinner.
Maggot's filth entry penis.
Yet ponging master's filth.
Torment selfish, piggy ant.
Empty not selfish grating.
It self-harming, petty song.

Got self-harming, tiny pest.
Grimy, potent angel shifts.
Mental piggery shifts not.
Neat shifts rompingly get.
Grim petty shifts on angel.
Meanly top fetish G-string.
My fetish strangling poet.
Graspingly met not. Fetish.
Fetish snarling potty gem.
Type malign strong fetish.
Shift gently strop enigma.
Shift prim, gentlest agony.
Shift graspingly meet not.
Thief posts rantingly. Gem.
O My! Thief strangling pest.
Snotty thief naggers limp.
Smear singingly top theft.
Theft groaning slimy pest.
Rompingly stages in theft.
No fighting masterly pets.
Sport seemly fighting ant.
Rant seemly fighting post.
Spot seemly fighting rant.
Stop seemly fighting rant.
Seemly fighting apt snort.
Tap seemly fighting snort.
Earn mostly fighting pest.
Slept on mastery fighting.
Mastery fighting on spelt.
Not fighting smeary spelt.
Fighting mean style ports.
Style fighting mean sport.
Style fighting Roman pest.
Slyest romp fighting neat.
Most fighting nasty leper.
Am frightening style post.
Am frightening style spot.
Not frighting measly step.
Payment lest so frighting.
Less frighting to payment.
Aptly frighting not seems.
Son's petty male frighting.
Son's petty meal frighting.
Top, mean styles frighting.
Rotten flashing pigsty me.
Empty tie strong flashing.
In-flight, sporty, neat gems.
Gayest, prominent flights.
Ratty flights pig on semen.
Gas sporty, eminent flight.
Pity resonant flight gems.
Frighten gays molest pint.
Tamely frighten top signs.

Mealy pongs frighten tits.
Frighten mostly tag penis.
Mostly frighten pint sage.
It frighten spongy metals.
Frighten stolen pigsty am.
Frighten Gipsy metals not.
Frighten simply stage not.
Simply frighten to agents.
Frighten stages imply not.
Frighten potty gems snail.
Frighten potty miss angel.
Frighten pity molests nag.
Frighten molest giant spy.
Nastily frighten post gem.
Pig not frighten slyest am.
Frighten nasty lisp to gem.
Frighten nasty slip to gem.
Frighten tasty, solemn pig.
Stay not frighten glimpse.
Frighten snotty lips game.
A snotty lips frighten gem.
Frighten testy mails pong.
Measly pong frightens tit.
Mangily frightens to step.
Pain frightens mostly get.
O My! Ant frightens piglets.
My lasting poet frightens.
Metal Gipsy frightens not.
Simply frightens to agent.
Gates imply not frightens.
Stage frightens not imply.
Nail petty smog frightens.
Spiny, total gem frightens.
Pliant gem frightens toys.
Toy frightens pliant gems.
Frights spite gently moan.
Eminently frights to gaps.
Eminently frights to gasp.
Aptly frights in gemstone.
Gently spit so mean fright.
Fright on mate piss gently.
Manly fright tenses to pig.
My elegant fright piss not.
Insolent fright patsy gem.
Potent fright slays in gem.
Empale fortnight's stingy.
Amen! Pig slyest fortnight.
Shifting, mangey plotters.
Gently tampers to fishing.
Me fights rantingly. Poets.
Eminently fights to grasp.
Manly poet fights stinger.
Fights stage prominently.

Temptingly fights on ears.
Temptingly earn so fights.
Temptingly fights so near.
Petty fights in a mongrels.
Nasties fight gently romp.
Limp fight sternest agony.
Fight strongly tame penis.
Top stingers fight meanly.
Fight raspingly meets not.
Fight prominently stages.
Patiently fight son's germ.
Partly fight in gemstones.
Fight types not malingers.
Leggy, potent, smart finish.
Straggle my potent finish.
A gem on thrift piss gently.
A thrift piss gently. Gnome.
Thrift glimpses net agony.
Spongely mangiest thrift.
Spongely steaming thrift.
Thrift times spongy angel.
Manly egg top thriftiness.
Shop-lifting, arty gems ten.
'e's shop-lifting tyrant gem.
Snigger shoplift natty me.
Shoplift teeny am G-string.
Shoplift yet ranting gems.
Thereof mangling typists.
Gaily froth temptingness.
Play-testing forth in gems.
Temptingly. Forth in gases.
Sanely spitting forth gem.
Temptingly rang to fishes.
Fishes gnat or temptingly.
Temptingly fish to ranges.
Temptingly fish on greats.
Agents fish or temptingly.
Petty mongrels fish giant.
Fish tasty, negligent romp.
Right! Flat, spiny gemstone.
Flatten in piggy smothers.
Falser, tiny, tempting hogs.
Frail, petty nothings gems.
Mighty flatters in sponge.
So getting frailest nymph.
Naggiest filters to nymph.
Flirt pithy gemstone nags.
Flirt pig nasty, honest gem.
Flies nag tempting shorty.
Stifle poets might granny.
Got stifle angriest nymph.
Earnest lifts mighty pong.
Horny, tempting sage lifts.

Lift spongy, earnest might.
Groin petty, smashing felt.
Hot tampering self stingy.
Not self pigsty nightmare.
This top fame grins gently.
Grotty fame piss in length.
Stingingly shot pert fame.
Sightly, sporting, net fame.
Shorty, glinting fame pest.
Fame hints spongy glitter.
Nights prig snotty female.
Yeah! Potent G-string films.
Film thorny, naggiest pest.
The forms tape stingingly.
This neat pigs from gently.
The paste from stingingly.
From tasty, sleeping night.
Gnash from sleeping titty.
Is pithy self-torment gang.
Right! Spiny, gentlest foam.
Gently ghost feminist par.
Feminist hogs gently. Trap.
Feminist parts hog gently.
Feminist traps hog gently.
Misfits earth gently pong.
Misfits heart gently pong.
Misfit thorny, gentle gasp.
Petty lightens as forming.
Garishly step not. Figment.
Pig trashy, stolen figment.
Sparsely. Figment to night.
Gosh! Ineptly star figment.
Hit angel's sporty figment.
Oh! Strangle tipsy figment.
Ghost spiny, alert figment.
Sap oily figment strength.
Phase snotty figment girl.
Trash nosy figment piglet.
I fragment gently piss hot.
Fragment the stingy spoil.
So sightly, inept fragment.
Fragment pig stylish tone.
Gently piss to the farming.
Farming poets shit gently.
Petty farming lightens so.
Ghost infirm, gentle pasty.
Tipsy, hot, negligent farms.
Slighting frame types not.
Atheist pongs gently firm.
Pig smelt farting honesty.
Seemly farting nights opt.
My gentle farting piss hot.
I'm the spongy lest farting.

The stings employ farting.
Manly tights fringe poets.
Temptingly fringe hot ass.
Fingers hottest manly pig.
Oh My! Sign flattering pest.
Ghost flattering, spiny me.
Empty in self-rating ghost.
Self-rating types on might.
Empty ghost sane flirting.
Heap flirting snotty gems.
My fleeting, tartish pongs.
My! This fleeting, star pong.
Rat fleeting, spongy smith.
Fleeting, spongy, hit smart.
Am fleeting, sporty things.
Nag fleeting, sporty smith.
Fleeting, pasty, strong him.
Fleeting, snotty, grim hasp.
Stifling, thorny, game pest.
A stifling, thorny pest gem.
O! Stifling, greatest nymph.
Stifling, terse nymph goat.
Nest stifling, mega trophy.
Sent stifling, mega trophy.
Stifling trophy as net gem.
Stifling trophy meets nag.
Stifling than germy poets.
Rat stifling, spongy theme.
Stifling, empty, north sage.
Nag stifling, sporty theme.
Stifling gnash or petty me.
Gosh! Stifling, pretty amen.
Stifling, pretty amen hogs.
Stifling patsy on the germ.
Phone stifling, tasty germ.
Phone stifling, tarty gems.
Stifling yet not sharp gem.
So lifting greatest nymph.
Feelings trim potty gnash.
I'm the petty organs flings.
Giftless, tenth, prim agony.
Meant giftless, thorny pig.
Giftless, thorny, inapt gem.
Not giftless, hyper mating.
Not typing giftless harem.
Right! On an empty, giftless.
Payment or giftless night.
Fast-settling, phoney, grim.
Pointless, neat frigg myth.
Spit mental frigg honesty.
Isn't the manly frigg poets.
Manly, potent frigg thesis.
Petty, sham, insolent frigg.

Saintly, potent frigg mesh.
I'm the snotty frigg planes.
Earthy, tempting sin flogs.
My right penitent flogs as.
My! The transient pig flogs.
Testier nymph giants flog.
Flog in merits gnash petty.
Masterings pity then flog.
Tyrannies might step flog.
Manly tights forget penis.
Spent in almighty forgets.
It stealing nymph forgets.
Tight penis forgets manly.
Is pithy tanglement frogs.
Shit! Frogs pity gentleman.
In the grotty, simple fangs.
Mightily stern poet fangs.
Fangs rent mightily. Poets.
Steep fangs torn mightily.
Rotten fangs spiel mighty.
Fangs meet thirstily pong.
Protestingly, I'm the fangs.
Prettily this gnome fangs.
Fangs might or inept style.
Imply the strong feasting.
Help snotty, grim feasting.
Gently sottish, prime fang.
Mightily. Fang pesters not.
Mightily strop tense fang.
Rotten fang spiels mighty.
Regiment stylish, top fang.
Fang hero sits temptingly.
Mightless fang in pottery.
Might rosy, pestilent fang.
Might fang plots serenity.
Stamp gently fisting hero.
Honestly! Part fisting gem.
Then fisting sporty gleam.
Sharply fitting gemstone.
Heroism gifts gently pant.
Gifts present on almighty.
Porn gifts hesitantly. Gem.
Gifts malign pert honesty.
Plainest, thorny gem gifts.
Not shrimpy, elegant gifts.
Telepathy gifts mornings.
Shy piglet gifts ornament.
Eminently gifts to graphs.
The gifts open smartingly.
The gifts name sportingly.
Rantingly gift poets mesh.
Glitter so gift sane nymph.
Gift malign trophy tenses.

The gift opens smartingly.
Temptingly gift on shares.
Gift hot penalty grimness.
Gift as smothering plenty.
Gift petty, smashing loner.
Smear gift snotty helping.
Fattiest hymen pongs girl.
I might gently safest porn.
Rompingly feast the sting.
Penitent hogs grimly fast.
No! Pesteringly might fats.
Might pongs entirely fast.
Ghost gently simper in fat.
Isn't prime fat hogs gently.
Gently promise nights. Fat.
Fat poser mights in gently.
Gently might fat poser sin.
Singingly strop fat theme.
Stingingly romp these fat.
Fat, motherly, singing step.
Fat ego-trip glints hymens.
Is fat nymph glitters gone.
Niggle monster's pithy fat.
Fat, stormy, sleeping night.
Sport fat, slighting enemy.
Openly fat, tight grimness.
The grim fat pongs in style.
The sly, meriting fat pongs.
Is fat, snotty helping germ.
The fat, stony gremlins pig.
Poser mights gently faint.
Shorty piglet gem infants.
Infants slight germy poet.
Infants grope might style.
Infant pest or sightly gem.
Hot merits pig gently fans.
Hero's git fans temptingly.
Safe, sightly, tempting nor.
Sportingly safe, tight men.
Nights safe, potty gremlin.
Nightly or tempting safes.
Hottest pan flimsy nigger.
Flimsy, hot, inept gangster.
Flimsy niggers patent hot.
Eat flimsy strength on pig.
Page to flimsy in strength.
Flimsy hats potent nigger.
Hat flimsy, potent snigger.
Flimsy pest than to nigger.
Nag flimsy, sporting teeth.
In the flimsy targets pong.
The potent, gas-ring flimsy.
Not spit the flimsy nagger.

Self-mastery hitting pong.
Firmly tightest, sane pong.
Mortifying length pets as.
A mortifying length pests.
The mortifying lent gasps.
The mortifying pets slang.
The missing flattery pong.
Right! Safely tempting 'n' so.
Safely grin not might pest.
Right! Tempting nose flays.
Might resets faintly pong.
Might pongs fattily sneer.
Fatly thirsting open gems.
Fatly shitting prone gems.
Fatly might sporting seen.
Fatly might sneering post.
Fatly might sneering spot.
Fatly stop sneering might.
I'm the stinger pongs fatly.
Fly segments hot pirating.
Fly might as not pestering.
Infantry host piglet gems.
Get hog simplest infantry.
Might egos slept infantry.
Might egos spelt infantry.
Infantry logs steep might.
Ferny, slighting, top mates.
Ferny, mightless, top giant.
This ferny, tempting goals.
Top, mangiest fry lightens.
Meanest, slighting, top fry.
Poets fry mangle shitting.
Sanest fry might on piglet.
Fry pig not mightless neat.
So fry this tempting angel.
I am this gentlest fry pong.
Not filthy spasm greeting.
Filthy, stringent ego maps.
Filthy mate pongs stinger.
Filthy, grit pong tameness.
Filthy pong mates stinger.
Filthy smog pestering ant.
Pig 'n' filthy gemstones rat.
Pig torments 'n' filthy sage.
Filthy gem stings not rape.
Strip nag filthy gemstone.
Filthy gems as potent ring.
Is filthy, potent germ nags.
Filthy enemas opt G-string.
Filthy, top segments grain.
Filthy pest mans to nigger.
Filthy pest as not merging.
Anger filthy gem spits not.

Spit filthy, strange gnome.
Thriftily. Pentagon's gems.
Thriftily gaps on segment.
Thriftily gasp on segment.
Freshly spitting not game.
It fortnightly semen gaps.
It gasp fortnightly semen.
Fortnightly penis at gems.
Fortnightly, mega pest sin.
Fortnightly pets as in gem.
Meat spots frighteningly.
Post teams frighteningly.
Spot frighteningly teams.
Stop frighteningly teams.
Shiftingly maps not greet.
Sponge shiftingly matter.
Me treats shiftingly pong.
Grasp shiftingly meet not.
Gape shiftingly torments.
Shiftingly state porn gem.
Shiftingly merges to pant.
Shiftingly pets to German.
Thrifty pongs stale in gem.
Thrifty pong lameness git.
Thrifty, genial stems pong.
Thrifty sons pig gentle am.
Thrifty, pleasing 'n' to gems.
Most thrifty, sleeping nag.
Spoilt gang thrifty semen.
Thrifty poet niggles mans.
Thrifty gem posts in angel.
Thrifty pests niggle moan.
Sort fishy, tempting angel.
Fishy, tempting gnat loser.
Fishy, giant, gentlest romp.
Fishy piglets torment nag.
Fishy, prattling gemstone.
Fishy, prone, tattling gems.
Hefty, limp, naggiest snort.
Hefty sting genitals romp.
Slime hefty, sporting gnat.
A hefty grimness plotting.
Is hefty, grim talent pongs.
Hefty strings malign poet.
Hefty, slim poets granting.
Got hefty, grim pliantness.
Split hefty, strong enigma.
Hefty spits torn gleaming.
Shifty, gentle giant romps.
Shifty angles torment pig.
Shifty pig torments angle.
Pig not strangle shifty me.
Name shifty, strong piglet.

Shifty gnome splattering.
Point strangle shifty gem.
Strangle in shifty, top gem.
Right! Nag lofty emptiness.
The lofty tampering signs.
Y-fronts help steaming. Git.
Slight inept Y-fronts game.
A Y-fronts slight inept gem.
Y-fronts gleam spite thing.
Them stealing Y-fronts pig.
Frosty, mean lighting pest.
Panel frosty shitting gem.
Frosty teething sampling.
Frosty, pleasing, net might.
Might frosty, pleasing ten.
Might frosty, elegant spin.
Frosty, spent, genial might.
Hint frosty, gleaming pest.
Forty as tempting English.
Forty tight plainness gem.
This negligent forty maps.
Pig menial softy strength.
Slighting, pert, mean softy.
I'm the grasping softy lent.
I'm the plane softy G-string.
Spit harm negligent softy.
Mights prettify on angles.
Songs prettify thin gleam.
Snore might self-pity gnat.
That self-pity snoring gem.
Mornings tag the self-pity.
Eh! Strong self-pity mating.
Honest, prim fatty niggles.
English fatty merits pong.
Fatty, sleeping, strong him.
Nifty sniggers tempt halo.
Slosh nifty, tempting rage.
Rape not slight nifty gems.
Gnash smelt nifty ego-trip.
Gate nifty, mirthless pong.
Might gnarl nifty poetess.
Pong rate nifty mightless.
Gate nifty, mightless porn.
Nifty piglets trash gnome.
Maggot's nifty hints repel.
Maggot's nifty, thin lepers.
The nifty, limp, strong sage.
Gremlin's to the nifty gaps.
Shit! Nifty pongs alert gem.
This nifty, alert pong gems.
This felon nags grim petty.
Felon shitting pasty germ.
Felon's naggish, trim petty.

Softer nymph stilting age.
Softer nymph git stealing.
Manly tighten softer pigs.
Softer pig tightens manly.
The manliest piggy fronts.
The tipsy gleaming fronts.
Front steaming shy piglet.
This front gleaming types.
Slight tempting oaf syren.
Thinly map softest nigger.
Thinly pig softest German.
Gently harming soft spite.
Sneeringly soft, apt might.
Soft, prim, negligent hasty.
Empaling soft, tight syren.
Soften grimly hating pest.
Fonts anger mightily. Pest.
Fonts pig hesitantly. Germ.
Hey! Smarting piglet fonts.
The fonts emit graspingly.
The fonts item graspingly.
Rashly spitting often gem.
Often smarting shy piglet.
Font germs pig hesitantly.
The font times graspingly.
Grime petty, slashing font.
Stray might sleeping font.
Gently meant of right piss.
Him of gently pig tartness.
Gently of the trim passing.
Gently simper of this gnat.
Glittery, spent of shaming.
Ingrately of spent mights.
Gayest strength of in limp.
Stringent of the gays limp.
Straying temple of nights.
Straying of tenth glimpse.
Slept of mightiest granny.
Granny of mightiest spelt.
Simplest, angry of tighten.
Pest of it hymenal G-string.
Hymen of starting piglets.
Pints of shatteringly. Gem.
Emptiness of rightly. Gnat.
Mangiest of rightly spent.
Rightly of steaming spent.
Temptress of nightly gain.
Tampering of nightly sets.
Lengthy of stingier stamp.
Lengthy of mangiest strip.
Lengthy of steaming strip.
Sightly of in gem patterns.
Emptiness of tightly rang.

Tightly of sneering stamp.
Spent of tightly smearing.
Sat nymph of elite G-string.
Shyest of glinting tamper.
Template of shiny G-string.
Mainly of the G-string pets.
Isn't strength of mealy pig.
Spent of gamely thirsting.
Grimly of nights neat pest.
Lengths of part stymieing.
Slept mangey of thirsting.
Smeary length of spitting.
My sharp of negligent tits.
Pitying of master's length.
Gather sins of temptingly.
Temptingly of a rightness.
Resist of temptingly hang.
Hearts of temptingly sign.
Thesis of temptingly rang.
Hits of temptingly ranges.
Implying of the strangest.
Emptying of star lightens.
Empty of in hints straggle.
The empty gits of snarling.
Payment of slighting rest.
Payment of gritless night.
Nights anger of slim petty.
Is petty mangler of nights.
Petty of this gremlin nags.
Typists of there mangling.
Gentler typist of shaming.
Typist of negligent harms.
The typist of snarling gem.
Smarten of slighting type.
Lighten of smarting types.
I'm gentler patsy of nights.
Is right spy of tanglement.
Right! Saintly of spent gem.
Strength of nastily pig me.
Intently sap of right gems.
Sly of the stinging tamper.
Nasty of tight, grim spleen.
Nasty might of gentler sip.
Nasty smith of gentler pig.
Isn't helping of tasty germ.
Isn't helping of tarty gems.
Syren of this tempting lag.
Slighting try of mean pest.
Tiny of the grasping smelt.
Gently pig smart fine host.
Gently shot smart fine pig.
Ghost gently trim fine sap.
Gently hog smart fine spit.
Mighty strongest, fine pal.
Pig fine myth to strangles.
Fine, trashy gems plotting.
Fine, slimy strength to gap.
Fine, pretty ghost maligns.
Hot spy rattling fine gems.
This fine gem pongs tartly.
Hot arms finest gently pig.
Ho! Finest gently pig smart.
Gently finest so might par.
Eh! Finest grotty sampling.
Finest opt gratingly mesh.
Finest part gnomishly get.
Finest slept mighty groan.
Finest spelt mighty groan.
Oh My! Straggle finest pint.
Oh My! Finest plate G-string.
Finest mates rightly pong.
Finest pong tightly smear.
Finest tent shaggily romp.
Finest shaggily potent Mr.
Get rompishly finest gnat.
Infest malign trophy gets.
Pong infest thirsty gleam.
Finest hast rompingly get.
Lights empty finest groan.
Finest play not right gems.
Pretty hog maligns finest.
Let's! Niftiest nymph aggro.
Fens might staringly. Poet.
Gosh! Gently if inept smart.
If inept hogs smart gently.
Right! Gently if mean posts.
Right! Gently if mean stops.
Gently top if nights smear.
I'm the stars if gently pong.
I'm the gross if gently pant.
Harems if gently spotting.
Gently tarnish if top gems.
Gently if this agents romp.
This stream if gently pong.
Pint if strangely hot gems.
Strangely hint if top gems.
Rantingly if the stops gem.
Isn't grotty if sane phlegm.
Strongly if pantheist gem.
Glossy if tenth tampering.
Gratingly if steep months.
Gayest strength if on limp.
If gritty gentleman shops.
Gnomishly if spent target.
Oh My! If gentlest pig rants.
Tampering if ghostly nest.
If ghostly tampering nets.
Sent if ghostly tampering.
Ghastly gem if inept snort.
Ghastly torn if inept gems.
Nightly if strangest poem.
Parts if nightly gemstone.
Traps if nightly gemstone.
If nightly gemstones part.
Trap if nightly gemstones.
Lengthy if impotent grass.
Lengthy if mangiest ports.
Lengthy if steaming ports.
Lengthy if mangiest sport.
Lengthy if steaming sport.
Lengthy if storming tapes.
Sightly if on gem patterns.
Thinly if mega, strong pest.
Rang if stylish, potent gem.
To nymph if latest niggers.
Gas nymph if gentlest riot.
Got if gritless, neat nymph.
If nymph gross elegant tit.
Strangle shitty me if pong.
Pest if namely hot G-string.
Strength if mealy posting.
Strength if not mealy pigs.
Smiley if not gap strength.
Strengths if mangily. Poet.
My! If angel's tightest porn.
My! That strong if sleeping.
Sportingly if the gem ants.
Spongy me if right talents.
Employ if strangest night.
If giant strength employs.
If tenth stages rompingly.
Horses if temptingly. Gnat.
If host ranges temptingly.
If shot ranges temptingly.
If stores hang temptingly.
Empty if to gnashers glint.
Empty if on hints straggle.
Play hot if stringent gems.
Plenty if shattering smog.
Angel's sporty if net might.
Angel's might if sporty ten.
Mangle if the sporty sting.
Spotty if negligent harms.
Honest petty if grim slang.
If petty 'n' strongish gleam.
If right sons mangle petty.
Gnash grim if stolen petty.
Petty hims if strong angel.
Slyer if to tempting gnash.
Might if steely rants pong.
Nasty if top germ lightens.
Strength if any molest pig.
Graph if snottily segment.
Might if snotty leper nags.
Might if snotty lepers nag.
Snotty sham if gentler pig.
Testy helping if strong am.
My! Hottest pilfering nags.
That stony gems pilfering.
Profits as negligent myth.
Pilfer tonight nasty gems.
The snotty gaming pilfers.
The splif tormenting gays.
Might enrage snotty splif.
The gassy flip tormenting.
Oh My! Neatest flip G-string.
Pong smartingly shit feet.
Grotty, mean helping fists.
Fists torment gay helping.
The top gem fits snaringly.
So fist lengthy tampering.
Lengthy tampering fits so.
Sift thorny, gleaming pest.
Hey! Fist piglet strong man.
The top fit sniggers manly.
Is open farts might gently.
Gently might in farts pose.
Gnomishly inept farts get.
Nightly poet farts in gems.
My sleeping tonight farts.
I'm honest pigs, gently fart.
Fart stingingly. Home pest.
Fart mighty log ineptness.
Mighty got penniless fart.
Fart step homely stinging.
On my sleeping tights fart.
Fart in spongy, steel might.
Empty stinging holes fart.
Empty on this fart niggles.
I'm the slyest fart ponging.
Maggot's finer plenty hits.
Finer petty glass on might.
Not slight finer, pasty gem.
Mighty talents pig on serf.
Pong tamely shitting serf.
Shit impotently gang serf.
Might stately pong in serf.
Might gently sap on strife.
Strife nets almighty pong.
Grotty meetings pin flash.
Grotty pest in gem in flash.
Flash tits empty on nigger.

Isn't empty flash to nigger.
It flash niggers empty not.
Grotty filth gaps in semen.
Gory filth emptiness gnat.
Gory, spent, mangiest filth.
Angry, emptiest filth song.
Is not angry filth pest gem.
Mangey stingers opt filth.
To my grasping, tense filth.
My sane filth poet G-string.
Filth spits to my gangrene.
Spongy, merest, giant filth.
Empty angriest filth song.
Sporty filth meanings get.
Petty filth ages mornings.
Rang tipsy filth gemstone.
Pity strong, sane filth gem.
Meetings pay strong filth.
Spy filth tormenting sage.
Pig filth or nasty segment.
I'm tasty filth pongs green.
Stray filth meetings pong.
Filth eyes tampon G-string.
Tiny, tempting go flashers.
To selfish, angry, tempting.
O My! Patient shelf G-string.
Ya! Flesh impotent G-string.
Stingingly pester fathom.
A petty fishmongers glint.
Top greeting shifts manly.
Fetish giants romp gently.
My! Pig not strangle fetish.
Nag gremlin's potty fetish.
Pity mangle strong fetish.
Ego-trip mans gently shift.
Shift gently mating poser.
Shift slimy, potent nagger.
Shift sore mangling petty.
Rantingly spot thief gems.
Rantingly stop thief gems.
Strongly inapt thief gems.
Angry, tempting thief loss.
Thief pongs grimy talents.
Graspingly stem not. Thief.
Aptly snorting thief gems.
Spit gremlin's theft agony.
I'm straggly theft on penis.
Manly theft piss to nigger.
Slimy, angriest theft pong.
Slimy, naggiest theft porn.
Graspingly times on theft.
Sportingly games in theft.
Tamely fighting pert sons.

Part fighting seemly snot.
Tersely fighting not maps.
Amen! Style fighting strop.
Fighting on slyest tamper.
Lose fighting natty sperm.
O My! Frightening, last pest.
Frightening pays to smelt.
Am frightening, top styles.
Salty, top semen frighting.
Style frighting pets moan.
Yet frighting not samples.
Types or lightning-fast me.
Lightning-fast, remote spy.
Petty, storming angelfish.
Pit grotty flashing semen.
Gritty, top flashing semen.
Protest tiny flashing gem.
Natty fleshing grim poets.
Grotty pain flights semen.
Is not empty anger flights.
Flights type on mastering.
Meaner, snotty flights pig.
Yes flights not tampering.
Flight stings mean poetry.
Masterings type on flight.
Flight types on mastering.
Top, mangiest flight syren.
Steaming top flight syren.
Frighten taste slimy pong.
Mangily frighten to steps.
My! Frighten to angel's spit.
Frighten impotently sags.
Frighten empty as so glint.
Frighten style among spit.
I'm sly poets frighten gnat.
Plot frighten sanity gems.
Frighten toy maligns pest.
Top mint frightens sagely.
Top mate frightens singly.
Is top get frightens manly.
My pest frightens in gloat.
Isn't empty goal frightens.
Frightens to type maligns.
I'm natty gospel frightens.
Sly, tempting as on fighter.
Fighter smiles natty pong.
Timely ant pongs fighters.
Patiently frights gnomes.
Empty son's genital fright.
Fortnight style pain gems.
Gently shifting to a sperm.
Top shifting greets manly.
So mangle pretty shifting.

Pest fights ignorantly. Me.
Ego-trip fights manly nest.
Ego-trip fights manly nets.
Ego-trip fights manly sent.
Top ranting fights seemly.
Protestingly mean fights.
Sage fights intently romp.
Amen! Pigs fights rottenly.
Arm-pits fight gently nose.
Stringently fight as poem.
Sneeringly fight to stamp.
Fight to germy pliantness.
Fight omnipresently tags.
Fight temptingly earns so.
Petty snores malign fight.
Fight spiny, tolerant gems.
Fight mangiest style porn.
Steaming fight style porn.
Fight snotty, genial sperm.
Fight plainer, snotty gems.
Straggly, potent finish me.
Amen! Leggy thrift piss not.
Many gentle thrift gossip.
Piggy, sanest thrift lemon.
So. Thrift Gipsy gentleman.
Thrift payments niggle so.
Spiny thrift gems to angel.
Slyest thrift pong enigma.
Thrift niggles nasty poem.
Shoplift any meet G-string.
Shoplift tasty 'n' emerging.
Shoplift giant entry gems.
Shoplift yet name G-string.
Stingy shoplifter gem ant.
Gaily. Forth temptingness.
Nag seemly spitting forth.
Shy, impotent niggers flat.
Pong flat mightiest syren.
Flatten smothering Gipsy.
False, inept, strong mighty.
Fail ghost tempting syren.
Flair segments hot typing.
Frailest pong nets mighty.
Flirt pithy gemstones nag.
I'm the spongy agents flirt.
Flies might not angry pest.
So stifle pregnant mighty.
My! Pong stifle shattering.
Neater, spongy lifts might.
Left tight agony primness.
Might spongy, nastier felt.
Left spongy, nastier might.
Left hating in sporty gems.

Oh! Straying, tempting self.
Self, natty, smothering pig.
Fame niggles trophy tints.
Fame hints sportingly get.
Protestingly nights. Fame.
Lights type snorting fame.
Son's pretty fame lighting.
Hot pig sly, stringent fame.
Pigsty or manifest length.
Right! Fameless, not typing.
The pitying, strong flames.
Flames pity on the G-string.
Flame so pitying strength.
Seething ratty films pong.
Film spite agony strength.
Hasty, potent niggers film.
Film or typesetting gnash.
Gently pissing the format.
Form pigsties than gently.
From hate pets stingingly.
From hasty in gentlest pig.
From genital's then pigsty.
Plenty from shitting sage.
From genitals type nights.
Form this negligent patsy.
Form gentle shitting pays.
Form tightest, spiny angel.
Spy from stinging athlete.
Nights pig from neat style.
Gently strop feminist hag.
Feminist helps grotty nag.
Gently misfit on sharp get.
Misfit gently hang or pest.
Misfit poetry nags length.
Eh! Piss! Gently formatting.
Sleepy, nights formatting.
Gently foaming the strips.
It, strangely posh figment.
The figment posts angrily.
Ghastly tin figment poser.
Ghastly risen top figment.
Ghastly iron figment pest.
Slash groin petty figment.
Figment lightens to spray.
The sporting figment lays.
Hot, rasping figment style.
Ghost nasty figment peril.
Singly fragment this poet.
Fragment nightly spite so.
Hotels fragment in pigsty.
Fragments pity so lighten.
Fragments pity to English.
Got engraftment syphilis.

Politest, shy, fragmenting.
It fragmenting posh style.
Frames shit gently pig not.
The frames opt stingingly.
Farm gently hoisting pest.
Tits farm seethingly pong.
Seethingly sting top farm.
Shaggily potent nets firm.
Gently farting posh times.
Farting hymens to piglets.
Sleeping farting to myths.
Gem pits honestly farting.
Pithy, stolen farting gems.
Seemly farting top things.
Gosh! Spent timely farting.
Farting hogs timely spent.
Might sleepy farting snot.
No type mightless farting.
Honestly! A tempting frigs.
The snotty grief sampling.
Tempting finger slays hot.
Tempting fringe slays hot.
Fringe potent might slays.
Smashingly fretting poet.
Flattering, shy gem points.
Flirting on the pasty gems.
A fleeting nymph gross tit.
Fleeting trophy mans gits.
Fleeting, pithy, smart song.
Fleeting, shitty arm pongs.
Fleeting, shitty ram pongs.
Fleeting than stormy pigs.
Harm fleeting pigsty snot.
Might sort fleeting pansy.
Man stifling, grotty sheep.
State stifling nymph goer.
My! The stifling, strong ape.
Ahem! Stifling, strong type.
The stifling germ pays not.
Hope stifling tyrant gems.
That spongy, trim feelings.
Right! Map snotty feelings.
Ornate pest flings mighty.
Flings gnash top temerity.
Shyest fling to tampering.
The steamy, sporting fling.
Amen! Thirty giftless pong.
Oh Man! Giftless, petty grin.
Flags on impiety strength.
Flag petty, smothering sin.
Pestilent frigg as on myth.
Shy, top, sentimental frigg.
Nymph flogs testier giant.

Petty gnash flogs in merit.
I'm the stingy parents flog.
I flog anything. Temptress.
Flog taste stingier nymph.
Flog that grimy ineptness.
Isn't nightmares type flog.
Spray eminent tights flog.
Teeny arm-pits flog nights.
Pin testy nightmares flog.
Forget gainless nymph tit.
Temptingly heats in frogs.
Fog ratty, penniless might.
Shitty poet gremlin fangs.
Temptingly its hero fangs.
Fangs sit temptingly. Hero.
The fangs groin slim petty.
Rottenly. Fangs, I'm the pigs.
Stingily mother fang pest.
Oh My! Fang glitters in pest.
Rightly. Fang to emptiness.
Fang meets thirstily pong.
Remissly tighten top fang.
Spot trimly seething fang.
Stop trimly seething fang.
Rompingly the fang testis.
Hot empty in gritless fang.
Tin mightless fang poetry.
Slosh petty, meriting fang.
Iron petty, mightless fang.
Fang shitting steely romp.
Partly fisting honest gem.
Almighty presents fig not.
Ape Shit! Norm gifts gently.
Gifts pig tolerant hymens.
Ant gifts seethingly romp.
Hoarsely 'n' tempting gifts.
Shy penitent gifts glamor.
Temptingly hears on gifts.
Temptingly gifts on share.
Trophies gift gently mans.
Gently gift phoniest arms.
Gift arm-pits shone gently.
Part gently gift hominess.
Ahem! Snortingly gift pest.
Gift homely, stringent sap.
Gift shy, pleasing torment.
Remissly gift potent hang.
Seemly gift snorting path.
Gift sporting than seemly.
Hot gift germy pliantness.
Gift pesteringly sham not.
Gift snotty, healing sperm.
Romp singingly fattest he.

Gently romping safest hit.
I'm safest 'n' grotty helping.
Niggle trim safest python.
Gently romping this feast.
Ogrishly 'n' tempting feast.
Fast shop gently meriting.
Ogreishly 'n' tempting fats.
Gently impish, strong fate.
Gently impish, strong feat.
Gently fate storming ship.
Gently fate sporting hims.
Stingingly feat, hot sperm.
Fate torments 'n' piggishly.
Feat torments 'n' piggishly.
Fate so implying strength.
So implying feat strength.
Gently might, is fat person.
Gently romping fat thesis.
This fat pongs mire gently.
Ho! Fat, girly temptingness.
Singingly tempt hero's fat.
Fat hymen glitters on pigs.
Honestly merging fat spit.
Hey! Gremlin's fat spotting.
The fat, slimy, open G-string.
Fat style 'n' smothering pig.
Eh! Pig gremlin's snotty fat.
Fat shrimps negligent toy.
Rely pong might fattiness.
Germy poets slight infant.
Mightier post fans gently.
Mightier fans spot gently.
Mightier fans stop gently.
I'm the fans get sportingly.
Shit! Gore fans temptingly.
I'm the fan gets sportingly.
Groin petty, mightless fan.
Hi! Safe, tempting, strongly.
Right! Temptingly safe 'n' so.
Gremlin's safe, potty thing.
No! Temptingly right safes.
Ago flimsy, inept strength.
Flimsy, potent thing rages.
Groan tighten flimsy pest.
Anger tight flimsy on pest.
Tenth raging flimsy poets.
Then gate sporting flimsy.
The flimsy nigger past not.
Mystifier nags top length.
Right! Gentle infamy stops.
Firstly the mangiest pong.
Top, singing flattery mesh.
Tight frailty semens pong.

Tempting flayer sings hot.
Flyers hog tempting saint.
Safely torment night pigs.
Might safely testing porn.
Presenting to might flays.
The pigs flays, tormenting.
Faintly tight person gems.
Fatly sting phoniest germ.
Fatly pin right gemstones.
Top sneering mights fatly.
Fatly pig not the grimness.
Fly tame phoniest G-string.
Hero's tempting giants fly.
Gnash potent, grimiest fly.
The fly masterings pig not.
Might not slang fiery pest.
Slope tight infantry gems.
Fairy, gentlest months pig.
Ferny mates spotlighting.
Ferny piglets might as not.
Tattling gems phonies fry.
Ghost tempting aliens fry.
Fry ghost sentimental pig.
Fry gloat might ineptness.
Fry not gleaming this pest.
Son's filthy, tempting gear.
Filthy tampons, greetings.
Filthy, neat G-string poems.
Filthy, sporting nets game.
A filthy, sporting gem nets.
Filthy, sporting me agents.
Filthy meeting pongs star.
Filthy, resistant pong gem.
Pig no filthy gem tartness.
Filthy gaps meet snorting.
Filthy, inept, strong games.
Gem prints not filthy sage.
A filthy, potent gems grins.
Is filthy, potent germs nag.
Filthy, potent miser gangs.
Filthy gem opens starting.
Poet men as filthy G-string.
Filthy tape in strong gems.
Filthy, snorting pets game.
A filthy gem pets snorting.
Some granting filthy pest.
Stem filthy pest groaning.
Tip filthy segments groan.
Gemstone gaps 'n' thriftily.
Gemstone 'n' thriftily gasp.
Torment fishily gang pest.
To flashy, tempting singer.
Grime flashy, potent sting.

Ant seems fortnightly pig.
Fortnightly past seeming.
Fortnightly pets in a gems.
Fortnightly spite me nags.
Sane gem pits fortnightly.
Mega net piss fortnightly.
Mega ten piss fortnightly.
Forty-eight plants in gems.
Frighteningly state mops.
Frighteningly. Stops meat.
Top at mess frighteningly.
Frighteningly most tapes.
Shiftingly. Sperm to agent.
Shiftingly stamp on greet.
Shiftingly map not greets.
Rats! Meet shiftingly pong.
Shiftingly open smart get.
Porn mates shiftingly get.
Shiftingly garment poets.
Shiftingly term poets nag.
Shiftingly neat post germ.
Shiftingly rent as top gem.
Shiftingly paste torn gem.
Shiftingly paste not. Germ.
Shiftingly pat not merges.
Shiftingly tap not merges.
Met thrifty, gainless pong.
Thrifty piglet mess on nag.
Thrifty poets slang in gem.
Thrifty pliantness gem go.
Fishy, tempting, strong ale.
Fishy attempts on niggler.
Fishy, potent, smarting leg.
Opt fishy, gentle smarting.
Fishy, storming, gentle pat.
Fishy, storming, gentle tap.
Hefty arm-pits niggle snot.
Hefty armpit niggles snot.
Isn't hefty tampering logs.
Hefty simpleton gratings.
I hefty strong man piglets.
Rattling hefty penis smog.
Hefty points lame G-string.
Apron hefty gems stilting.
Isn't hefty gleaming ports.
Hefty poets malign string.
Shifty, tempting, large son.
Trim shifty as gentle pong.
Shifty talents pig on germ.
Fogey tints smart helping.
Stain limp fogey strength.
Felonry mans tightest pig.
Apt stingers might felony.

Pat stingers might felony.
Shame lofty, stringent pig.
Y-fronts pig slight neat me.
Eight pliant gems Y-fronts.
Y-fronts negate lips might.
A Y-fronts might gentle sip.
A Y-fronts pig gentle smith.
A Y-fronts pig gentlest him.
Egg hesitant Y-fronts limp.
The Y-fronts impaling, gets.
The Y-fronts pig malign set.
Might frosty, giant spleen.
I'm the niggers plant softy.
This softy prig gentleman.
Prettify nights gas lemon.
Prettify might lesson nag.
Prettify the SOS, mangling.
Prettify slang this gnome.
Petrify hot mangle stings.
Alignments petrify ghost.
North, giant self-pity gems.
Might groan nest self-pity.
Might groan sent self-pity.
I'm the self-pity gang snort.
Self-pitying gem 'n' hot star.
Self-pitying gems 'n' hot rat.
Self-pitying term nags hot.
Hat self-pitying, strong me.
Then rat self-pitying smog.
So inserting fatty phlegm.
I'm fatty sniggers help not.
Fatty, honest, limp snigger.
Fatty, slighting person me.
The fatty mongrels pig sin.
Nifty, posh, gentler stigma.
Nifty, sharp get molesting.
Meet nifty, grasping sloth.
Nifty loathing pets germs.
Nifty loathing germ pests.
Gosh! Smarten nifty piglet.
Nifty hogs smarten piglet.
Nifty lengths as grim poet.
I am nifty strength gospel.
I'm a nifty strength gospel.
Nifty hag to gremlin's pest.
Nights gap nifty molester.
Nights nifty, steep glamor.
Nifty gemstones prig halt.
Nifty presents might goal.
Nifty might gets personal.
Nifty, mightless pant ogre.
Nifty sham or gentlest pig.
The nifty limp aggress not.

The nifty, grim pongs stale.
The nifty, gormless pig ant.
Shit! Nifty telegram pongs.
Shit! Pong alert nifty gems.
Mighty spit strange felon.
Felon thirsting empty gas.
Leg frostiest, giant nymph.
Nag frostiest, tiny phlegm.
Softer pin as gently might.
Mightily spent softer nag.
Softer, genital nymph gits.
Manly pig the softer sting.
Might nasty, sleeping fort.
I am the pigs fronts gently.
Front sagely might in pest.
Shaggily 'n' emptiest front.
For neat piss gently might.
Temptingly for it gnashes.
Temptingly for the assign.
Fatso nymph titles nigger.
Fatso niggers title nymph.
The gremlin's fatso typing.
Soft, large hymen spitting.
Soft nymph sage in glitter.
Primly seething soft gnat.
Right! Soft penalty in gems.
Ineptly hating soft germs.
Nights type soft maligner.
Enlighten soft, grim patsy.
Softie nymph nags glitter.
Fonts heap timely G-string.
I'm the fonts get raspingly.
My often priggish talents.
Gently misshape grit font.
Tigerish font maps gently.
Gently of right amen spits.
Gently of prim, sane tights.
Gently harming of its pest.
Pig gently smart of the sin.
Gently of the grim ant piss.
Pest of staringly hint gem.
Pest of staringly thin gem.
Strangely of this pint gem.
Shit! Gem of rantingly pets.
Pest of rantingly hits gem.
Pest of rantingly hit gems.
Pest of snaringly tight me.
Searingly tempt of nights.
Stringently of eight maps.
Stingingly of there stamp.
Three of stingingly stamp.
Gay of inept, slim strength.
Mighty of gentler ant piss.

Pets of nightly mastering.
Trim lengthy of sanest pig.
Mans of tightly pestering.
Eighty of tempting snarls.
It a G-string of steel nymph.
Isn't pithy of strangle gem.
Print gems of shitty angel.
Transmit shy of gentle pig.
Namely spit of the G-string.
Pest of nights manly tiger.
Smiley of the pant G-string.
Smartingly of steep thing.
Smartingly of spent eight.
Stymie of pregnant slight.
Theme of graspingly tints.
Graspingly of tenth items.
Graspingly of tenth times.
Piggy of mirthless tenant.
Pigsty of lightest manner.
Gipsy of strength ailment.
Springy gem of this talent.
Temptingly of nights arse.
Sight of temptingly earns.
Heats of temptingly grins.
Earth of temptingly signs.
Heart of temptingly signs.
Temptingly of theirs nags.
The ass of temptingly grin.
Payment of light stingers.
Things of patiently. Germs.
Grimness of aptly tighten.
Smith of pertinently gags.
Presently of giant mights.
Presently might of a sting.
A plenty of thirsting gems.
Slashing petty of grim net.
Slashing petty of grim ten.
Petty of halting grimness.
Nightmare's types of glint.
Pansy of its gentler might.
The pansy of stilting germ.
Patsy of merest lightning.
Pasty might of gentler sin.
Right! Spiny of gentlest am.
Rats! Spiny of gentle might.
Instantly prig of the gems.
Sly shit of tempting anger.
Nasty of trim helping gets.
Lighten of nasty, grim pest.
Tasty helping of grim nest.
Tasty of grim helping nets.
Syren of a tempting lights.
Fine, hot pig smarts gently.

This fine, grotty gem plans.
Strongly pat this fine gem.
Strongly tap this fine gem.
Fine pots strangle mighty.
Mighty strangle fine tops.
Shaggily tempt fine snort.
Straggle sit to fine nymph.
Fine nymph to gritless tag.
My fine pest hogs rattling.
My! Pig fine, strong stealth.
Simply fine strength goat.
Fines pig gently smart hot.
Finest gently rompish tag.
Shrimp gently infest goat.
Infest sap or gently might.
Finest grotty, simple hang.
Finest gnomishly pert tag.
Motherly pint gags finest.
Finest remit ghastly pong.
I infest straggle to nymph.
Finest lasting trophy gem.
Tamely infest right pongs.
The top nags finest grimly.
Finest raging empty sloth.
Petty logs finest harming.
Finest might longer patsy.
Finest tarty helping smog.
Niftiest, large myths pong.
Ghastly meriting top fens.
Sperm if gently hot giants.
Gently if hot, apt grimness.
Gently if something. Parts.
Gently if something. Traps.
Posers if gently might ant.
Them if sporting as gently.
Harm if gently sting poets.
Gently hat if top grimness.
Pest if rantingly shot gem.
Rantingly step if hot gems.
Ha! Stringently if top gems.
Tight if permanent glossy.
I'm the straggly if not pens.
Straggly hint if top semen.
If stingy as rotten phlegm.
Pest if mighty snort angel.
Pigs if motherly tangents.
If smothery planting gets.
Myth if sane glitters pong.
Myth penis if not straggle.
If top gems 'n' shatteringly.
In pest if not ghastly germ.
Post if lengthy mastering.
Spot if lengthy mastering.

Stop if lengthy mastering.
Stealthy if grim nets pong.
Spring if not stealthy gem.
Rashly sting if potent gem.
Pest if hotly mean G-string.
Nymph if logger tattiness.
Nymph if agents glitter so.
Git or gentlest if as nymph.
Shrimpy if to gentlest nag.
Trophy if gentleman's gits.
Python if it strangle gems.
Son's hyper if tattling gem.
Shy if top, stringent gleam.
Measly strength if it pong.
If masterly pong tightens.
If a timely strengths pong.
The set if smartingly pong.
If tenth games sportingly.
If spongy anthem glitters.
Spongy themes if rattling.
Pigsty if the ant mongrels.
Gipsy if short tanglement.
If range hosts temptingly.
If songs earth temptingly.
If songs heart temptingly.
Empty if strongish tangle.
Right if longest payments.
Semen if aptly hot G-string.
Ghost trim if gentle pansy.
Trim pansy if gentlest hog.
Slight pansy if rotten gem.
Angel's spy if rotten might.
Porn if nights stately gem.
Might if steely pongs rant.
Nasty phlegm if to stinger.
Nasty if prim, gentle ghost.
Nasty if prim, gentlest hog.
Snottily gnash if pert gem.
Tasty gems 'n' hot pilfering.
Then pilfering tasty smog.
Ghastly profit in segment.
Torment shy, naggiest flip.
That feet romps singingly.
Nasty, slighting feet romp.
Fists nag temptingly. Hero.
Fist gently storming heap.
Fits heap gently storming.
Sift gently storming heap.
Gently fist smarting hope.
Fits hope gently smarting.
Ahem! Gently sporting fist.
Ahem! Gently sporting fits.
Fist grotty, insane phlegm.

Grotty, insane phlegm fits.
Ragingly fist potent mesh.
Ragingly potent fits mesh.
Fist hymenal poet G-string.
Me fits shatteringly pong.
Nymph fits soggier talent.
Temptingly fist hero's nag.
Temptingly sift hero's nag.
Then fist sporty gleaming.
Sporty gleaming fits then.
Mangling hero's petty fist.
Mangling hero's petty fits.
Straggly, posh, eminent fit.
O My! Pleasing fit strength.
Gosh! Temptingly saner fit.
The nasty mongrels pig fit.
No fair pests might gently.
So fair, gentlest nymph git.
Fair spy on gentlest might.
Them farts singingly. Poet.
Seemly night farts not pig.
Farts pig not slight enemy.
Farts opt slighting enemy.
Farts pity on gem lightens.
Farts pity gnome lightens.
I'm negligent farts spy hot.
Singingly top themes fart.
Nightly poets fart in gems.
Fart pin sightly gemstone.
Fart gossipingly tenth me.
Emptying fart lightens so.
Tipsy fart lightens on gem.
Fart lightens tipsy gnome.
Fear nymph egotists glint.
Finer, ghastly pint to gems.
Thinly. Maggot's finer step.
Goatishly tempting ferns.
The spotty serf maligning.
The snotty, malign serf pig.
First, shy, potent gleaming.
My! Point self-hate G-string.
Flash trying nepotist gem.
Flash grey, impotent sting.
Flash not pig gritty semen.
Flash regiment top stingy.
Flash potty gem inserting.
I'm one flash, petty G-string.
Temerity stings half pong.
Filth signs grotty ape-men.
Soggy, penitent filth arms.
Not spite angry filth gems.
Pig not germy, sanest filth.
O My! Gang filth prettiness.

Pong stymie strange filth.
Not anger tipsy filth gems.
Pity strange filth on gems.
So type mean filth G-string.
Type snorting filth games.
A filth types snorting gem.
Maggot's inner filth types.
Filth merging nasty poets.
Tasty, groping filth semen.
Pig snotty, sane filth germ.
Filth pongs ratty seeming.
Testy, mangier filth pongs.
Testy filth on grasping me.
Pity nag thriftless gnome.
Any pig not thriftless gem.
I'm heart-felt stingy pongs.
Selfish, gory, tempting ant.
Flesh tempting orgy saint.
Is not gray, tempting flesh.
Is not gray, tempting shelf.
Torment piggy shelf saint.
Flesh potty gem straining.
Isn't self-harming, petty go.
Stringently top game fish.
Gently man ego-trip shifts.
Gently margin poet shifts.
Geometry shifts planting.
Temptingly shifts no rage.
Strongly paint fetish gem.
Fetish grants timely pong.
Many strong fetish piglet.
Amen! Glittery shift pongs.
Neat shift gets rompingly.
Presently shift in maggot.
Gently smart thief on pigs.
Thief pongs smatteringly.
Sportingly. Thief gems ant.
Temptingly rag son's thief.
Thief snags or temptingly.
Heftiest, manly, strong pig.
Gently grim theft passion.
Pig measly, snorting theft.
Theft to gems in raspingly.
Lame sporty, singing theft.
Sporty, gleaming theft sin.
Tamely fighting not. Press.
Mostly fighting a present.
My posers fighting talent.
Empty losers fighting ant.
Penalty stems or fighting.
Sporty, steel man fighting.
Romp sanely fighting test.
Sanely fighting top terms.

Lay no fighting temptress.
Tersely fighting on stamp.
Not fighting a style sperm.
Neatest, sly romp fighting.
Only fighting pest master.
Try fighting top lameness.
Frightening, spotty males.
Frightening, spotty meals.
Frightening metals to spy.
Meanly frighting top sets.
'e's pest to manly frighting.
No! Tamely frighting pests.
Seemly frighting post ant.
Frighting to messy planet.
Ants empty lose frighting.
O Man! Less frighting petty.
Molest nay frighting pest.
Frighting on testy sample.
'e's lightning-fast or empty.
Germy 'n' pottiest flashing.
Empty to resting flashing.
Pretty flashing into gems.
Try flashing nepotist gem.
Itsy, potent flashing germ.
Flashing yet torment pigs.
Trim potent gays fleshing.
A pigsty fleshing torment.
Type fleshing to smarting.
Amen! Grotty penis flights.
Flights may not pestering.
Poetry flights mean sting.
Flights 'n' mangiest poetry.
Poetry flights 'n' steaming.
Flight torments gay penis.
Mangey, rotten flight piss.
Spongy, neat flight merits.
Tipsy, resonant flight gem.
Ratty semens pig on flight.
It frighten gently maps so.
Frighten post aims gently.
Frighten spot aims gently.
Frighten aims stop gently.
Singly frighten top mates.
Frighten slimy pest on tag.
Timely frighten past song.
Mangily frighten top sets.
Frighten pain gets mostly.
Frighten on my stalest pig.
Frighten piglet as my snot.
My! Frighten lasting poets.
Frighten in my pest gloats.
Frighten to my angel spits.
Lament so frighten pigsty.

Frighten lame pigsty snot.
Frighten as molten pigsty.
It frighten gems plays not.
Frighten molest pansy git.
Pasty gits frighten lemon.
Frighten saintly tops gem.
Frighten tasty lisp on gem.
Frighten tasty slip on gem.
Frighten lamest, stony pig.
Frighten mental pigs toys.
Mealy pong frightens tits.
It frightens penalty smog.
Aptly frightens into gems.
I'm sly poet frightens gnat.
Pint frightens toys gleam.
Mail testy pong frightens.
Fighter son as temptingly.
Tempting fighter slays no.
Sly, impotent fighter nags.
Testy fighter on sampling.
Sly, impotent fighters nag.
Fighters plain snotty gem.
Frights nag potent smiley.
Temptingly frights as one.
Temptingly frights on sea.
Empaling on testy frights.
My fright on genital's pest.
Petty fright smiles on nag.
Only, mangiest fright pest.
Only steaming fright pest.
Fortnight's meetings play.
I'm a fortnight's gentle spy.
Empty freight ton signals.
My sane fortnight piglets.
My! Spite angel's fortnight.
Fortnight piss neatly. Gem.
Pile nasty fortnight gems.
Am shifting pest or gently.
Pong seemly shifting tart.
Shifting geometry plants.
Shifting plays rotten gem.
Sporty fishing gem talent.
Armpit fights gently nose.
Gently import sane fights.
Amen! Potent grisly fights.
My pestilent fights groan.
Permanently fights so. Git.
Tempting fights on layers.
Ya! Gremlin's potent fights.
Fight strongly spite amen.
Manly poets fight stinger.
Steep fight on smartingly.
Pesteringly fight to mans.

Permanently fight so. Gits.
Neat fight sets rompingly.
It fight sleepy strong man.
Fight pig slyest ornament.
Soggy, mental thrift penis.
Soggy, pliant thrift semen.
Leggy thrift moans in pest.
Many thrift niggles poets.
My! Is elegant thrift pongs.
Man gossipy, gentle thrift.
Entail spongy thrift gems.
Emit angel's spongy thrift.
Item angel's spongy thrift.
Thrift payment niggles so.
Spiny, elegant thrift smog.
My thriftiest angles pong.
Tempting father in glossy.
Temptingly star-fish gone.
Not gleaming fresh typist.
Ran shop-lifting, testy gem.
It shoplift angry segment.
Shoplift nag gritty semen.
My! Shoplift stringent age.
Entry giants shoplift gem.
Tiny agents shoplift germ.
Singingly tame forth pest.
Temptingly froth in gases.
Fish mealy, potent G-string.
Empty not straggle in fish.
Fish petty, gleaming snort.
Fish tempting style organ.
Mighty presenting so flat.
My sporting flat seething.
Flat empty hero's stinging.
Piggy hint torments false.
False piggy torments thin.
Fleas type snorting might.
Right! False, nosy, tempting.
Fails empty on the G-string.
Mighty, snorting flea pest.
Mighty, snorting leaf pest.
I'm the spongy gin flatters.
Poet flirts anything. Gems.
Empty nothings flirt sage.
Flies than piggy torments.
File the pigsty strong man.
The life pigsty strong man.
Stifle horny, tempting gas.
Hey! Stifle tampon G-string.
Stifle shy, tempting groan.
Might granny stifles poet.
Left shitting agony sperm.
Straying might opens left.

Trophy mates left singing.
Hasty pongs left meriting.
The felt ransoming pigsty.
Nights sporty felt enigma.
Left name snotty priggish.
Left ageing snotty shrimp.
Left simpering snotty hag.
I'm the stony, grasping felt.
I'm the stony, grasping left.
Pong left arty mightiness.
Feel shitty, smarting pong.
Rights fame points gently.
Sightly, potent fame rings.
Fame sets glinting trophy.
Pithy, stringent fame logs.
Fame gets sportingly hint.
Thin fame gets sportingly.
Ineptly shot fame G-string.
Slight petty fame snoring.
Rottenly nights. Fame pigs.
Tiny fame helps to G-string.
Spiny, tight, strong female.
Flame on the tipsy G-string.
Film on the piggy tartness.
Right! Neatest, spongy film.
Eh! Stingingly format pest.
Forms type slighting neat.
Ghastly form sentient pig.
Form shitty, negligent sap.
Form slighting neat types.
Shit! Form negligent patsy.
From spiny, elegant tights.
Gays pig thin self-torment.
Ha! Pig stingy self-torment.
Gosh! Gnarl petty feminist.
Feminist hogs petty gnarl.
Lengths misfit pert agony.
Groan misfit lengthy pest.
Misfit presently hog gnat.
Misfit lengths nag poetry.
Halo stringy figment pest.
Sightly figment rapes not.
Rang stylish figment poet.
Pig holy figment tartness.
Shapely gits torn figment.
Figment or shy talents pig.
Sanely spot right figment.
Sanely stop right figment.
Hang sisterly, top figment.
Figment style to phrasing.
Sly, garish, potent figment.
Sly, sporting figment hate.
Hissingly fragment to pet.

Nightly fragment to spies.
Tightly fragment on spies.
Top fragment gets shinily.
Hey! Top listings fragment.
Fragment pity nights lose.
Eh! Snottily fragment pigs.
Pigsty fragments in hotel.
Hostile fragments typing.
Ghastly sting top firemen.
Slight tasty firemen pong.
Tit farms seethingly pong.
Farms enlighten to pigsty.
Gently ghost panties firm.
Firm not shaggiest plenty.
Tasty, posh, negligent firm.
Home spits gently farting.
Pong meet stylish farting.
Met honestly farting pigs.
Ghost seemly farting pint.
Manly poet fingers tights.
Posh flattering stingy me.
Flattering mighty pens so.
Gosh! In my flattering pest.
In my flattering pest hogs.
So fleeting, star nymph git.
Opt fleeting, shy smarting.
Fleeting, shy, storming pat.
Fleeting, shy, storming tap.
Fleeting spy on star might.
Got fleeting, nasty shrimp.
Fleeting, snotty, sham prig.
Fleeting, arty smith pongs.
Stifling, apt honesty germ.
Stifling, pat honesty germ.
Tap stifling honesty germ.
Paste stifling, thorny gem.
Reset stifling nymph goat.
Part ghost stifling enemy.
My! Together stifling span.
Stifling 'n' empty shortage.
Stifling, arty theme pongs.
Top feelings rants mighty.
Feelings might snotty par.
Top earnest flings mighty.
Nymph flings rattiest ego.
I'm the petty flings groans.
Natty gem flings trophies.
Is greatest fling to nymph.
Riot giftless nymph agent.
Giftless, pithy magnetron.
Giftless, empty nor hating.
Giftless than empty groin.
Giftless, petty, minor hang.

Shy, potent, meriting flags.
Faggot slimy thinner pest.
Presently faggot in smith.
Stain steel frigg to nymph.
Station steel frigg nymph.
Spy hot sentimental frigg.
Sample in the snotty frigg.
The snotty, limp, sane frigg.
The floating, stingy sperm.
Floating myths pestering.
Mirth flogs penitent gays.
Enemy flogs part shitting.
My! This penetrating, flogs.
Earn empty shitting flogs.
Empty shitting flogs near.
Pity flogs tenth smearing.
I'm a type flogs in strength.
Type flogs in the smarting.
Flog shit emptiest granny.
Angry, emptiest hints flog.
Empty hesitant grins flog.
Empty angriest hints flog.
Pity nightmare's nets flog.
I'm a types flog in strength.
Shit! Pretty meanings flog.
Tyrannies golf might pest.
Patient syren mights flog.
Temptingly forgets in ash.
The tiny sampling forgets.
Neat frogs spent mightily.
Thinly patient gems frogs.
Meanly spitting the frogs.
Temptingly shit sane frog.
Sporting, elite myth fangs.
Fangs romp seethingly. Tit.
Mire sightly, potent fangs.
Slimy, tenth ego-trip fangs.
Timely, tight person fangs.
Petty heroism fangs glint.
I'm the pretty, losing fangs.
Only tightest, prime fangs.
Might feasting style porn.
I'm hotter fang piss gently.
Gently strip homiest fang.
Mightily stern fang poets.
Mightily snort steep fang.
Reptile's mighty fang snot.
Fang tits romp seethingly.
Seethingly trim fang post.
Thirty pointless fang gem.
Seemly spit not right fang.
Fang or nights timely pest.
Temptingly its hero's fang.

Temptingly sit hero's fang.
Fang glints petty heroism.
Nights pity fang molester.
Pig trim honest fang style.
Tip smothering fang style.
Motherly pest fisting nag.
Thorny pest fisting gleam.
Shit! Fig sporty gentleman.
Hit man gifts gently. Poser.
Tense porn gifts almighty.
Homely pest gifts ranting.
Rent smashingly gift poet.
Gift ports manly seething.
Manly gift tenth gossiper.
Manly gift sporting sheet.
Gift in the masterly pongs.
Sportingly gift neat mesh.
Gift permanently sight so.
Gift sporty amen lightens.
Snotty gremlins gift heap.
Snigger oil fattest nymph.
Fattest nymph or I niggles.
My fattest helping groins.
Safest trophy glinting me.
Feasts might not replying.
Hot typing safest gremlin.
Shit! Feast gently romping.
I'm lengthy, sporting feast.
Fast penis or gently might.
Gently might fats in poser.
Homely, inept fats G-string.
Fast! Polite hymen G-string.
Feat, limp honesty G-string.
Feat, slimy strength on pig.
Hint sportingly fate gems.
Sportingly fate thin gems.
Rompingly feat tightness.
Fate mongrels pity nights.
Feat mongrels pity nights.
Gently smother fat in pigs.
Gently pissing fat mother.
Them, stingingly fat poser.
Fat might or stingy spleen.
Fat lepers might on stingy.
Is fat, strong hymen piglet.
Pig honestly nest grim fat.
Pig honestly sent grim fat.
Fat nymph niggers, toilets.
I'm fat, gentle trophy signs.
Hey! Not fat, simple G-string.
Hey! Fat grimness plotting.
Fat, sporting enemy lights.
Fat, messy, rotting helping.

Pesteringly hint fat smog.
Not replying this fat gems.
No! The gremlin's fat pigsty.
Re-typing fat on mightless.
Ineptly fat gems or nights.
The fat, singing style romp.
I'm snotty niggers help fat.
Stingier, fat, stony phlegm.
Fat gremlins hog tiny pest.
Yet ponging mirthless fat.
Hog grim fattiness plenty.
Nightly, grim fatness poet.
Fatness replying to might.
Rompingly the fatness git.
Faint, grotty helping mess.
Faint, sprightly gemstone.
Infants might steep glory.
I'm the leggy infants sport.
Infants might poetry legs.
Infant, grey, top mightless.
Tightly infant poser gems.
Infant, tight leprosy gems.
Shit! Grim poet fans gently.
Is the tempting glory fans.
Hero fans temptingly. Gits.
Mighty, sporting, steel fan.
Safe myth in strong piglet.
Rompingly safe, tenth gits.
Great! Nothing flimsy pest.
Right flimsy 'n' potent sage.
Flimsy, inapt strength ego.
Step not flimsy gathering.
Flimsy, potent hag stinger.
Flimsy, strange night poet.
Not grasp flimsy teething.
Tenth ageing flimsy strop.
Family pest on the G-string.
Lengths nag top mystifier.
Fertility hasn't pongs gem.
Firstly the poignant gems.
Pig nest gnomish flattery.
Pig sent gnomish flattery.
Frailty tenses might pong.
Ghost tempting flayer sin.
Flyer hogs tempting saint.
Safely potent mights grin.
Hi! Safely tempting, strong.
Tightest porn flays in gem.
He flays impotent G-string.
Person gets faintly might.
Then, sporting falsity gem.
Tempting hero sings fatly.
Fatly right semens pig not.

Fatly spin right gemstone.
Fatly pig smothering nest.
Fatly sent smothering pig.
Fly smart seething not pig.
Fly nights mastering poet.
Fiery, tempting songs halt.
Infantry piglets shot gem.
Infantry lest hot pig gems.
Stem infantry hogs piglet.
Hottest malign ferny pigs.
Might genital's ferny post.
Might genital's ferny spot.
Stop genital's ferny might.
Ferny egotists might plan.
Potent insights fry gleam.
Malign tightest opens fry.
Fry so pig this tanglement.
Shiftily tempt on naggers.
Map filthy, stringent egos.
Filthy, impotent 'n' aggress.
Meanest, filthy grit pongs.
Filthy termite pongs nags.
Filthy, saner spotting gem.
It sprang filthy gemstone.
Filthy semens pig to grant.
Filthy, merest pig nags not.
Filthy gaps in rotten gems.
Filthy gasp in rotten gems.
Strongest, filthy, mega pin.
Filthy, pert, mangiest song.
Steaming filthy, pert song.
Filthy gem as potent rings.
Filthy, potent, remiss gang.
Filthy, open, starting gems.
Filthy gems gnat pointers.
Strop filthy, naggiest men.
Filthy, patient germ songs.
Filthy, patient song germs.
Filthy, mega, snorting step.
Filthy pest staring on gem.
So ranting filthy pest gem.
Filthy pest staring gnome.
Amen pongs thriftily gets.
Mega pongs nest thriftily.
Mega pongs sent thriftily.
Gems opens thriftily. Gnat.
Freshly so tempting giant.
Freshly tame top stinging.
Am fortnightly, tense pigs.
Fortnightly met sane pigs.
Fortnightly, inept gem ass.
Fortnightly pain sets gem.
Fortnightly meet nag piss.

Frighteningly mat so. Pest.
Shiftingly temper not gas.
Tempt shiftingly anger so.
Shiftingly tempt on rages.
Shiftingly tee smart pong.
Part shiftingly note gems.
Shiftingly segment to par.
Shiftingly strop mean get.
Poet 'n' shiftingly star gem.
Poet 'n' shiftingly rat gems.
Shiftingly. Poet ant germs.
Shiftingly smart top gene.
Shiftingly stem top anger.
Shiftingly or apt segment.
Shiftingly segment or pat.
Tap or shiftingly segment.
Pest gem or shiftingly. Ant.
Thrifty poem stings angel.
Is thrifty, gentle am pongs.
I'm thrifty, steel nags pong.
Thrifty, gentle pig mans so.
Amen! Thrifty piglet songs.
Ton thrifty, pleasing gems.
Spin to angel's thrifty gem.
Pin to angel's thrifty gems.
Thrifty, mean post niggles.
Thrifty, mean spot niggles.
Spot in angel's thrifty gem.
Stop in angel's thrifty gem.
Opt in angel's thrifty gems.
Lisp nag thrifty gemstone.
Slip nag thrifty gemstone.
Thrifty pest maligns gone.
Thrifty gleaming steps no.
Pit on angel's thrifty gems.
Tip on angel's thrifty gems.
No fishy template G-string.
Pig sort fishy tanglement.
Talents pig not fishy germ.
Meant fishy, strong piglet.
Fishy, potent meal G-string.
Opt fishy, negligent smart.
So glinting hefty tampers.
Hefty sampling to stinger.
Limp so hefty, neat G-string.
Hefty limp to sane G-string.
Son's hefty, glittering map.
Hefty, stinging, stale romp.
Hefty G-string tampons lie.
Hefty, meriting pongs last.
A gremlin's hefty spotting.
Hefty, meriting lasts pong.
Hefty pigs on grim talents.

Hefty torments align pigs.
Mangling to hefty priests.
Hefty poser, mangling tits.
Hefty porn as stilting gem.
Strop lame hefty stinging.
Plot hefty gems straining.
Hefty, top, meriting slangs.
Hefty, ignorant splits gem.
Hefty, grim angel spits not.
Hefty spit in strong gleam.
Shifty tampers niggle not.
Name shifty glitters pong.
Shifty germs pig on talent.
Shifty, potent rings gleam.
Shifty, potent, grim angles.
Shifty, top, mental niggers.
Rattling. Fogey shipments.
Inapt, slim fogey strength.
Signify top, gentlest harm.
That gentle romps signify.
Might prig lofty neatness.
Lofty earnings might pest.
I'm the lofty, grasping nest.
I'm the lofty, grasping nets.
Lofty ape-men shit G-string.
I'm gentle Y-fronts spit hag.
Y-fronts tag limp seething.
Y-fronts impale nights get.
Sight Y-fronts name piglet.
Y-fronts might pest in gale.
Ahem! Y-fronts sting piglet.
I'm the Y-fronts tangle pigs.
Y-fronts hast piglet in gem.
Y-fronts hat piglet in gems.
Piglet hints Y-fronts game.
Y-fronts hint piglet as gem.
Y-fronts as thin piglet gem.
The Y-fronts pig lame sting.
Nights frosty, inept gleam.
I mangling the frosty pest.
Shit! Frosty, negligent map.
His frosty pig tanglement.
Forty tempting gnash lies.
Nights plainest forty gem.
Forty pleasing might nets.
The forty empaling stings.
This forty pigs gentleman.
Softy 'n' nightmare's piglet.
Prettify 'n' gleaming hosts.
Gosh! Prettify malign sent.
Prettify nights lame song.
Amen! Prettify nights logs.
Prettify angel's thin smog.

Prettify mangle this song.
Hog smarting self-pity ten.
Self-pity nags not right me.
Self-pity granting to mesh.
No! Am the self-pity G-string.
Rant shot self-pitying gem.
Self-pitying terms nag hot.
Hast self-pitying, torn gem.
Self-pitying germ hats not.
Hat snort self-pitying gem.
Hat self-pitying, torn gems.
Tenth simplify to naggers.
Satisfy tenth pig mongrel.
Fatty, honest pigs gremlin.
Nifty germs toast helping.
Rattling nifty sheep smog.
Nifty piglet as north gems.
Hot misspelt nifty nagger.
Together nifty samplings.
Nifty loathing gets sperm.
Gosh! Nifty lest tampering.
Gosh! Nifty, tempting laser.
Nifty, tempting laser hogs.
Gosh! Nifty, emptiest gnarl.
Nifty, emptiest hogs gnarl.
Nifty pest hogs trim angel.
Hog align nifty temptress.
Nifty, ghastlier pongs met.
Nifty length as grim poets.
Nifty porn as lightest gem.
Nifty poets mangle rights.
Nifty, agile strength mops.
Nifty, elegant sight romps.
Nifty poets sight mangler.
Nifty might relates pongs.
Nifty might enrages plots.
Opt anger nifty mightless.
Nifty light meter pongs as.
Nifty smothers pig tangle.
Nifty smothers niggle pat.
Gang nifty, poetless mirth.
Nifty glimpses or the gnat.
The nifty tampering gloss.
The nifty, top, slim naggers.
Smart pig the stingy felon.
Mighty stingers pat felon.
Mighty stingers tap felon.
Typists might anger felon.
Felon patsy thirsting gem.
Might testy, rasping felon.
Felon's pithy, tame G-string.
Angel's softer, mighty pint.
Anything smelt softer pig.

Softer, petty, slim hanging.
Shit! Mangling softer type.
Front stealthy pig in gems.
I'm front, shaggiest plenty.
Shit! Pigsty for gentleman.
Gipsy for this tanglement.
Gently prime fatso things.
Lengthen tipsy, grim fatso.
I'm softest graph in gently.
Hip! Rantingly softest gem.
Gently soft, mightier span.
Met soft, straying helping.
Soft, stingy, grim elephant.
Title soft nymph greasing.
Agree soft nymph stilting.
Soft nymph tiger stealing.
Soft, shrimpy, gentle giant.
Try soft, mangiest helping.
Strangle softie nymph git.
Ragingly. Fonts, I'm the pest.
Fonts pig shatteringly. Me.
The pigsty maligner fonts.
The fonts tag simperingly.
I'm the often, straggly spin.
Smartingly the often pigs.
Gently praise font mights.
Font pets searingly might.
Mightily. Font press agent.
Shaggily merit spent font.
Gently phase of trim sting.
Tangiest of gently shrimp.
Isn't might of gently parse.
Gently misprint of the gas.
Gently shit of giant sperm.
Shit of gently smarten pig.
Shit of gently margin pest.
Eh! Gently of smarting spit.
I'm glittery of spent gnash.
Grisly of tempting as then.
Gratingly of the pint mess.
Gratingly of this pest men.
I'm the straggly of spent in.
Stingingly of the pest ram.
Trying of nastiest phlegm.
Mighty strangle of in pets.
Largest hymen of spitting.
Hymens of taping glitters.
Stealthy gem of sprinting.
Nymph of gangster elitist.
Nymph of it stalest nigger.
Leg nymph of stingiest rat.
Strangle pig of shitty men.
Strangle pin of shitty gem.

Gem of shitty angel prints.
Gamely spit of in strength.
Length of stymieing sprat.
Mastery of spent lighting.
My right of pestilent nags.
My shitting of gentler sap.
My negligent of this sprat.
Smith of pesteringly. Gnat.
Ash of temptingly. Stinger.
Empty G-string of the snail.
Empty of this lane G-string.
Empty G-string of this lean.
Payments leg of thirsting.
Reply of tight assignment.
Ineptly of nights star gem.
Petty of as gremlin's thing.
'e's petty might of snarling.
Nightmares of petty sling.
Petty hasn't of slim nigger.
Pretty thesis of mangling.
I'm gentler pansy of tights.
I'm spiny of tenth straggle.
A slyer, tempting of nights.
Rely of tempting as nights.
Sly might of stringent ape.
Tiny strength of lame pigs.
Tiny harm of gentlest pigs.
Yet of impaling strengths.
Might of yet snarling pest.
Fine, hot gasps trim gently.
Gently might a fine sports.
Fine mights opt strangely.
Grossly patent fine might.
Fine myth points straggle.
Not fine, ghastly, grim pets.
Spit ghastly torn fine gem.
Rattling fine, shy, top gems.
Fine hosts rag temptingly.
A fine, empty, strong slight.
Fine, straight plenty smog.
Fine, sporty length stigma.
That fine, sly, sporting gem.
Rottenly mights fine gaps.
Finesse might grotty plan.
Grotty phlegm fines saint.
Fines might strongly tape.
Masterly, tight fines pong.
Fines might rottenly gaps.
Fines might rottenly gasp.
Finest graphs gently omit.
Infest months pig greatly.
Infest grotty as in phlegm.
Finest tempting glory ash.

Finest ghastly pig on term.
Ghastly rip not infest gem.
Large gits infest to nymph.
Infest nymph gloats tiger.
Nymph gits finest gloater.
Trophy glints finest game.
Infest trophy sting gleam.
Finest later spongy might.
Hat finest employ G-string.
Might slang infest poetry.
Potty gremlins infest hag.
Gosh! Finest malign pretty.
Snort niftiest, gay phlegm.
Gnome if gently sharp tits.
Pest if gently hot margins.
Smart gently hog if in pest.
Right! O Man! Pests if gently.
Ahem! Gently if strong spit.
If merits hast gently pong.
Master's hit if gently pong.
Glittery pongs if the mans.
Staringly if then, top gems.
If top gem hints strangely.
Grotty if mean length piss.
Strongly meant if the pigs.
I'm the straggly if spent on.
Straying pong if the smelt.
Angel's mighty if torn pest.
If pets strangle on mighty.
Smothery pest if tangling.
Ghastly if inept, strong me.
If pest 'n' torment shaggily.
Plotters if anything. Gems.
Stealthy terms if ponging.
I'm thorny if gentlest gaps.
I'm thorny if gentlest gasp.
To nymph if latest snigger.
Nymph if tits strangle ego.
Storming if neatest glyph.
Strangle gem if pithy snot.
Shitty panel if strong gem.
Shitty plane if strong gem.
Gem if shirty talent pongs.
Piglet if shy torments nag.
Right testes if manly pong.
Trimly gang if honest pest.
Gamely spit if on strength.
Smatteringly if the pongs.
If this germy talent pongs.
Army if this gentlest pong.
Many pongs if the glitters.
Strangle if the misty pong.
My! The starlets if ponging.

Hat if sportingly segment.
Spongy if it lame strength.
I'm spongy if late strength.
Spongy might if steel rant.
Shit! Germ if spongy talent.
Gipsy if not lame strength.
Harm gentlest Gipsy if not.
If shots anger temptingly.
If the snags or temptingly.
Hotels if an empty G-string.
Empty not if gritless hang.
Eh! Empty if to stranglings.
If stringent gem plays hot.
If maggot hints presently.
Shame plenty if to G-string.
The sporty set if mangling.
Spotty length if smearing.
Gosh! If gremlin's petty ant.
If gremlin's petty ant hogs.
If petty mongrel as nights.
Strong man if the legs pity.
Slyer if potent might nags.
Style if snorting path gem.
If torments hang pig style.
If might pongs tensely rat.
Ahem! Sly if potent G-string.
If snotty green light maps.
Might if snotty nags repel.
Nosy might if gentle sprat.
Toy if empaling strengths.
Yes malign if top strength.
Mighty profiles tangents.
Flop might tasty sneering.
Sane profit mights gently.
Nasty tights pilfer on gem.
Nasty tights pilfer gnome.
Not pilfers mangey tights.
Nasty, tight gnome pilfers.
My! Hottest enraging splif.
Manly sight sporting feet.
Am negligent trophy fists.
I'm the fist, strangely pong.
Pong hesitantly fist germ.
Sift pig shorty gentleman.
Nymph fits terse gloating.
Hasty, negligent fits romp.
The masterly fist ponging.
The masterly fits ponging.
The gem fits raspingly not.
Sift empty strong healing.
Pong fist style nightmare.
Style fits nightmare pong.
Fist ratty helping on gems.

Fair, nightly, top segments.
No! I'm the pigs farts gently.
I'm the son farts gently pig.
Slimy teething farts pong.
Empty on this farts niggle.
Gnomishly pig fatter nest.
Gnomishly sent fatter pig.
Gently after on might piss.
One might piss gently fart.
Them fart singingly. Poets.
Fart gnomishly get in pest.
Seemly things pig not fart.
Fart pongs slimy teething.
Fart spot slighting enemy.
Fart stop slighting enemy.
My! Nights sleeping to fart.
Fart empty slighting nose.
Fart ineptly ghost in gems.
Fart pity on gems lightens.
Fear mops gently shitting.
Safer might points gently.
Temptingly fears so. Thing.
Finer, top mights as gently.
Finer mighty pongs latest.
Finer hasty plotting gems.
My finer talents ghost pig.
Finer shags to temptingly.
Typist frees hot mangling.
Almighty sing potent serf.
Nightly steaming top serf.
On a sightly, tempting serf.
Thinly. Maggot's inept serf.
May slighting, potent serf.
First, snotty, mega helping.
Talents fire mighty pongs.
Mighty fires talents pong.
Typists free hot mangling.
Emptying rotting flashes.
It my potent niggers flash.
It flash empty not snigger.
Flash empty to signet ring.
Isn't potty flash emerging.
Flash in most petty nigger.
Flash typist emerging not.
Flash tempting, grit nosey.
Flash yet tempting groins.
It half gory temptingness.
Half stingy termites pong.
Is half petty, snorting gem.
Gassy filth in potent germ.
Pertinent filth smog gays.
Filth gays print gemstone.
Filth poet 'n' straying gems.

Got angry filth emptiness.
Greasy, tempting filth son.
My! Gas not pestering filth.
Piggy filth to semens rant.
Piggy filth on tense smart.
Not piggy filth mare's-nest.
Filth nags spongy termite.
Empty sanest filth goring.
Got empty filth angriness.
Filth nags sporty meeting.
Filth gross petty meaning.
Enter maggot's spiny filth.
Filth ego-trip 'n' nasty gems.
Grip nasty filth gemstone.
Snotty, germane filth pigs.
Filth toys G-string ape-men.
Yes tempting filth organs.
Filthiest, spongy germ ant.
Tasty, meriting shelf pong.
Flesh ratty pointing gems.
Fathomless petty ringing.
Self-harming yet top sting.
A trim fetish pongs gently.
Gently sap not grim fetish.
Grimy fetish talents pong.
Shift gently merit as pong.
Shift gently pig on master.
Meanly shift poet G-string.
Angel's grimy, potent shift.
Shift on angel's grim petty.
Yet empaling strong shift.
Snortingly. Thief past gem.
Snortingly apt thief gems.
Snortingly pat thief gems.
Snortingly tap thief gems.
Thief pongs timely grants.
Thief snarling petty smog.
Sly, tempting thief organs.
Glossy theft in tampering.
Straying theft on glimpse.
Is masterly theft ponging.
It spongy theft malingers.
Sly, sporting theft enigma.
Theft mongrels pig sanity.
Yes impaling strong theft.
Sort meanly fighting pest.
O My! Patternless, fighting.
Partly fighting not seems.
Man petty losers fighting.
Son's pretty lame fighting.
Pretty, mean loss fighting.
Fighting pert style moans.
Lamest, top syren fighting.

Frightening pet as mostly.
Stop frightening style am.
Am sly frightening to pest.
Not frighting mealy steps.
Ants opt seemly frighting.
Ape nets mostly frighting.
Empty on lest as frighting.
An empty lest so frighting.
Empty so frighting as lent.
Let's! So frighting payment.
Style frighting pest on am.
Sly, potent me as frighting.
Am snotty sleep frighting.
Lame stony pest frighting.
Metal nosy pest frighting.
Grotty flashing pest in me.
Petty flashing gems in rot.
Petty flashing into germs.
Flashing gets petty minor.
Prig meet snotty flashing.
Flashing pongs mere titty.
Grotty, mean spit fleshing.
Pity not fleshing star gem.
Flights torment gay penis.
Grimy, potent, sane flights.
Tempting flights on years.
Flight on a petty grimness.
Rip nasty flight gemstone.
O My! Frighten lasting pest.
Stymie frighten top slang.
Amen! Frighten lost pigsty.
Amen! Lots frighten pigsty.
Frighten pigsty lest moan.
Frighten empty stain logs.
I'm pasty legs frighten not.
Frighten molest spiny tag.
Slay so frighten tempting.
Frighten inapt style smog.
Frighten only pest stigma.
Frighten snotty mile gaps.
Mile frighten snotty gasp.
Toys frighten piglet mans.
Frighten plot as tiny gems.
Frighten testy mail pongs.
It frightens gently map so.
Post frightens gently aim.
Spot frightens gently aim.
Aim frightens gently stop.
Aims opt gently frightens.
Atom frightens gently sip.
I'm gay spelt frightens not.
Stingy frightens top male.
Stingy frightens top meal.

Namely frightens top gits.
Mealy tit frightens pongs.
Apt song frightens timely.
Timely song frightens pat.
Song frightens timely tap.
Top set frightens mangily.
Mangey, top list frightens.
May piglet frightens snot.
My pig frightens not steal.
My! It's top angel frightens.
It frightens spongy metal.
Neat frightens simply got.
Its gnome frightens aptly.
Nail spotty gem frightens.
Lame potty sign frightens.
Am longest pity frightens.
It frightens not spy gleam.
Neatly frightens most pig.
I'm nasty, top leg frightens.
O Man! Fighter spits gently.
On a sly, tempting fighters.
A frights nose temptingly.
Tipsy, gentle frights moan.
Patient gems frights only.
Glassy, top, eminent fright.
Gently not. Fright impasse.
Net simplest fright agony.
Fright pongs steamily net.
Fright typing to lameness.
'e's fright nags impotently.
Fright 'n' tense polygamist.
Saintly pongs meet fright.
Top fright style meanings.
Sly fright on patient gems.
Emptiest fright nags only.
Fright yet manliest pongs.
My genial fortnight pests.
My! Piss! A gentle fortnight.
Angel's tipsy fortnight me.
Pig sanely stem fortnight.
Fortnight slays inept gem.
Fortnight mans steely pig.
Play shifting, rotten gems.
Poet fights snaringly met.
A poem fights stringently.
Pesteringly fights to man.
Prominently fights gates.
Neat set fights rompingly.
Alien strong fights empty.
Gems fights nor patiently.
Mean song fights prettily.
Poetry fights alignments.
Malign potty fights sneer.

Means fights rottenly pig.
Names fights rottenly pig.
Fight gently spite ransom.
Potent fight mess angrily.
Seemly paint strong fight.
Fight seemly snorting pat.
Fight not imply greatness.
Fight in strangest employ.
Empty so strangle in fight.
Fight on gritless payment.
Fight or lay temptingness.
Fight simper snotty angel.
Finish mangle grotty pest.
Shiftier 'n' maggot's plenty.
Slap soggy, eminent thrift.
Leggy mentions sap thrift.
Thrift opens stingy gleam.
Seemingly. Thrift gaps not.
Seemingly gasp not. Thrift.
My! Pig son's elegant thrift.
To my sleeping thrift nags.
My! So sap negligent thrift.
Let's! Spongy thrift enigma.
Gang empty thrift lioness.
Empaling nosy thrift gets.
Man leggy, top thriftiness.
My! Stilting feathers pong.
Father stings timely pong.
Temptingly nags to fisher.
Stingingly fresh, top mate.
Temptingly so fresh giant.
Treaty 'n' shop-lifting gems.
Shop-lifting, stray, net gem.
Segment shop-lifting tray.
Tiny germs shoplift agent.
Strongly inept faith gems.
Nigger shafts impotently.
Shaft slimy, potent nigger.
Forth spits gently. Enigma.
Stringently top, mega fish.
Egos fish temptingly rant.
Fish sporty, gentle mating.
Fish snotty, pert gleaming.
Trim spongy flat seething.
Hot empty in sniggers flat.
Sporty engines might flat.
Potent mighty grins false.
False met stinging trophy.
Shy, impotent flea G-string.
Shy, impotent leaf G-string.
Pong mighty tensest flair.
In might flatters yes pong.
Frailest pongs net mighty.

Frailest ten pongs mighty.
Frailest, spongy, net might.
Might frailest, spongy ten.
Sight infernal, petty smog.
Fertile nymph nags to gits.
Oh! Flirt tempting gayness.
Flirt shyest, poignant gem.
Gosh! Petty meanings flirt.
Flirt some gnashing petty.
Flirt petty, smashing gone.
Pig flirt on the nasty gems.
Flies gnash not grim petty.
Payments file hot G-string.
Stifle rotting nymph sage.
Stifle shy, tempting organ.
Stifle grimy, potent gnash.
Lifts harm soggy penitent.
Earnest lift pongs mighty.
Payment sniggers hot lift.
Left angry, top mightiness.
Left trophy stings enigma.
Shit! Mangey, sporting felt.
Shit! Mangey, sporting left.
It left spongy nightmares.
Not left nightmare's Gipsy.
Any piggish felt torments.
Any piggish left torments.
Feel might snorting patsy.
Sporting ant feels mighty.
Tame self, stinging trophy.
Ghost self, tiny tampering.
Strongly spite fame thing.
Strongly pig this net fame.
Potent fame signs rightly.
Sightly, sporting fame ten.
Pretty, singing fame sloth.
Stony, slighting, pert fame.
Fameless, grotty, ninth pig.
Gently formats in the pigs.
Forms slight gay penitent.
Elegant forms pity nights.
Form gently tag pithiness.
Gently. Pigs from the saint.
Pig tightly form neatness.
Shaggily form intent pest.
Form neat pigsty lightens.
Gainless petty from thing.
Steely path from stinging.
From nasty, tight, sleeping.
The formless giant typing.
Self-torment hats in piggy.
Ha! Isn't piggy self-torment.
The formal stinging types.

Leftmost syren hating pig.
Greatly then misfits pong.
Misfit grants gently hope.
Misfit gently note graphs.
Misfit graphs gently tone.
Misfit than gently gropes.
Misfit gently gas the porn.
Misfit hang grotty spleen.
Misfit horny, gentlest gap.
Misfit gas gentler python.
Figment or gently sap shit.
Ha! Strongly spite figment.
Strongly ape figment hits.
Ogrishly. Figment pest ant.
Ghastly figment penis rot.
Figment ties ghastly porn.
Figment nor stealthy pigs.
Rashly sting figment poet.
Hey! Salt sporting figment.
This figment poetry slang.
Ho! Strangle tipsy figment.
Pasty, honest figment girl.
Gosh! Saintly, pert figment.
Saintly, pert figment hogs.
Testily graphs on figment.
Nasty, light figment poser.
Try slashing figment poet.
Genital's trophy figments.
Tightly fragment so. Penis.
Is not pithy legs fragment.
Hey! So fragment splitting.
Fragment ineptly sight so.
Fragment hot style in pigs.
She fragment snottily pig.
Sightly pie fragments not.
Gosh! Tipsily. Engraftment.
Tipsy hotels fragmenting.
Testy polish fragmenting.
Infirm, pasty, gentlest hog.
This frames pig gently not.
It is the farms pong gently.
Spit gently ghost fireman.
It is the farm pongs gently.
Farm stingy, honest piglet.
Pong farm steely shitting.
Gently firm so hating pest.
Farting pongs slimy teeth.
She, temptingly farting so.
Gem hosts ineptly farting.
Manly tights finger poets.
Finger temptingly hot ass.
Manly fingers tight poets.
Point flattering, shy gems.

In flattering, shy, top gems.
It flattering spongy mesh.
Mesh not flattering Gipsy.
Flattering, spiny, shot gem.
Shit! Spy flattering gnome.
Ghost payments filtering.
Fleeting, pithy smog rants.
My fleeting, posh starting.
Greyest, stifling phantom.
Stifling myths anger poet.
Stifling, thorny tapes gem.
State stifling nymph gore.
Start stifling, phoney gem.
Stifling, phoney, smart get.
My! Hot anger stifling pest.
Stifling Germans type hot.
Stifling German types hot.
The stifling germs pay not.
Feelings smart hot typing.
Feelings might torn pasty.
I'm greatest python flings.
My shattering flings poet.
Poetry flings mean tights.
The nasty, grim poet flings.
Trophy fling nastiest gem.
Ape Shit! Snotty fling germ.
Giftless hymen to parting.
To giftless, tearing nymph.
Great! I, not giftless nymph.
Rat giftless python in gem.
Giftless, mangey, hot print.
Right! An empty, giftless no.
Giftless or an empty night.
Flag smothery intents pig.
It isn't east flogger nymph.
Prime faggots nest thinly.
Prime faggots sent thinly.
Ineptly forgetting smash.
Oh My! Penitent frigg lasts.
Honestly! Frigg mates pint.
Spit honestly meant frigg.
Ole! Frigg nymph tattiness.
Neatest, slim frigg python.
Shy, mental frigg nepotist.
Pasty, eminent frigg sloth.
I'm the talents spy on frigg.
Impotent frigg slays then.
Posh frigg mates intently.
Tensely tampon this frigg.
This sly, potent, mean frigg.
Earnest pint flogs mighty.
Temerity flogs nights pan.
Ahem! Stringent pity flogs.

Pity flogs then mastering.
Pasty flogs then meriting.
Her tempting sanity flogs.
Tiny, tempting share flogs.
Teeny armpit flogs nights.
Flog mighty present saint.
Flog in a tempting shyster.
My interesting paths flog.
Flog my prettiness hating.
Flog might as petty sinner.
A petty sinners might flog.
Thirsting mean types flog.
Flog in the nasty, grim pest.
Forget manly spite nights.
It's genital nymph forgets.
An emptiest, nightly frogs.
The frogs spent malignity.
Eh! Saintly, tempting frogs.
I'm the pests fog rantingly.
Tigerishly tempt on fangs.
Fangs opt merely shitting.
Together slimy pint fangs.
Thirteen fangs pig mostly.
Isn't fangs imply together.
Temptingly shire to fangs.
Fangs ghost prettily mine.
Hot, grimiest plenty fangs.
I'm the fangs pig torn style.
The trim fangs pig on style.
I'm the sly, rotten fangs pig.
Feasting hits gently romp.
Fang romps seethingly. Tit.
Shitty fang gremlin poets.
Lose shirty, tempting fang.
Tightest, slimy, prone fang.
Slimy, sporting fang teeth.
My thorniest fang piglets.
Pesteringly. Fang to smith.
The fang emits sportingly.
Hot typing meritless fang.
Fang merits ghost ineptly.
Ineptly might fang tosser.
Gently honest armpit figs.
Gently hesitant figs romp.
Trophies man gently gifts.
Gently arm phoniest gifts.
Phoniest ram gifts gently.
Armpit gifts gently shone.
I'm the porn gifts as gently.
Potent men gifts garishly.
A nymph gifts strong elite.
Manly gifts together spin.
Gosh! It gifts permanently.

It gifts permanently hogs.
Plenty gifts hot smearing.
A smothering plenty gifts.
Honestly gift giant sperm.
Gift honestly smarten pig.
Gift honestly margin pest.
Apt gremlins gift honesty.
Pat gremlins gift honesty.
Gift thorny neat glimpses.
Gift gnarliest nymph toes.
Generalists gift to nymph.
Nymph orgies gift talents.
So gift nightmare's plenty.
Gift on the pasty gremlins.
Nasty, rompish, gentle gift.
No! Priggishly fattest men.
Fattest gem grins phonily.
O My! Fattest helping grins.
Eh! Fattest rompingly sign.
Thinly prig not safest gem.
My safest helping rotting.
Oh! Temptingly safest grin.
Feast nymph stilting ogre.
Fast! Homely, pert stinging.
Nymph gets fast loitering.
Pong merely shitting fats.
Penitent fats hogs grimly.
Sportingly. Fats in the gem.
Fats pongs entirely might.
Fast might only pestering.
Grime snotty fats helping.
My! Fate strength spoiling.
My feat strength spoiling.
Gently fat, gnomish priest.
Fat penis mights or gently.
Stingily the fat porn gems.
Stringently fat home pigs.
Snortingly fat theme pigs.
Fat mother pets singingly.
Mightily present fat song.
Fat pint greets gnomishly.
Fat nymph to stingier legs.
Fat python in gritless gem.
Son's pithy, grim, gentle fat.
I'm shirty, gentle fat pongs.
Seemly pin fat, hot G-string.
Right! Isn't fat, seemly pong.
Nights prig not seemly fat.
Hint seemly pig strong fat.
Seemly pig thin strong fat.
Fat, slimy strength pigeon.
Grimy fat lightens on pest.
Fat employs in the G-string.

Rompingly fat seen tights.
Fat, empty lighting snores.
Fat sores empty lightning.
Lighten sporty fat in gems.
Fat, petty, mongrel hissing.
I'm right fat pongs tensely.
Fat, sly, top, sneering might.
I'm fat, snotty nigger helps.
The fat, tinny, gormless pig.
The fat, tiny pigs mongrels.
The fat, itsy gremlins pong.
Eh! Grotty infant glimpses.
Rightly infant gems poets.
Infant, sightly poet germs.
It the gem fans sportingly.
Piggish fans met rottenly.
Mightier fan posts gently.
Pesteringly mights to fan.
Gently might its safe porn.
Safe nymph or stilting get.
Safe python stilting germ.
Grimly safe, potent, nights.
Grimly safe, potent things.
Rompingly safe ten tights.
Hi! Safe, strong, temptingly.
Empty snort safe lighting.
I'm safe, hot plenty G-string.
Spy torment safe lighting.
Foamy strengths in piglet.
Not flimsy greeting paths.
Hot presenting flimsy tag.
Hog flimsy, stringent tape.
Right! Flimsy pest on agent.
Pig flimsy strength on ate.
Pig flimsy strength on tea.
Ape flimsy strength on git.
Flimsy, star teething pong.
Tightest, flimsy, prone nag.
Flimsy tights negate porn.
Their potent flimsy gangs.
Flimsy tenth as top nigger.
Flimsy pongs in the target.
The flimsy spotting anger.
Great! Isn't the flimsy pong.
The flimsy treats ponging.
Isn't the flimsy, top nagger.
Pant to the flimsy snigger.
Firmly ghost penitent gas.
Right! Longest infamy pest.
Firstly pig than gemstone.
Might flattery penis song.
Pong might nastiest flyer.
Safely thirsting 'n' top gem.

Safely sight tempting nor.
Torment piggish net flays.
Torment piggish ten flays.
Right pint flays gemstone.
The printing flays to gems.
Faintly meet posh G-string.
Mesh faintly. Poet G-string.
Pig faintly snort the gems.
Eh! Faintly tempting gross.
Might fatly pestering son.
Green piss fatly might not.
Stringent homes pig fatly.
Fly hottest spraining gem.
Fly seething top smarting.
I am the fly pest on G-string.
I'm the strangest fly on pig.
Infantry gets hot glimpse.
Infantry tights slope gem.
Slight ferny, impotent gas.
Tempting, genial hosts fry.
Hot empaling settings fry.
Isn't impotent haggles fry.
Hang gentle optimists fry.
Mangle shittiest fry pong.
The gleaming spits not fry.
Filthy, tempting songs ear.
Filthy nor emptiest gangs.
Filthy, naggiest tens romp.
Negate filthy stings romp.
Filthy niggers tampon set.
Gas filthy, stringent poem.
Filthy pong smearing test.
Filthy, strange items pong.
Filthy, strange times pong.
Pig filthy, torn, sanest gem.
Filthy pig segments no rat.
Filthy pig on star segment.
Filthy penis grants to gem.
Spent not filthy, grim sage.
Not print filthy gems sage.
Filthy, potent gem in grass.
Filthy, potent germs in gas.
Filthy, potent miss nagger.
Filthy, smarting opens get.
Spot filthy enema G-string.
Stop filthy enema G-string.
Filthy, top, sane me G-string.
Sap filthy, strong meeting.
Filthy tapes in strong gem.
Filthy gemstone grins pat.
Filthy, apt gemstones grin.
Filthy, pat gemstones grin.
Filthy gemstones tap grin.

Filthy pest in strong game.
Filthy pest on grim agents.
Filthy spit on strange gem.
Tip filthy gemstones rang.
Semen tags thriftily pong.
Gem nets as thriftily pong.
Net gems as thriftily pong.
Gnat seems thriftily pong.
Gemstones gap 'n' thriftily.
Gem on pests nag thriftily.
Pests nag thriftily. Gnome.
Freshly stinging top mate.
Regiment flashy spotting.
Fortnightly sap semen git.
Gas fortnightly tip semen.
Isn't forty-eight gem plans.
Frighteningly maps to set.
Frighteningly map to sets.
Frighteningly met as post.
Frighteningly spot as met.
Frighteningly stop as met.
Shiftingly temper to nags.
Shiftingly torment gapes.
Gem opens shiftingly. Tart.
Shiftingly. Germ ant poets.
Shiftingly merge past not.
Step shiftingly rat on gem.
Step shiftingly rat gnome.
Thrifty, genial stem pongs.
Slime thrifty agents pong.
Thrifty gleam opens sting.
Mangle thrifty poet sings.
Thrifty poets niggle mans.
Thrifty man niggles poets.
Mangling thrifty, top sees.
Thrifty pest niggles on am.
Align thrifty pest on gems.
Thrifty pest smog in angel.
O Man! Thrifty pests niggle.
Germs pig not fishy talent.
Is hefty or tempting slang.
Impale hefty G-string snot.
Impale hefty, strong sting.
Groin simplest, hefty gnat.
Is not hefty, limp gangster.
Pongs hefty tits malinger.
Not trim angel's hefty pigs.
Is hefty, mental, strong pig.
Hefty, strong piglet mains.
Hefty, smarting piglet son.
I'm hefty pin straggles not.
Print hefty gloating mess.
Molest hefty, stinging par.

Hefty, top smiles granting.
Gremlin's hefty giants opt.
Hefty pests or it mangling.
No hefty gem piss rattling.
Gas shifty, tempting loner.
Shifty, sporting, net gleam.
Met shifty, sporting angel.
I'm shifty, gentle pongs rat.
Mangle shifty, rotten pigs.
Pig sort shifty gentleman.
Shifty, Roman, gentlest pig.
Shifty piglet rants on gem.
Shifty piglet rants gnome.
Am shifty, negligent strop.
Gremlin's shifty, top agent.
Leapt shifty, snorting gem.
Slept shifty, ignorant gem.
Spelt shifty, ignorant gem.
Not shifty, grim pest angel.
Flaying to presents might.
This potent germs flaying.
Slept not gratifying mesh.
Mesh not gratifying spelt.
Signify to ample strength.
Frostily pig than segment.
Pests might giant felonry.
Might spit strange felony.
Trash felony spitting gem.
Softly might pat sneering.
Softly pig tenth smearing.
Lofty, pressing, neat might.
The lofty gnat impressing.
Y-fronts metal piggish net.
Y-fronts metal piggish ten.
Y-fronts lame piggish tent.
Piggish mate lent Y-fronts.
Y-fronts hating me piglets.
Y-fronts malign eight pets.
Y-fronts might spiel agent.
I might pest angel Y-fronts.
I'm the Y-fronts page glints.
It the Y-fronts mangle pigs.
The Y-fronts pig slime gnat.
This Y-fronts gleam pig ten.
This Y-fronts pig met angel.
This Y-fronts tip gem angel.
Frosty, plane shitting gem.
I'm the frosty pant niggles.
Forty sleeping ants might.
The forty maligning pests.
Shit! Forty pigs gentleman.
This spent, gleaming forty.
Hang pestilent, grim softy.

Might rent pleasing softy.
Tenth, pleasing, grim softy.
Prettify sloth nags in gem.
Prettify ghost mangle sin.
I'm a songs prettify length.
I'm a lengths prettify song.
Prettify nights 'n' so gleam.
Prettify longest, shaming.
Prettify along gems hints.
Prettify smog hints angel.
Shit! Prettify mangle song.
Petrify to smelt gnashing.
The slim gangs petrify not.
Self-pity 'n' smothering tag.
Self-pity organs might ten.
Hat strong self-pity in gem.
Self-pity gem on this grant.
This self-pity gnome grant.
Hi! Torments gang self-pity.
Throat 'n' self-pitying gems.
Self-pitying, hot germ ants.
Simplify neat strength go.
Fatty, slighting poser men.
Nifty sampling greets hot.
Nifty, hot, simple gangster.
Ghost nifty, genital sperm.
Nifty, slashing potter gem.
Right! Nifty, top angel mess.
Nifty strength as limp ego.
Spoil nifty, game strength.
Not haggles nifty permits.
Politest, nifty germs hang.
Pig slash nifty, rotten gem.
Pest mights or nifty angel.
Nifty lepers might not gas.
Pest or nifty angles might.
Nifty might glares on pest.
Nifty might as longer pest.
Pong tear nifty mightless.
Nifty piglets smother nag.
Nifty piglets trash on gem.
Not nifty, rash piglet gems.
Great! The nifty, slim pongs.
Am the nifty, gritless pong.
The nifty, grim poet slangs.
Mighty staring felon pest.
Felon gets pithy smarting.
Felon spitting hasty germ.
My tightest, rasping felon.
Isn't the piggy, smart felon.
Empty sign straight felon.
Might pasty felon stinger.
Natty felon piss right gem.

Felon's pithy mate G-string.
This felon's empty grating.
Might felon's petty grains.
Float stingier nymph gets.
Float pithy semen G-string.
The angry, tempting fossil.
Niggle at frostiest nymph.
Temptingly softer hag sin.
Might sign softer penalty.
His mangling softer petty.
Pain forests gently might.
The piggy fronts ailments.
I'm the front pigs as gently.
Sane piglets front mighty.
Hesitantly front pigs gem.
Front shy, mangiest piglet.
Front timely naggish pest.
Glassy for penitent might.
Thinly for tempting gases.
Shy for tempting stealing.
Genital's empty for nights.
Tempting for yet hassling.
Mighty spin gentler fatso.
Oaf sets glittering nymph.
Softest nymph gnat girlie.
Sap soft, glittering hymen.
Hey! Soft tampering glints.
Nights grime soft penalty.
Ahem! Ineptly soft G-string.
Might soft, sleepy ranting.
Gremlin's soft type hating.
Right! I'm soft, gentle pansy.
The soft, sly, impregnating.
Pairs soften gently might.
Gently map tigerish fonts.
Fonts resent almighty pig.
Often angel strips mighty.
Stingers play often might.
Often, petty, smashing girl.
Font praises gently might.
Reptile's font nags mighty.
Thirsty, pleasing font gem.
Gently of neat git shrimps.
I'm straight of gently pens.
Pest of gently right mains.
Gently of nights permit as.
Penis mights of gently rat.
It smashing, pert of gently.
Master hints of gently pig.
Gently of the margins spit.
This sign of gently tamper.
Gently of this mega prints.
Gently of this German spit.

Stingily of the sperm gnat.
Singly of tempting haters.
Shipment of glittery nags.
I'm tenth pigs of strangely.
I'm then pests of gratingly.
I'm tenth pests of ragingly.
Theme of stingingly. Sprat.
Stringy of the pliant gems.
Helping of stingy matters.
Prints of gentle as mighty.
Hymens of great splitting.
Myths of negligent rapist.
Lengthy of tampering sits.
Pit of lengthy masterings.
Tip of lengthy masterings.
Tampering of sightly tens.
Sightly, tempting of earns.
Gnarliest nymph of it gets.
Shitty of gentleman's prig.
Simplest of they granting.
Hey! Pest of smart glinting.
Strength of tamely pig sin.
Smiley of pig strength ant.
Timely snap of the G-string.
My! Sap gentle of thirsting.
Male pigsty of in strength.
Hater of temptingly sings.
Temptingly of in rash gets.
Empty lightest of snaring.
Isn't angel's right of empty.
Empty as of slighting rent.
Slighting of an empty rest.
Isn't large of nights empty.
Gritless of an empty night.
Strangle empty of in sight.
Empty of in hint straggles.
Empty in of thin straggles.
Penalty of grim tightness.
Isn't gems of prettily hang.
Ineptly of strange mights.
Plenty games of thirsting.
Plenty of asserting might.
I'm that plenty of sniggers.
Angel's petty of grim hints.
I'm petty he of stranglings.
Type of nightmare's glints.
Spy might of gentler saint.
Style of nights prime gnat.
Gems of intently sharp git.
Intently of the grim gasps.
Might rants of tensely pig.
Right! Sly of tempting, sane.
I'm the sly pest of granting.

Sly of the tempting grains.
Nasty shrimp of gentle git.
Tasty phlegm of in stinger.
Pig tyrant of slight semen.
Ray of light temptingness.
Master's length of tiny pig.
Right! Tiny of gentle spasm.
Tiny strength of a glimpse.
Testy of trim helping nags.
Yet mangling of the strips.
I'm fine parts ghost gently.
I'm fine traps ghost gently.
Gently romps a fine tights.
Fine hogs tempt staringly.
Strongly stamp fine eight.
Fine songs prattle mighty.
Fine myth straggles point.
In fine, top myth straggles.
Fine, ghastly terms pig not.
Smartingly ghost fine pet.
Fine, germy, tattling shops.
Fine, pasty, mongrel tights.
Hot map fine style G-string.
Right! Fine, nasty gem plots.
Fine phlegm or tasty sting.
Starlet fines mighty pong.
It straggle to nymph fines.
Fin poets might strangely.
Stealthy, sporting fin gem.
Finest gently sap trim hog.
Finest strongly map eight.
Finest shop gratingly met.
Finest strop leggy hit man.
Finest mighty anger plots.
Motherly pit gangs finest.
Finest tip motherly gangs.
Myth organs finest piglet.
Finest ghostly, prime gnat.
Finest mate pongs rightly.
Finest prig not ghastly me.
Finest tightly apron gems.
Finest mastering to glyph.
Trophy games finest glint.
Trophy gem as finest glint.
Pong finest light mastery.
Finest sportingly met hag.
Finest typing harlot gems.
Finest hat rompingly gets.
Empty light groans finest.
Finest phlegm or nasty git.
Gently hog fitness armpit.
Pong mighty alert fitness.
Fitness hag or temptingly.

Niftiest than leggy romps.
Niftiest, gay lengths romp.
Timely, straight fens pong.
Gently stage if not shrimp.
Gently if to agents shrimp.
I'm the arts if gently pongs.
I'm the gaps if gently snort.
I'm the gasp if gently snort.
In if gently trash top gems.
Gently if the porn stigmas.
This song if gently tamper.
Strangely if thin, top gems.
If hot gem steps rantingly.
Pest if stringently hog am.
Stringently has if top gem.
Agony if lengths trim pest.
Helping if grotty ant mess.
Pest if snortingly hat gem.
Isn't top hymen if straggle.
Gropes if tattling hymens.
Merit nest if ghastly pong.
If merit nets ghastly pong.
If termites 'n' ghastly pong.
If lengthy masterings opt.
Isn't stealthy germ if pong.
Stealthy porn if sting gem.
If gem nets tartishly pong.
Net gems if tartishly pong.
Thinly if top, strange gems.
Temptingness if hotly rag.
If thorny as tempting legs.
Pigs if thorny gems talent.
Title nymph if not aggress.
Note nymph if it straggles.
Nymph straggles if it tone.
Nymph if egos strangle tit.
If a nymph or gentlest gits.
Gemstone if sprightly ant.
Trophy if gentle am stings.
Pithy if gormless tangent.
Shitty if gentle romps nag.
Angel's shy if tempting rot.
Shy if tempting, large snot.
Timely pongs if the grants.
Mostly if the grasping net.
Mostly if the grasping ten.
Many if the strong piglets.
My elephants if to G-string.
Male pigsty if on strength.
The mental if strong Gipsy.
Springy gems if hot talent.
Sportsmanly if tight gene.
If stern hog as temptingly.

Temptingly if on rash gets.
Empty if so align strength.
Is empty if along strength.
If goals empty in strength.
Empty if so strangle night.
Strangle empty if on sight.
Empty if on hint straggles.
Empty on if thin straggles.
Empty if the strong signal.
Gems if prettily hangs not.
Plenty if the storming gas.
This mega if strong plenty.
If sleepy might grants not.
Length if sporty gem saint.
Sporty tanglement if sigh.
Spotty, gentler if shaming.
Length if petty organisms.
Nights if so petty mangler.
If thing as petty mongrels.
Steely might if strong pan.
I'm the style if grants pong.
Intently if to gems graphs.
Hero's sly if tempting gnat.
Tasty phlegm if on stinger.
Snottily gang if the sperm.
Pig if snotty gem enthrals.
If tampering toys lengths.
Might if ratty lenses pong.
Try if hassling potent gem.
Testy angel if nights romp.
Testy porn if nights gleam.
Pilferage 'n' snotty mights.
On my tightest leaf spring.
Neat gems profits nightly.
Pilfer nights tasty gnome.
Maggot's tiny then pilfers.
Might rotten flip gayness.
Might gay flip rottenness.
Not straying the flip gems.
Fee strongly map shitting.
That fee romps stingingly.
Feet pongs mightily rants.
Ghastly pin storming feet.
Manly pig this strong feet.
Oh! Gently tampering fists.
Strangely fist open might.
Fits might strangely open.
Strongly fist the mean pig.
Strongly sift the mean pig.
Fist gays torment helping.
Gays torment helping fits.
Gnat fits seethingly romp.
Sift so lengthy tampering.

Hey! Sift piglet strong man.
Fist prettily gnash gnome.
Prettily gnash gnome fits.
Sift prettily gnash gnome.
Gently shape storming fit.
Fit hopes gently smarting.
Empty strongish fit angel.
Fit style nightmares pong.
Fair might steps on gently.
Steel farts pong in mighty.
Nightly gem farts in poets.
I'm shy, top, negligent farts.
Seemly farts in tight pong.
Farts empty stinging hole.
I snotty helping farts gem.
No spies might gently fart.
Themes fart stingily pong.
Home pets stingingly fart.
Steel fart pongs in mighty.
Gentle mighty piss no fart.
Nightly pig to semens fart.
Tightly pig on semens fart.
Git segments phonily fart.
Seemly fart in tight pongs.
Messy fart lightning poet.
Imposingly gets then fart.
Empty singing hotels fart.
Oh! Fear stings temptingly.
Temptingly nights so. Fear.
Empty slighting fear snot.
Finer, glassy, hot, tempting.
Mighty stalest, finer pong.
Ghastly spotting finer me.
Finer mates pongs tightly.
Thinly finer maggot pests.
Might so slang finer petty.
Might longest, finer pasty.
Finer phlegm as snotty git.
Gently hang serf optimist.
Might in angel's potty serf.
Gentleman hogs first pity.
Talent fires mighty pongs.
Free stingingly stamp hot.
No type-setting, grim flash.
Meet pitying, strong flash.
Flash not empty its nigger.
Flash niggers empty on tit.
I'm flash, petty nigger snot.
Flash pity strong meeting.
I'm flash, teeny, top G-string.
Print meanest, soggy filth.
Soggy, eminent filth parts.
Soggy, eminent filth traps.

Steamy, open filth G-string.
Filth enraging top system.
Smartest filth piggy none.
Filth tapestrying on gems.
So emptying, strange filth.
Great! Son's emptying filth.
Spotty, mean filth snigger.
Amen! Spotty filth niggers.
Filth as snoring petty gem.
Petty filth messing groan.
Tipsy filth on strange gem.
Tipsy, strange filth gnome.
Pay strongest filth in gem.
Groin nasty filth pest gem.
Snotty empires gang filth.
Snotty, gasping, mere filth.
Snotty filth nags mere pig.
I'm potent filth gags syren.
Filth gaps yes tormenting.
Filthiest, germy ant pongs.
Rang potty filthiness gem.
Gory, tempting shelf saint.
Piggy tits flesh ornament.
Fetish pongs grimy talent.
Shift gently pig not smear.
Enigma ports gently shift.
Shift gently margin poets.
Gem pets ignorantly shift.
Seemly granting top shift.
Shift employ neat G-string.
Thief pongs staringly met.
Spongy glitters man thief.
Theft agony stingers limp.
Pig snortingly seam theft.
Theft rests moaningly pig.
Saintly pongs grime theft.
Manly fighting terse post.
Manly fighting terse spot.
Manly fighting steep sort.
Measly portents fighting.
Measly, torn pest fighting.
Mostly fighting as repent.
Mostly fighting pat sneer.
No fighting messy prattle.
Lasers empty not fighting.
Let's! Payments or fighting.
Lame sporty nest fighting.
Lame sporty nets fighting.
Let's! Sporty amen fighting.
Some fighting petty snarl.
Only fighting steep smart.
Mostly frightening a step.
Mealy pest frighting snot.

Messy plot frighting neat.
My potent sales frighting.
My toneless pat frighting.
My toneless tap frighting.
Frighting sane lots empty.
Empty sane slot frighting.
Petty lemon frighting ass.
Frighting on lamest types.
No frighting steely stamp.
Steely, top mans frighting.
Amen! Style frighting post.
Amen! Style frighting spot.
Amen! Stop style frighting.
Slyest, top amen frighting.
Flashing tints empty ogre.
Insert potty flashing gem.
Petty flashing or tin gems.
Petty, grim flashing onset.
Flashing tones grim petty.
It's petty flashing on germ.
Flashing yet not grim pest.
Steaming fleshing top try.
Yet fleshing top smarting.
Flights merit spent agony.
Stringy, mean poet flights.
Meaner pigsty flights not.
Am potty sneering flights.
Ratty penis flights on gem.
Ratty penis flights gnome.
Sporty, giant flight semen.
Flight pottery manginess.
Type storming, sane flight.
Frighten posts aim gently.
Aim gently frighten stops.
Frighten atoms sip gently.
Frighten gay, not misspelt.
Frighten pests got mainly.
Frighten manly spit so get.
Tamely frighten pigs snot.
Frighten slimy agents opt.
Timely frighten apt songs.
Frighten timely songs pat.
Frighten timely songs tap.
Frighten mangey, top lists.
My! Spot frighten stealing.
My! Stop frighten stealing.
Frighten spongy am titles.
Frighten potty lame signs.
Frighten mean typist logs.
Spy steaming frighten lot.
Frighten salty gem points.
SOS! Frighten tempting lay.
Frighten sly, top gem saint.

Stonily frighten past gem.
Stonily frighten apt gems.
Stonily frighten pat gems.
Tap stonily frighten gems.
Frighten stony pig metals.
Stony piglets frighten am.
Frighten toys malign pets.
Frighten tiny gap molests.
Top sing frightens tamely.
It's mangey plot frightens.
My! Not frightens a piglets.
Am spongy title frightens.
A molten pigsty frightens.
Stating employ frightens.
Stain empty log frightens.
It frightens not play gems.
Mangle to tipsy, frightens.
I'm pasty leg frightens not.
Any piglet frightens most.
Snotty gap frightens mile.
Metal stony pig frightens.
Tip stony gleam frightens.
Toys man piglet frightens.
Tiny plot frightens as gem.
Tiny pals frightens to gem.
Tiny slap frightens to gem.
Tiny pal frightens to gems.
Gleam spin snotty fighter.
Meanly spotting fighters.
Fighters pig on my talents.
Fighters empty not signal.
Fighters malign petty son.
Fighters pan snottily. Gem.
To penalty frights in gems.
Pong steamily nest fright.
Pong steamily sent fright.
Pig messy fright on talent.
Fright on my sanest piglet.
Is my angel's potent fright.
Mean, stolen fright pigsty.
A fright noses temptingly.
Fright penalty to messing.
So pity gentleman's fright.
I'm gentlest fright on pays.
Fright pongs stately mine.
Any molesting fright pest.
Snottily gap fright semen.
Fright toy piss gentleman.
Fortnight mess neatly pig.
Sanely tip fortnight gems.
Yes malign fortnight pest.
Am shifting, grotty spleen.
Seemly shifting top grant.

Empty angel's shifting rot.
Shifting, empty, large snot.
Shifting glares empty not.
Shifting, sporty, net gleam.
Met shifting, sporty angel.
Spy shifting, tolerant gem.
So timely, pregnant fights.
Fights malign poetry nets.
Isn't fights mangle poetry.
Pasty, gentle fights minor.
Tempting slayer fights no.
Ant promises gently fight.
Its ape-men fight strongly.
Fight as stringent employ.
Presently fight on stigma.
Mean songs fight prettily.
Fight so mastering plenty.
Sanely fight not grim pest.
Shiftier pongs mat gently.
Gently soap thrift in gems.
Soggily spent mean thrift.
Sat seemly ponging thrift.
Mangey, losing thrift pest.
Stem spongy, genial thrift.
Spy thrift semen gloating.
Farthest sing timely pong.
Farthest smiling yet pong.
Strategy 'n' shop-lifting me.
Shop-lifting yet garments.
Shoplift stingy, mere gnat.
Shoplift 'n' temerity gangs.
My! Shoplift tense grating.
Trim teeny gangs shoplift.
Sign natty shoplifter gem.
Snortingly. Faith pest gem.
Ineptly strong faith gems.
Regions shaft temptingly.
Fish gently sporting meat.
Fish gently storming tape.
Rantingly fish pest to gem.
Mine straggly, potent fish.
Gingerly fish on attempts.
Flat stingiest nymph goer.
Fail mighty sternest pong.
Fail potent myth sniggers.
Gosh! Tiny, tempting flares.
Mighty pigs flatters none.
Piggy flatters on this men.
Mighty nest frailest pong.
Mighty sent frailest pong.
Infernal pests got mighty.
Empty not naggish stifler.
Top, naggiest hymen flirts.

Maggot's tinny sheep flirt.
Oh Man! Petty files G-string.
Pong mighty file tartness.
Stifle angry might on pest.
Strop anything stifle gem.
Anything stifle top germs.
Stifle empty, snorting hag.
Top germ stifles anything.
Hey! Tempting organs lifts.
I'm the spongy, strange lift.
Tight felt agony primness.
Nastier felt pongs mighty.
Nastier left pongs mighty.
Left mighty resonant pigs.
It's left or naggiest nymph.
Left may phoniest G-string.
Pity nags left smothering.
Ya! Left imposing strength.
Stony nightmares pig left.
Partington's mighty feels.
Ho! Straying, tempting self.
That spongy, meriting self.
Gently right fame in stops.
Right! Gently sins top fame.
Fame shitting spent glory.
This leggy fame prints not.
Sportingly sight net fame.
Not lightest, springy fame.
Try slighting fame on pest.
Manifest hogs trip gently.
This strong female typing.
Flame in the strong pigsty.
The strong filament Gipsy.
Film ratty pongs seething.
The piggy informs talents.
Shit! Neat forms gently pig.
Piggy forms in the talents.
Petty forms sane lighting.
From gently as tight penis.
From panties sight gently.
Gently stain from the pigs.
Gently shit from neat pigs.
Heat stingingly form pest.
Stingingly sap from teeth.
Pestilent stingy from hag.
Form shitty, sleeping gnat.
Form petty healing stings.
It formless, petty hanging.
It pin shaggy self-torment.
Straggly, hot feminist pen.
Lengthy feminist to grasp.
Grant hopes gently misfit.
Misfit gently graph notes.

Misfit gently graph stone.
Misfit sang gentle trophy.
They misfit strangle pong.
Misfit spongy, gentler hat.
Pithy, gentlest as forming.
Oh! Staringly. Figment pest.
Oh! Strangely spit figment.
Figment than grisly poets.
Ghastly figment in poster.
Figment pets in or ghastly.
Stealthy figment on grips.
Honestly sap grit figment.
Raspingly hot figment set.
Shortest figment playing.
Spongy hits alert figment.
Shit! Sporty figment angle.
Spray on lightest figment.
To figment graphs in style.
Right! Sap figment on style.
Pig trash figment on style.
Snotty lies graph figment.
SOS! Ratty figment helping.
Fragment in ghostly spite.
Fragment sightly poet sin.
Fragment shinily got pest.
Egos fragment thinly spit.
Fragment the pitying loss.
This gits fragment openly.
Lighten so tipsy fragment.
Fragment to tipsy English.
Hot fragment in slyest pig.
Shinily top fragments get.
Fragments pig thinly toes.
Ego fragments thinly spit.
Gosh! It fragments ineptly.
It fragments ineptly hogs.
So pithy, gentlest farming.
Shit! Sly poet fragmenting.
Gnash filmsetting poetry.
Ghost infirm, gentle patsy.
Frames ghost intently pig.
Snotty helping frames git.
Hot frame pets stingingly.
Farm gently shitting pose.
Farm on this gentle pigsty.
This poet nags gently firm.
Firm shaggily potent nest.
Shaggily sent potent firm.
Firm, naggish, potent style.
Firm ghost sleeping natty.
Gently farting posh items.
Gently farting this poems.
Farting gets limp honesty.

Seemly farting nightspot.
O My! Ship gentlest farting.
Farting system to helping.
Ineptly farting shot gems.
Steely months pig farting.
Finger slays potent might.
Almighty fingers not pets.
Piss! Got flattering hymen.
Spit flattering, shy gnome.
Flattering, shiny, top gems.
My! This flattering sponge.
My! Nights self-rating poet.
Empty gas honest flirting.
Oh My! Fleeting spit grants.
Fleeting myth groans spit.
O My! Nights fleeting sprat.
Right! Fleeting many posts.
Right! Many fleeting stops.
Fleeting, sporty hims gnat.
Stay nights fleeting romp.
Fleeting strays pig month.
Stifling myth gropes neat.
Stifling myth ranges poet.
Rag stifling symphonette.
Name stifling trophy gets.
A stifling trophy nets gem.
Meet stifling, trashy pong.
Stifling, hasty, pert gnome.
Stifling nags empty other.
Meet stifling, sporty hang.
A stifling, sporty, then gem.
Together man stifling spy.
Stifling, testy harem pong.
Tasty mirth feelings pong.
Angry, hot, emptiest flings.
Flings as tempting theory.
Flings rat pithy gemstone.
So earthy, tempting flings.
Straight, top enemy flings.
The potty flings smearing.
I'm petty fling to gnashers.
Great! It, on giftless nymph.
Not a giftless nymph tiger.
Mine giftless trophy gnat.
Pong harm giftless entity.
My strength failing poets.
Smothery pigs flattening.
Flag in the potty grimness.
Flag hot petty in grimness.
The simpler, tinny faggots.
Is stale nymph forgetting.
Slimy frigg as potent then.
Mostly has penitent frigg.

Mesh nastily potent frigg.
Sanely potent frigg smith.
Shit tensely tampon frigg.
Snotty frigg impales then.
I'm the stingy parent flogs.
Trim steep anything flogs.
Great! Tiniest nymph flogs.
Thirty-nine flogs past gem.
Thirty-nine gems flogs pat.
Enemy flogs pat thirsting.
Nightmare's net pity flogs.
Tiny nightmare flogs pets.
Flog mighty trip neatness.
Thirsty, eminent gaps flog.
Hey! Is tempting rants flog.
Impregnate shy tints flog.
Flog in typesetting harms.
An impiety strengths flog.
Flog ran petty mightiness.
Tipsy nightmares net flog.
I'm a pity strengthens, flog.
Shit! Flog a tempting syren.
Emptiest frogs nag thinly.
Sane frogs hit temptingly.
Any pestilent frogs might.
Temptingly this sane frog.
Fog gentle nymph satirist.
Right! Fog petty manliness.
Is the fangs import gently.
Not sightly emptier fangs.
Hotly meriting pest fangs.
I'm its gentle trophy fangs.
Fangs type meriting sloth.
Fangs might entirely spot.
Fangs might entirely stop.
Tonight prime style fangs.
Tight fangs on prime style.
I'm the fangs prig not. Style.
Testily romping the fangs.
This fangs pig rottenly. Me.
Strop thinly feasting gem.
Thinly feasting top germs.
Stingily. Fang to the sperm.
I'm this grotty fang spleen.
Tense fang ports mightily.
'e's motherly fang spitting.
Spite motherly fang sting.
Merit sightly fang on pest.
Thirstily meet fang pongs.
Right! Timely fang on pests.
'e's this fang or temptingly.
Empty stingier fang sloth.
Ineptly might sorest fang.

Sporty fang lightens item.
Mile petty, strongish fang.
Fang lest smothering pity.
This gremlins type to fang.
Nights prime fang to style.
Tempting fang hits sorely.
Gently fisting to sharp me.
Temptingly hot, saner figs.
Hesitant fig romps gently.
Fig ghastly torment penis.
Threateningly gifts mops.
Sharp gifts got eminently.
Eminently grasp hot gifts.
Meanly the sporting gifts.
Poser gifts manly tighten.
Posh enemy gifts rattling.
I ghost permanently gifts.
The gifts gas prominently.
Gifts enlighten sporty am.
On the sly tampering gifts.
Gently gift torn emphasis.
Gently gift a hot primness.
Gift pest homes rantingly.
Gift sneeringly stamp hot.
Mesh ignorantly gift pest.
Strongly gift inept shame.
Almighty presents gift no.
Gift almighty porn tenses.
Gift hymenal, top stingers.
Gift top, gnarliest hymens.
Gift ant romps seethingly.
Phonily gift gem tartness.
Right! Gift moneyless pant.
O My! Gift helping tartness.
Gift presently as on might.
Gift in the pasty mongrels.
Shop transiently gift gem.
Tartly gift phoniness gem.
Hoarsen sly, tempting gift.
Gift tasty gremlins phone.
Gift snottily graph semen.
Only nightmares gift pest.
Grin phonily fattest gems.
My strong helping fatties.
Trim safest, gently hoping.
Not meriting safest glyph.
Gently shop meriting fats.
Fast might sneeringly opt.
Fast sleeping mighty torn.
Fast timely phone G-string.
Fast enlighten stormy pig.
The pitying fats mongrels.
Fast! The tiny mongrels pig.

Gently ship storming feat.
My sporting fate lightens.
My sporting feat lightens.
Fate gem hints sportingly.
Feat gem hints sportingly.
Imply fate honest G-string.
Gently prime fat signs hot.
Gently ghost fat, prime sin.
Fat mothering piss gently.
Pig gently smother fat sin.
Shit! Grim fat opens gently.
Hi! Fat glory temptingness.
Fat theme ports singingly.
Is fat hymen glitters pong.
Fat gemstone grips thinly.
Honestly! Isn't fat pig germ.
Fat, thorny piglets in gems.
I'm fat, thorny pest niggles.
I'm fat, horny, gentlest pigs.
Nymph titles so fat nigger.
Fat seems glinting trophy.
Then pitying gormless fat.
So typing the fat gremlins.
Fat stingers employ night.
Fat teeth signs rompingly.
Rompingly sting these fat.
Temptingly horse fat sign.
Fat songs hire temptingly.
Fat sloths empty in nigger.
Fat niggers empty in sloth.
Fat, sleepy, storming thing.
Mornings sleepy, tight fat.
Fat mongrels type insight.
Fat mights entirely pongs.
Sly fat hogs grim penitent.
Sly gem in the sporting fat.
Fat mights only pestering.
Fat entry on mightless pig.
Fat syren mights on piglet.
Fat yet this gremlins pong.
Faint, homely G-string pets.
Leggy smothers tip infant.
I'm the infant, leggy sports.
Infant, motherly pigs gets.
Infant, sightly germ poets.
Infant poetry gems lights.
Infant germs pig hot style.
Fans, I'm the glittery pongs.
Grotty, impish, gentle fans.
Rotten fans met piggishly.
Fans pong slight temerity.
Shit! Gem fans rottenly pig.
Tight fan promises gently.

Mightily steep, strong fan.
Stylish, tempting fan goer.
Gently nights safe import.
Safe myth glitters in pong.
Safe sight nor temptingly.
Met safe, sporty lightning.
Temptingly hot safes grin.
Flimsy, top gathering nets.
The flimsy point gangster.
Eh!Flimsy, top, neat G-string.
Hang lest mortifying pest.
Pest than mortifying legs.
Gentlest infamy grips hot.
Infamy gross tenth piglet.
Shop stinging flattery me.
Posh met singing flattery.
Flattery night piss on gem.
Flattery night piss gnome.
'e's flattery pongs in might.
Flayer sings potent might.
Fairly nights potent gems.
Nights steaming top flyer.
Grin safely tempting host.
Safely shot tempting grin.
Tight gnome prints safely.
Tempting singer flays hot.
Faintly reset might pongs.
Might pongs faintly trees.
Green posts faintly might.
Imposing fealty strength.
Merest nothings pig fatly.
Romp fatly seething sting.
This pongs regiment fatly.
Tempting star hogs finely.
Fly hot impregnate stings.
Gosh! Tempting, nastier fly.
Tempting, nastier fly hogs.
Gnashers fly impotent git.
Tight sons impregnate fly.
Fly pretentions might gas.
Shit! Impotent naggers fly.
This fly, penetrating smog.
Fiery, tempting hasn't logs.
The infantry lots pig gems.
Most ferny, piggish talent.
Ferny pig maligns hottest.
I'm ferny talents ghost pig.
Amongst this ferny piglet.
Slashing, impotent fry get.
Fry gleam on shitting pest.
Sane piglets might not fry.
Might inelegant posts fry.
Fry shit so tempting angel.

Shiftily nag not pert gems.
Filthy, sporting name gets.
A filthy, sporting, net gems.
Filthy, sporting seem gnat.
I'm filthy 'n' greatest pongs.
Filthy merits, agents pong.
Filthy termites sang pong.
To filthy, rasping segment.
A filthy segments pig torn.
Filthy agents pig monster.
Filthy gasps in rotten gem.
Gasp meet filthy snorting.
Print maggot's filthy seen.
Part sign filthy gemstone.
Got filthy, pert manginess.
Rag filthy, potent messing.
Filthy, open smarting gets.
Filthy meat opens G-string.
Filthy, top 'n' angriest gems.
Filthy gemstone past grin.
Filthy, apt gem on stingers.
Filthy, apt gnome stingers.
Filthy segments groin pat.
Filthy segments groin tap.
Filthy niggers man to pest.
Filthy pest snaring to gem.
Maggot's filthy, inner pets.
Filthy smarting pets gone.
Filthy pest on giant germs.
Filthy, naggiest norm pets.
Filthy grants spite gnome.
Filthy segments pit groan.
Serfishly tempting go ant.
Pongs meet thriftily nags.
A gems nets thriftily pong.
Thriftily meets nags pong.

953906

Printed in Great Britain by
Amazon.co.uk, Ltd.,
Marston Gate.